SAGE was founded in 1965 by Sara Miller McCune to support the dissemination of usable knowledge by publishing innovative and high-quality research and teaching content. Today, we publish over 900 journals, including those of more than 400 learned societies, more than 800 new books per year, and a growing range of library products including archives, data, case studies, reports, and video. SAGE remains majority-owned by our founder, and after Sara's lifetime will become owned by a charitable trust that secures our continued independence.

Los Angeles | London | New Delhi | Singapore | Washington DC | Melbourne

The contemporary world experiences an ever fast pace of social transition caused by globalization, penetration of information and communication technologies, new and social media, and emergence of knowledge economy. These have ushered several new social institutional arrangements, values, norms, customs, and the new culture of social movements; and have profoundly altered the pre-existing arrangements affecting the essence, construction and reconfiguration of identity in fundamental ways. This book undertakes an in-depth analysis of the essence, construction, transformation and rejuvenation of identities. It examines these dynamics of identity in the contexts of collective mobilizations and social movements; transformation of tribal and peasant societies; emergence of a globalized knowledge society; intersectionalities of ethnicity, nationality and citizenship; and articulation of patriotism through lived-in experiences of alienhood in a perceived alien land and thereafter growing up and acquiring adulthood in India. The book also covers the process of rejuvenation of identities of the indigenous people of Australia in the context of introduction of the policy of reconciliation by the Australian state on the one hand and the articulation of environmental concerns by the indigenous people on the other.

IDENTITY, SOCIETY
and
TRANSFORMATIVE SOCIAL CATEGORIES

Debal K. SinghaRoy

IDENTITY, SOCIETY and TRANSFORMATIVE SOCIAL CATEGORIES

Dynamics of Construction, Configuration and Contestation

Los Angeles | London | New Delhi
Singapore | Washington DC | Melbourne

Copyright © Debal K. SinghaRoy, 2018

All rights reserved. No part of this book may be reproduced or utilized in any form or by any means, electronic or mechanical, including photocopying, recording, or by any information storage or retrieval system, without permission in writing from the publisher.

First published in 2018 by

SAGE Publications India Pvt Ltd
B1/I-1 Mohan Cooperative Industrial Area
Mathura Road, New Delhi 110 044, India
www.sagepub.in

SAGE Publications Inc
2455 Teller Road
Thousand Oaks, California 91320, USA

SAGE Publications Ltd
1 Oliver's Yard, 55 City Road
London EC1Y 1SP, United Kingdom

SAGE Publications Asia-Pacific Pte Ltd
3 Church Street
#10-04 Samsung Hub
Singapore 049483

Published by Vivek Mehra for SAGE Publications India Pvt Ltd, typeset in 10/12 pt Times New Roman by Fidus Design Pvt. Ltd., Chandigarh and printed at Chaman Enterprises, New Delhi

Library of Congress Cataloging-in-Publication Data Available

ISBN: 978-93-528-0462-7 (HB)

SAGE Team: Abhijit Baroi, Vandana Gupta, Abhinav Singh and Ritu Chopra

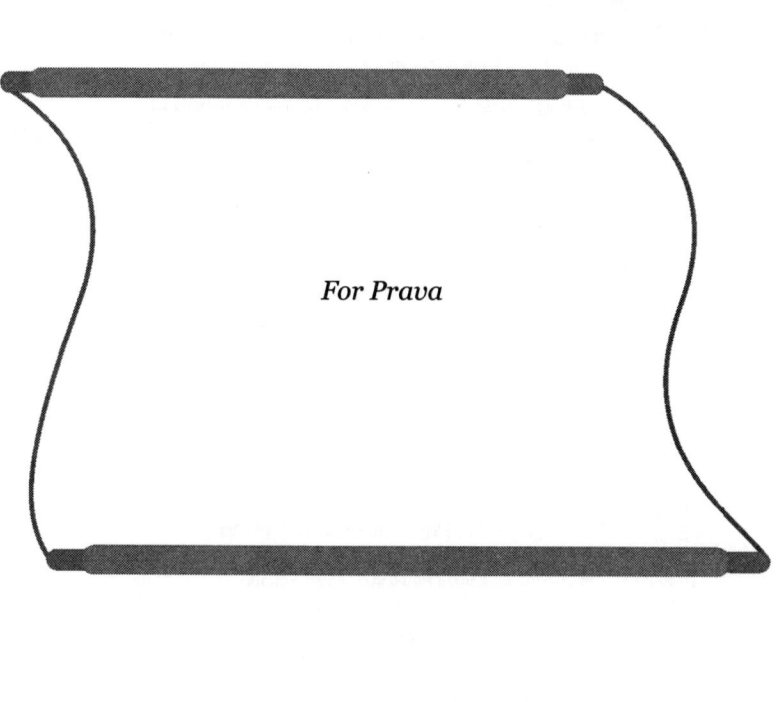

Thank you for choosing a SAGE product!
If you have any comment, observation or feedback,
I would like to personally hear from you.

Please write to me at **contactceo@sagepub.in**

Vivek Mehra, Managing Director and CEO, SAGE India.

Bulk Sales

SAGE India offers special discounts
for purchase of books in bulk.
We also make available special imprints
and excerpts from our books on demand.

For orders and enquiries, write to us at

Marketing Department
SAGE Publications India Pvt Ltd
B1/I-1, Mohan Cooperative Industrial Area
Mathura Road, Post Bag 7
New Delhi 110044, India

E-mail us at **marketing@sagepub.in**

Get to know more about SAGE

Be invited to SAGE events, get on our mailing list.
Write today to **marketing@sagepub.in**

This book is also available as an e-book.

Contents

List of Tables	ix
Preface	xi
Introduction	1
1 Dynamics of Identity: Essence, Construction and Transformation	11
2 Identity, Social Movements and Collective Mobilizations: Dynamics of Transformation and Reconfiguration	43
3 Peasant, Caste, Class and Identity: Contesting Marginality	70
4 Environment, Development and Indigenous People's Identity: Annihilation, Reconciliation and Resistance in Australia	97
5 Globalization, ICTs, Networks, Work, Culture and Identity: Reflexivity in an Emerging Knowledge Society	127
6 Ethnicity, Nationality, Citizenship and Identity: Accelerated Binaries and Complementarity of Differences	159
7 Partition, Alienhood, Migration and Shaping Up of an Indian Identity: The Cost and Joy of Being Patriotic	197
Bibliography	236
Index	247
About the Author	254

List of Tables

2.1	Typology of Social Movements	53
2.2	Major Facets of Social Movements in Independent India	60
3.1	Percentage Distribution of Rural Households	80
3.2	Availability of Per Household Land in 1961–62, 2002–3 and 2012–13 at All India Level	81
3.3	Availability of Per Capita Land in India in 1951, 1981, 2001 and 2013	82
3.4	Changing Work Participation Patterns of Peasants in Agriculture since 1951	82
3.5	Percentage of Main and Marginal Workers among Total Workers, India, 1981–2011	83
3.6	Landholding by Caste/Ethnic Backgrounds	84
3.7	Landholding and Employment	85
3.8	Changing Trends of Collective Mobilizations and Construction of Peasant Identities	91
4.1	Diversity in the Orientation	123
5.1	Comparative Features of Agricultural, Industrial and Knowledge Societies	129
5.2	Level of Education by Caste and Gender in the Metro Cities, District Towns and Villages	137
5.3	ICTs Penetration in the Selected Metro Cities, District Towns and Villages	138
5.4	Proportion of Knowledge Workers in Relation to the Service/Business and Total Workers	139
5.5	Proportion of Knowledge Workers in Relation to Total Workers in Metro Cities, District Towns and Villages by Caste and Gender	140
5.6	Dominant Patterns of Integration with Knowledge Society	149

Preface

Contemporary societies are experiencing an unprecedented pace of social transformation widely caused by globalization; profound transition in the economic order; spread of information and communication technologies (ICTs) and new and social media; increased physical and social connectivity; and fast transference of goods and services, images and messages across the globe. These developments have made social transformation very disruptive and have caused many of pre-existing human thoughts and actions to become disoriented and decontextualized. Consequently, a sharp decline in the significance of many old institutions and arrangements, norms and values, and social practices and processes on one hand, and the formation of new ones on the other hand have become the dominant order of the day. Societies now experience the formation of new frontiers for solidarity and networking, arrival of new social norms and values, consumerism and desires, strategies for new repressions and dominations, marginalization and bondage, and the articulation of new protests and resistance. Objective social realities and subjective perceptions are now constructed on a daily basis in terms of these transformations taking shape in the wider contexts of the society and at the grass-roots level through ICTs and social and new media. The conventional social collectivities such as those of caste, class, ethnicity, gender, peasants, farmers and workers have acquired new forms of reflexivity and have become resilient for self-articulation and collective assertions of various forms. The increased social mobility and fast pace of communication in both the real and the cyberspace have produced a good deal of flexibility in these social collectivities to be posited with solidarity at one end and fluidity at the other. In this interactive world, these collectivities have emerged to be reflexive and transformative by undergoing new processes of their construction, transformation and reconfiguration for rejuvenated self-expression and self-assertion and for development of contestation against varieties of social arrangements that stand for their domination and marginalization in society. Such reflexivity and transformative dynamics produce new collective identities out of pre-existing social selves.

The process of identity formation is linked to transformation from a structure to an agency that emanates with the resilience of a social collectivity. Such transformation is linked to social structure and culture and its politics. The disruptive social transformation, achieved by affecting the whole gamut of culture, economy, technology and politics, has widely made the conventional social categories in their given form inadequate to represent their transformation. Efforts are now being made to put the dynamics of identity in operation as an explanatory device to inquire into the transformative resilience of these social categories.

An inquiry into the process of identity construction needed not only thorough engagement with the existing body of available literature but also an in-depth empirical observation on these processes. My previous academic engagement with the study of social movements, social development, marginalization and tribal and peasant societies was of great help in reformulating my thoughts on the dynamics of identity. I also got the opportunity to share my thoughts and understanding in front of challenging academic audiences when I was invited to deliver keynote, plenary and theme addresses at some important national and international seminars and conferences in India and abroad in the last couple of years. The following of my presentations were modified and improvised for this book: 'Marginalization, Social Movements and Empowerment through Local Self Government' at the International Conference on Marginalization, Poverty and Decentralization, organized by the Kerala Institute of Local Administration (KILA), Kochi, 19–22 November 2016; 'Agrarian Development in the Neo-liberal India: Emerging Research Concerns', organized as a public lecture by the Department of Sociology, University of Allahabad, 5 August 2016; 'Identity and Social Movements', at the National Seminar of Social Movements, organized by Department of Sociology, Savitribai Phule University, Pune, 13–14 June 2016; 'Dynamics of Culture in a Changing Society' at the National Seminar on Dynamics of Culture, organized by the Department of Sociology, University of Kalyani, Kalyani, Nadia, 27–28 March 2016; 'Development, Marginalization and People's Movements' at the 41st All India Sociological Conference, organized by the Indian Sociological Society in Bhubaneswar, Odisha, 27–29 December 2015; 'Knowledge Society in India', at a national conference titled 'Knowledge Society: India's New Revolution', organized by the India International Centre, New Delhi, 9 January 2015; 'Caste, Class and Identity: Facets of Resilience and Resurgence', at a national conference titled 'Making of a Casteless Society in India: Discourses and Mobilizations', organized by Jawaharlal Nehru

University (JNU), New Delhi, 7 April 2014; 'Environmental Issues in the Indigenous Movement in Australia', organized by the Civil Society Research Centre, University of Technology, Sydney, as theme lecture on completion of my Endeavour Fellowship Programme in Australia, 6 September 2010; and 'Social Movements: The Emerging Dimensions in a Developing Society' at the World Congress of Sociology, Gothenburg, 9–17 July 2010. In addition, the chapters 'Dynamics of Identity: Essence, Construction and Transformation', 'Ethnicity, Nationality, Citizenship and Identity: Accelerated Binaries and Complementarity of Differences', and 'Partition, Alienhood, Migration and Shaping Up of an Indian Identity: The Cost and Joy of Being Patriotic' are written afresh based on additional research and readings.

I am extremely thankful to the organizers of the aforementioned seminars and conferences, especially to Professor S. Balan, the former Director, KILA, Kochi; Professor A. Satyanarayana and Professor Ashish Saxena, Department of Sociology, University of Allahabad; Professor Shruti Tambe, Department of Sociology, University of Pune; Professor Samita Manna, Department of Sociology, University of Kalyani; Professor Anand Kumar, former President, Indian Sociological Society, New Delhi; Dr S. Majumdar, Librarian, India International Centre, New Delhi; Dr Rajiv Kumar, Centre for Policy Research, JNU, New Delhi; Professor James Goodman, University of Technology Sydney; and Professor Benjamin Tejerina, Universidad del País Vasco, Spain, for inviting me to these events as a keynote/plenary/theme speaker. I am sincerely thankful to the scholars, friends and colleagues who commented on my papers.

The chapter 'Environment, Development and Indigenous People's Identity: Annihilation, Reconciliation and Resistance in Australia' is based on a research project titled 'Environmental Movements and the Indigenous People in Australia', sponsored by the Department of Education, Employment and Workplace Relations, Government of Australia, under the auspices of the Endeavour Award undertaken at the University of Technology, Sydney. I am thankful to the Endeavour Fellowship Foundation, Australia, for awarding me the fellowship and allowing me to undertake research on this topic. It was an exciting experience to undertake fieldwork among the indigenous people of Australia. I am especially thankful to my respondents, particularly Uncle Dootch Kanedy, a community elder and elected Chairperson of Illawarra Local Aboriginal Land Council; Aunty Carol Ridgeway-Bissett, a community elder, Worrimi Land Council; Andrew Smith, Chairperson of Worrimi Land Council; Sister Karol Brown, Gandangara Land Council; and numerous indigenous people who helped to organize my visits and fieldwork among them. I am also sincerely thankful to Professor Heather Goodall and Dr Heidi Norman, University of Technology, Sydney, and Professor Stuart Rosewarne, University of Sydney for their profound encouragement and insights.

I am also thankful to Professor Maitrayee Chaudhuri, School of Social Sciences, Centre for the Study of Social Systems, JNU, New Delhi; late Professor D. N. Dhanagare, former Vice-chancellor, Shivaji University of Kolhapur; Professor Shruti Tambe, Department of Sociology, University of Pune; Professor V. Xaxa, Department of Sociology, Tezpur University, Assam; Professor Partha Nath Mukherjee, former Director, Tata Institute of Social Sciences, Mumbai; and Dr Vibha Arora, Professor, IIT Delhi, for their sustained encouragement. Moreover, I am thankful to my departmental colleagues Professor Nita Mathur, Dr Rabindra Kumar, Dr B. Kiranmai, Dr Archana Singh, and Dr R. Vashum for their encouragement and support. I am also grateful to all my research students for keeping me engaged with my academic zeal.

I am grateful to the library staff of IGNOU for extending their all-out support in providing me very quick access to all the library resources such as books, documents, journals and other related literature. It would have been very difficult to bring out this book without the selfless support of my dear colleagues Mr Joginder Kumar, Mr Naresh Kumar and Ms Sonia Singh who worked very sincerely for finalizing the script and introducing series of corrections, modifications and upgrades to the manuscript. In fact, without their intelligent effort, it would have been impossible to retrieve the manuscript after it lost its essence because of system malfunction several times. I am also thankful to Ms Poonam Ahuja for her cooperation.

I am greatly thankful to my children, Dr Purbali SinghaRoy and Mr Anirudh SinghaRoy, for bearing with my obsession and for developing critical and constructive arguments on the theme of this book on several occasions. My wife, Dr Prava Debal, has always been a great friend and stands beside me in both pleasant and difficult times with thoughtful guidance, appreciation and criticality.

Lastly, I am thankful to SAGE Publications for accepting the manuscript of this book, getting it timely evaluated by reviewers and publishing it. I am especially thankful to the SAGE team for their quick appreciation and action and for the pains they took in bringing out this book by introducing the necessary corrections and modifications in due time.

Introduction

Identity is concerned with change and transformation, resonance and resilience, and reflexivity and dynamism of self in society. It has always remained central to the social, cultural and political expressions of human beings. It is an expression of solidarity and uniqueness reflective of its individual and collective ontology. However, despite being an expression of solidarity, identity has not always remained a straitjacketed single, given, fixed and unaltered phenomenon, paving the way for its multiple and transitional manifestations. Thus, while on the one hand, it has remained culturally inherited, fixed, unified and locally circumscribed, on the other, it has also become constructed, reformulated and fragmented and part of a fluid entity in society. The contemporary world experiences a host of paradoxes in the manifestation of social identity in the wake of increasing interconnectivity across the globe on the one hand and simultaneous fragmentation in society on the other. These have caused the processes of formation, sustenance, change, transformation and essentialization of identity and its interrelationship with those of 'other' identities to become complex. These complexities are often accentuated by the movement of identity from collective to individual, primordial to secular, cultural to civic, essentialization to construction, dormant to active, and an end to a means or vice versa.

In a fast, transitional, plural and multicultural society, while identities are essentialized on the basis of primordial considerations, they are also constructed on the basis of non-primordial considerations, cross-cutting each other's inherited and constructed boundaries that have provided the space for the coexistence of old identities along with constructed new ones. On many occasions, old identities are rejuvenated in new contexts and new identities are formed for collective expression, which may be complementary at one end and contradictory at the other. Furthermore, as all social identities are to make their presence felt by becoming socially relevant and purposeful both to its members and to others for their substance, they undergo the process of their essentialization, rejuvenation and constructions situationally by making their social texture quite complex.

Thus, identities as social expressions are not simply the reflection of our language, our food, our region and religion, or our social groups in the form of caste, race, class, gender, ethnic group and nation, but these are also the expressions of the roles these entities perform, subjective meanings they produce, and symbols they represent either individually or collectively. Although identities are used as a cover term for a range of social personae, including social statuses, roles, positions, relationships and institutional and other relevant community expressions (Ochs 1993), they are specifically described as internalized role designations (Stryker 1990) and as a source of meaning (Castells 1997) to provide legitimacy to the decisions, actions and unity of a group's existence (Cerutti 2001). Moreover, though identities are social constructs, they also function as agencies by developing an intrinsic relation between society and self, wherein the society shapes the self and the self shapes the society (Stryker 1990). In recent years, with the spread of information and communication technologies (ICTs) and media, within local and global interactive processes, 'identity has become a reflexive project that organizes self-planning ... (and) becomes a central feature of the structuring of the self-identity' (Giddens 1991, 53).

Identities are formed within the structural arrangements of society and are linked to the exercise of power and action; moreover, they are continuously re-legitimized through 'habitus'—the legitimized norms and tendencies that guide behaviour and thinking (Bourdieu 1986). Identity is deeply linked to the system of power and domination in a 'disciplinary society' through a scientific discourse that shapes the social structure that in turn shapes the culture which decides social control and the acceptability or non-acceptability of behaviour (Foucault 1989).

The contemporary world experiences growth individualism that doubts the importance of collective meaning and action and control over people and looks for reworking social living and integration of individualized individuals into broader social relations through varieties of innovation (Beck 2009) and continual self-actualization and instant self-reinvention (Elliott and Lemert 2006). The growth of individual self, however, is not a revolt of an individual against society or his/her emancipation in society. He/she is as much the product of social change and transformation in society as the producer of the same. Man is an agent and the creator of historical processes which change the shape of the world and the thoughts of man (Carr 1961, 55). Despite the product and producer relationship, individual identity has remained a reality in society. However, the individual identity evolves from the whole package of individualized experience, and in the event of formation of collective identity, the individual identity is placed at the backdrop (Bradley 2016; Coleman and Collins 2004). The dynamics of identity acquire added complicities as identities are subjected to fragmentation and multiple manifestations since everyone consciously or not identifies with more than one identity (Lawler 2008; Stryker 1990). Individuals as rational beings take advantage of alternative identities to suit different conditions (Eminov 2007), through reasons and alternative choices (Sen 1999, 21).

Identities undergo the processes of reconstruction along the transformation of society caused by modernization, colonization, globalization and penetration of ICTs. Modernization has reconstructed new identities by bringing in new logics of self-determination. Society has transformed through the process of calculating the numerical size of identities—many small, approximate and tentative forms of social universe—into the typical modern image of mapped and counted identities. This has created majorities and minorities and provided the fuzzy communities a good deal of concrete identities (Kaviraj 1995). Enactment of laws, especially personal laws founded on religious affiliations that govern the aspects of marriage, inheritance, etc., also creates the identities of majority and minority. Similarly, the constitutional provisions for collective/group rights contribute to such formations. The spread of colonisation also helps construct a larger identity through the arousal of the nationalistic spirit by submerging several indigenous identities, including majoritarian, minoritarian or other fuzzy ones, under its flow. Since the middle of the last century, when most of the colonies of Western Europe got swayed by the spirit of nationalism, most of the colonized countries articulated their national identity against colonial forces for independence. Most of the newly liberated states, by accepting a welfare state philosophy, initiated technological modernization, rapid industrialization and expansion of education and mass-communication networks across their societies, and injected the identity of citizenship for nation-building under the ambience of nation-state.

However, a vast section of the Indian society has only been partly integrated with the nation-building process, for one reason or the other, as economic stagnation and downward mobility, political segregation and disempowerment, and cultural isolation and social inequalities has remained part of their everyday lived-in experience. For this vast section, their marginalized economic and political status has remained intertwined with their primordial status. The inherited primordial collective identities of caste, religion, region, etc., which were overshadowed by the identity of nationality in the urgency of attaining freedom by driving away the British, have resurfaced and been reinvented in the post-Independence era with full potential across the country. With sustained inequalities and divides between the rich and the poor, increased interconnectivity among the marginalized people, and growing awareness at the grass-roots level about historical injustice and neglect towards them, societies now experience the extensive proliferation of discontent, resistance and social movements for social equality, justice and sustainable livelihood. These processes have been furthered with the practice of democracy at the grass-roots level that provides the space for rejuvenation and construction of multiple social identities in public space.

In the contemporary world, the processes of construction of new collective identities and rejuvenation of old identities have acquired additional space with the revolution and phenomenal expansion of ICTs, social and mass media, expansion of education, economic globalization, migration and movement of ideas and objects at an unprecedented speed across the globe, and a tendency of homogenization of culture and economy with increasing consumerism. Despite making people phenomenally interconnected, these factors have made people substantially fragmented through unequal access to ICTs, education and other opportunities, and have transfigured and replaced the earlier facets of stable group membership (Bococks 1993, 31) through their manifestation of flux and fluidity in the identities. Moreover, these forces have converted the society to half flow and half being (Castells 1997), have visibly produced fluidity in identities (McDonald 2002) and proliferated multiplicity of 'other' cultures and identities (Sassen 1996, 211–20) through the transnationalization of space. In the wake of increasing instability in the pre-existing relations and the tendency to create an amount of 'otherness' from within, there has been the proliferation of multiple identities along with consolidation of primordial identities across the space. Along the line, there has been the frequent twisting of identities—from locating them as an end in itself to posit them as a means to an end—in contemporary society. Within the emerging flows of instability some scholars, for example, Castells (1997), find self-reflexivity of people becoming a questionable proposition, and the manifestation of flux and instability emerging to be a never-complete process (Hall 1990; Weeks 1990). However, many find identity to have emerged as a self-reflexive project (Giddens 1991), a reflection of individualized individuals looking for justification, re-elaboration and integration with broader networks (Beck 2009). At this stage, the relationship between society and self has acquired new intensity to shape the society and its historical journey as a change agent.

Significantly, the emerging sociocultural processes and fast economic, technological, as well as political transformations have not only injected complexity in the formation, transformation and fragmentation of identities but have also made their descriptions complex. Sociologists have widely used social groups of various forms in their analyses of social structure. The dynamics of identity are at times used to add the value of construction, meaning and agency to those social groups in the context of their collective mobilizations and social movements. Such usage has covered those identities that are formed on the basis of subjectively précised or imagined unity and also those that are formed on the basis of objectively defined goals in society. Hence, the descriptions of the dynamics of identity have remained at times as contentious as the realities are.

The processes of essentialization, construction and rejuvenation of identity in India, which were deeply impacted by Westernization, colonization, modernization and various social movements, have been impacted further, in recent years with the expansion of the forces of neoliberal globalization, penetration of ICTs and emergence of knowledge economy across the globe. Here, the transitional trajectory of contemporary society experiences the consolidation of old identities on the one hand and manifestation of fuzziness and fluidity in identity on the other, along with the emergence of new patterns of intersectionality between individual and collective; local and global; peasant, caste and class; and ethnic, national and citizenship and various such other identities. In the same vein, debates on the changing texture of identity have also intensified. However, all these debates have avoided discussion on the understanding of the essence, construction and transformation of identities. Hence, debates on identity ought to focus on the following questions: What are the basic dynamics of the formation of identity? How are identities constructed and reconfigured? How and why is a specific social identity privileged over another within the dynamics of rejuvenated multiple identities? How are new identities constructed in social movements and get transformed with the transformation of social movements? What have the emerging patterns been of intersectionality between caste, class and tribal identities in the peasant society in India? How do the indigenous people reconstruct their identities through social movements, negotiate their identities with the developmental initiatives of the state, and reconfigure them against the state and the civil society over time? What have been the emerging patterns of identity formation in a knowledge society? How do ICTs and social media influence the formation and transformation of identity in contemporary India? How are the identities of ethnicity, nationality and citizenship constructed and intersected with each other? How do the childhood experiences of trauma, alienhood, migration and resocialization and the process of growing up affect the formation of national identity and the identity of citizenship of people? This book is an attempt to answer these questions through an in-depth analysis of the conceptual formulation of identity and by applying those formulations on the formation, fragmentation and rejuvenation of new identities in the contexts of collective mobilizations and social movements; transformation of tribal and peasant societies; emergence of a globalized knowledge society; intersectionalities between ethnic, national and citizenship identities; and articulation of nationalism through lived-in experiences of alienhood, migration, re-socialization and contestation to domination in Indian society. The book also covers the process of rejuvenation of identities of the indigenous people of Australia in the context of introduction of a policy of reconciliation, developmental initiatives and their intersectionality with the indigenous culture and environment. This book is organized into seven chapters.

Chapter 1 is titled 'Dynamics of Identity: Essence, Construction and Transformation'. While elaborating the fundamental nuances of identity, the chapter clarifies the location of social identity within the dynamics of social roles and meaning, and elaborates the interrelationships between individual and collective identities, essentialist and constructionist views on identity, role of reasons and choice in determining identity, processes of consolidation of identities in social movements, and their transformation with the transformation of social movements in the wake of colonization, modernization, Westernization, penetration of ICTs and expansion of globalization. It also presents the postmodernist critiques on identity and issues of reflexivity, and elaborates the relationship between individualism, self and society. This chapter in essence provides a conceptual backdrop for the analysis of the formation and transformation of the identities of caste, class, tribe, ethnicity, nationality, citizenship, etc., in the subsequent chapters of this book.

Chapter 2 is titled 'Identity, Social Movements and Collective Mobilizations: Dynamics of Transformation and Reconfiguration'. Social movements occupy the core of social dynamics by integrating social tension, crisis, conflict, change and transformation with the process of progression of society. The chapter analyses the major theoretical

Introduction 7

perspectives on social movements and highlights as to how social movements produce social space for challenging the existing values, norms and societal arrangements, and paves the way for the emergence of new cultures, ideas, interests, knowledge, societal arrangements and identities over time and space. Although each historical phase is marked by the appearance of distinctive social movements, collective actions and collective identities, not all theoretical perspectives on social movements have acknowledged the formation of new identities to be a key dynamic of social movements. Against this backdrop, this chapter elaborates the significance of the perspective on new social movements that emphasizes on the formation of a new collective identity as the key function of social movements to develop fundamental and common humanitarian concerns, intersubjectivity, emotions and a higher degree of cognition, knowledge and ideas in society. The chapter also elaborates as to how in the wake of globalization and planetarianization of common concerns, there have emerged the phenomena of social movements, formation of social movement societies and the proliferation of anti-globalization and social anti-movements—phenomena that have contributed to the formation of not only multiple identities and fluidity of identity in social movements but also a reactionary communitarian social order. Further, this chapter examines the changing facets of identity formation through the changing trajectory of social movements in India since Independence by positing the socio-historical context of manifestation of issues involved in the participation of primordial groups in social movements, the kind of response it invoked from the state, and the new identities and solidarities these groups produced through their participation in the movements. The chapter also discusses, by presenting empirical evidence, the dynamics of transformation of social movements from radicalization to institutionalization, the emerging interface between solidarity and fluidarity in identity, reconfiguration of primordial collective identities, and multiple collective assertions through multiple protests and processes of solidification of new collective identities on the one hand and their deconsolidation on the other.

Chapter 3, titled 'Peasant, Caste, Class and Identity: Contesting Marginality', narrates the emergence of an interface between peasants, caste and class in India in the process of fostering their common identity through peasant movements and transformation of these movements. Against the backdrop of historically inherited social, economic and cultural denials and deprivations, subjugation and domination, and legitimization and reproduction of marginality of peasants, the chapter describes various types of collective mobilization and protests that have remained integral parts of peasants' life and have contributed to the formulation of a distinctive identity of peasants in the Indian society. Moreover, the chapter discusses the emerging patterns of political mobilization of peasants in contemporary India by providing a background of declining land–man ratio, preponderance of semi-landlessness and marginal holding, and un/ underemployment in agriculture on the one hand, and fast penetration of mass media and education, road and transport facilities, connectivity afforded by ICTs, state- and civil-society-sponsored developmental initiatives, expansion of the scope and conditions of occupational diversification, and increasing spatial and horizontal mobility of peasantry on the other hand. The central thrust of this chapter is to delineate the emerging intertwining between peasant, caste and class identities in contemporary India and the processes of construction of new identities, thereby highlighting the change and transformation in the agrarian society in India since Independence, transformation of radical peasant movements into reformative ones, and the emerging facets of formation of new identities and their fragmentation through the emergence of multiple and cross-class identities. Methodologically, the chapter is based on both macro-level and empirical micro-level data.

Chapter 4, titled 'Environment, Development and Indigenous People's Identity: Annihilation, Reconciliation and Resistance in Australia', focuses on the identity of the indigenous people in Australia with reference to their association with their environment and response to the state initiative for reconciliation and their development. On the basis of both primary and secondary sources of information, the chapter describes the historically inherited symbiotic relationship between the indigenous people's identity and their environment, and the process of destruction of this relationship by the colonial forces through their economic and environmental dispossession, cultural and political subordination, physical annihilation and forced assimilation with the colonial way of life. It elaborates the indigenous people's struggle against the continuing subordination, injustice and neglect in the Australian society. It shows that in recent years, these struggles have taken multidimensional shapes with the interpenetration of several exogenous forces among the indigenous people on the one hand and increasing heterogeneity among them on the other; moreover, the emerging relationships between the state, civil society, indigenous identity, and their culture and environment are diversely perceived by the indigenous people themselves. Against this backdrop, the chapter examines the emerging dynamics of identity of the indigenous people in Australia from a socio-historical perspective based on selected case studies of development and welfare initiatives of local land councils, and resistance against development projects and sand mining in New South Wales.

Chapter 5 is titled 'Globalization, ICTs, Networks, Work, Culture and Identity: Reflexivity in an Emerging Knowledge Society'. As India stands today at the epochal transition towards a knowledge society characterized by mass production of knowledge for wealth and employment by cultivating human mind, large-scale economic transformation, replacement of traditional workers by knowledge workers, and gradual displacement of agricultural and industrial workers by knowledge workers, this society has brought varieties of discontinuity, disorientation, conflict and has produced series of new identities. The chapter elaborates the process of construction of identity in the emerging knowledge society in India in the context of economic neoliberalism, advancement of economic globalization, and proliferation of ICTs and new and mass media— phenomena that have brought new economic momentum, mobility and new socio-cultural milieu on the one hand and new patterns of marginality of vast sections of population on the other. The chapter shows that by creating conditions for the emergence of varied patterns of social integration, by sustaining pre-existing social divisions, by bringing in diverse opportunities for social networking, and by keeping a vast section of population at the periphery, the emerging knowledge society has greatly contributed to the construction of multiple identities and fluidity in identity in a pre-existing part-agrarian and part-industrial society in India. The knowledge society has brought a mix of despair and hope in the Indian society. Though by reinforcing primordiality and pre-existing forms of marginalization, the knowledge society has brought despair instead of hope and aspiration, by upsetting many of the pre-existing arrangements and by bringing in new work, work relations, networks and social and occupational choices, it has also ushered a brave and smart world that enables even the marginalized to construct a new identity enabling them to challenge the structure of domination imposed on them. In many ways, the knowledge society has produced reflexive self-identity by igniting the human mind through new knowledge and connectivity.

Chapter 6, titled 'Ethnicity, Nationality, Citizenship and Identity: Accelerated Binaries and Complementarity of Differences', examines from a socio-historical perspective the interrelationships among these identities that have become eclectic across the space as the essence of these identities has been negotiated and constructed through social, cultural and political considerations in contemporary India. Ethnicity is founded on primordial and cultural orientation and is the oldest among all these identities.

Notwithstanding the claim that nationality is as ancient as human civilization, as an imaginary construction of the political and emotional unity of people in its modern incarnation it has started taking shape only in the 17th century. Citizenship, founded on rational and legal orientation, in its modern form has evolved from Western Europe through several stages since the 17th century and subsequently spread to other parts of the world. In operational term in India these identities are neither compartmentalized nor free from each other's influence. These factors make the relationships between these identities more complicated and unpredictable at times. Further, these identities operationally are still not fixed—they are getting evolved, transformed and contextualized over time and space. This chapter analyses the text and the context of the emergence of interface of these identities in terms of their situational contradictions and complementarities.

Chapter 7 is titled 'Partition, Alienhood, Migration and Shaping Up of an Indian Identity: The Cost and Joy of Being Patriotic'. It narrates the processes behind the construction and transformation of alien, immigrant identities to a liberal–patriotic one though biography of an individual, who migrated to India in his childhood in the aftermath of India's partition in 1947. The chapter documents the lived-in experiences and memories of alienhood of this individual and his family in East Pakistan in the wake of the Partition and post-Partition turmoil in the Indian subcontinent; persisting communal tension in then East Pakistan; immigration and disintegration of his family during the Indo-Pak war in 1965; their reunion during the Bangladesh War of Independence in 1971; socialization, upbringing and early education of this individual as a child and an adolescent in a remote Indian village; and his schooling and education in a multicultural environment therein. Through the experiences and memories of this individual, this chapter describes the processes of construction and transformation of his identity from an alien religious minority in East Pakistan to a migrant and refugee in India, and subsequently to a citizen and a liberal patriot. Moreover, the chapter describes how even in threat situations, his family survived with the help and cooperation of native Muslim families in the neighbourhood, and how his re-socialization and upbringing in a liberal multicultural village helped him encounter the forces of communalism and fundamentalism in the later part of his life in a cosmopolitan city.

1
Dynamics of Identity
Essence, Construction and Transformation

Identity is an agency for the change and transformation of a structured entity; it resonates with the resilience of such an entity. It forecasts and ushers change and transformation in society, and its movement results in the arrival of a new order by transforming a given structure into an agency. It reflects the arousal of reflexivity and the identification of purpose and meaning of an entity, and echoes the self-awareness of ontology of an entity. Identity, however, does not connote a fixed or static entity. Rather, as a dynamic and complex social reality, it interweaves through multiple foundations of its essence; undergoes frequent processes of construction, transformation and reconfiguration; and expresses itself through diverse modes of solidarity, fuzziness and fluidity. It intersects with the dichotomous logics of individual freedom and collective conscience, objective condition and subjective perception, and an end in itself and a means to an end for its expression, sustenance and reproduction. Furthermore, the dynamics of identity often acquire added complexity due to the very paradoxical nature of human beings themselves who are time and again described in contradictory terms to be moral, rational, sacrificing, considerate, social and intelligent on the one hand, and crooked, nasty, brutish and selfish on the other. In fact, the complexity of identity is as much linked to the realities of identity itself as to the descriptions of its reality that have not remained universal and singular in essence or in construction due to its socio-cultural specificity. However, despite such complexities and fuzziness, identity has always remained an important aspect of social reality and social analysis as it is essentially a social phenomenon, and there is good degree of underlying consistencies in the dynamics of identity.

In recent years, with the fast social transformation and increasing interconnectivity and mobility of people across the globe on the one hand and consolidation of new forms of social collectivities, manifestations of new forms of domination, marginalization and various types of discontent and protests at the grass-roots level on the other, the contours of contraction and configuration of identities have undergone phenomenal change. Simultaneously, there have also emerged diverse perspectives to analyse the dynamics of identity. Against these backdrops, this chapter is an attempt to develop an understanding of the nuances of identity in terms of its role, meaning, essence and construction within given socio-cultural arrangements; its formation, transformation and configuration within the broad processes of social transition such as those of collective mobilizations, modernization, colonization, globalization and penetration of ICTs and mass and social media; the emerging contexts of exercise of power, domination and marginalization; its strategic use as an end in itself and as a means to an end; and its interface with individualism, social self, reflexivity and individuation.

Identifying Identities: Intersecting with Role, Meaning, Legitimacy, Solidarity and Structural Arrangements

Though, in general parlance, identity is understood as an abstraction, in everyday life, it is evidently depicted through the performance of social roles, derivation of meaning and legitimacy, projection of social solidarity, and individual and group positions in the society. Within the structural arrangement of society, identity is usually described as a person's sense of self both as an individual—reflective of his or her interpersonal skills and distinctiveness—and as part of the larger society—focusing on the reference groups to which people belong and suggesting something about the ways people view the world (Bennett 2015, 405). Identity is often used as a cover term for a range of social personae, including social statuses, roles, positions, relationships and institutional and other relevant community identities, one may attempt to claim or assign in the course of one's social life (Ochs 1993, 288). Identity thus represents a complex connotation.

In society, every identity interacts in an interactive plural situation as 'I', 'we', 'our', 'he'/'she', 'they', 'their' or 'others', etc., by acquiring specific descriptive individual or collective names. While individually they are represented by individual characters, collectively they are represented by the collectivities of caste, class, gender, race, ethnicity, age set, language, religion, nation, citizenship, peasants, farmers, workers, countrymen, etc., and many other such entities. These identities are socially and culturally grounded within specific socio-cultural traditions, interactional patterns and the institutional arrangements of society. All identities are distinctive and differentiated from each other through their role performances, products, expression, assertion and representation as individual or collective entities located within the given social structure and processes of society. They simultaneously possess the potential to act as agencies in society through the roles they perform; the new meaning, individuation and solidarity they produce; the legitimacy they derive; and the self-perception they develop through their actions.

Identities as Social Role, Meaning and Self-Discovery

Members of society are posited in multiple role sets, and many of these roles are interconnected. Though all identities are distinctively differentiated both by their essence and the processes of construction, they are also interlinked and interconnected, especially through the roles they perform in society. Stryker (1990) points out that in a differentiated society, identities represent themselves 'as organized systems of encompassing interactions and role relationships cross cutting each other's boundaries. They also simultaneously function as sets of discrete identities or internalized role designations'. As social beings, people possess and represent multiple identities; they can invoke different identities in different situations or can invoke a given identity in a variety of situations. Hence, identities 'can be defined as differential probability'. In society, while social actors make choices for assertion of or association with specific identities, the choices reflect the relative location of the identities associated with those roles. Thus, according to Lawler (2008),

> No one has only one identity, in the sense that everyone must either consciously or not, identifies with more than one identities. This is more than combining multiple identities in an additive way ... Different forms of identity, then should be seen as interactive and mutually constitutive rather than additive. (3; cf. Bradley 2016, 43–44)

It should also be seen as constitution or interweaving of multiple roles through association with multiple identities. However, identities cannot simply be understood in terms of objective role performance. There are in-depth subjective meanings attached to them for their substance and transformative expression.

According to Castells (1997), there are differences between identities and roles. While roles recognize functions, identities recognize the source of meaning, that is, the symbolic identification of the purpose of action by a social actor. He also adds the process of 'individuation'—the process of bringing unconscious to a level of consciousness and integrating this consciousness with the whole personality, to find meaning for the formation of identity of people. To him, identities are, in essence, sources of meaning for actors themselves who also construct these identities through a process of individuation. Individuation refers to the process of construction of meaning on the basis of cultural attributes. Although identities can also originate from dominant institutions, they can become identities only when and if social actors internalize them and construct their meaning around their individuation (Castells 1997, 7).

Cerutti (2001) has gone further by observing that the process of construction of new identities leads to self-discovery of the actor(s). It creates new meaning out of newly formed self-perception and self-recognition of the actor. This new meaning plays a crucial role in the formation, transformation and resurgence of identity. This signifies a shift in their essence from structure to agency, gives birth to a new worldview and provides legitimacy to the development of the actor's newly acquired self-perception, his actions, his transformations and his undoing. Moreover, Cerutti (2001) has emphasized two important dimensions related to the establishment and transmission of identity: (a) it creates a source of meaning to provide legitimacy to the decisions, actions and unity of a group's existence, and (b) it also defines the outer limits of the group's solidarity.

The patterns of role performance and the processes of acquiring meaning, individuation, self-perception, recognition and solidarity, which play crucial roles in transforming an essence to an agency of identity are, however, not autonomous. Rather, these encounter the conditionality of the structural arrangements of the society and the dynamics of configuration of power, knowledge and culture therein. Let us discuss the location of identity with these arrangements and configuration.

Social Structural Arrangements, Power and Identity

Men as social animals are conditioned by the structural arrangements and processes of society. Within these arrangements, society, its norms, values, etc., get deposited in a person, making him accept and endure social distinctiveness and differentiation. These arrangements are deeply linked to the exercise of power and political action. Hence, Bourdieu's (1984, 1986) concept of *habitus* is rather very crucial. According to Bourdieu, power is culturally and symbolically created and continuously re-legitimized through an interplay of agency and structure that takes shape through *habitus*: 'the socialized norms and tendencies that guide behavior and thinking'. To him, it is through *habitus* that the society becomes deposited in people in the forms of lasting dispositions, or trained capacities and structured propensities to think, feel and act in determinant ways, which then guide them (Wacquant 2005, 316). These dispositions, which are shaped by past events and structures and which shape current practices and structures, importantly condition our very perception of these arrangements. Hence, *habitus* is created and reproduced unconsciously 'without any deliberate pursuit of coherence ... without any conscious concentration' (Bourdieu 1984, 170). Further, according to Bourdieu, social order is progressively inscribed in people's minds through social, cultural and symbolic capital 'melding the system of education, language, judgments, and values, methods of classification and activities of everyday life. These altogether lead to our unconscious acceptance of social differences and hierarchies, sense of one's place and behavior of self-exclusion' (1986, 241). These many ways essentialize a social entity within a given structure, constraining it to be transformed into an agency of identity.

For Foucault, identity is deeply linked to the system of power and domination within a given framework of culture. For him, the configuration of discourses, knowledge and power in human sciences has deeper social implications. Though the discourses aim to reveal truth, in essence, they control an individual. Foucault's genecology of knowledge and power suggests that the subject, form and extent of social control and the forms of authority, form and extent of acceptability of behaviours are defined by culture that is shaped by the social structure; moreover, the social structure itself is shaped by scientific discourses and discipline. Hence, individual identity is interwoven with the genecology of knowledge and power and its reproduction that control individual identity in this 'disciplinary society' (Foucault 1989).

Though the structural arrangements of society produce distinctive tendencies in the formation of identities, they do not always remain unaltered. There are always the possibilities of self-discovery and reconstruction of identity through encounter and intersectionality with varieties of phenomena and processes. This opens up the possibilities of choice and exercise of reasoning in getting associated with identities. In this regard, Sen's (1999) observation is very crucial.

Reason, Choice and Identity

To Sen (1999), though identity is central to the community life of humans and they tend to comprehend identity in absolute and subjective terms, especially in the context of primordial bondage and community living, identity does not remain subjective and absolute all the time. The centrality of human life, according to Sen, is conditioned by inherited socio-cultural processes on the one hand and by reasons and alternative choices on the other. In an interactive world, individuals are faced with varieties of choices. While extensively examining the question as to whether our identities are constructed/shaped by choice or by reasoning or by passive recognition, Sen accepts that neither the choice to be identified is permanent in society nor are there unlimited choices to identify with. Even as one discovers his/her identity at a certain stage or in certain conditions of life and even though the scope of his/her choices widens, he/she has to make the choices.

> Choices have to be made even when discoveries occur. The unquestioning acceptance of social identity may also involve a radical shift in the identity having accepted as discovery rather than reasoned choice. For example, a shift from the holistic to sectarian identities may be a product of unquestioning acceptance of coercive arrangement. (Sen 1999, 21)

Ideally, identities are formed in contexts of plurality, choice and reasoning. According to Sen (1999, 22), 'to deny plurality, choice and reasoning in identity can be a source of repression; choice is possible and important in individual conduct and social decisions even if we remain oblivious of it'. However, at times, one identity is privileged over and even tyrannized by the other. The phenomena of 'new tyrannies' emerge in the form of a newly asserted identity that tyrannizes by eliminating other identities. These identities may have a political role.

isolated in his or her inner world and going his or her own way without caring about others' ways. To Sartre, whenever and wherever individuals do something—even just walking in the street—they are accompanied by the silent companion of 'social control' as the public space is wholly under the control of the established power. Every individual, whatever he/she thinks of the manifest public discourse, is conditioned to accept that 'all is well' and 'nothing can be changed'. Whether he/she looks at all the others to work, comply and keep quiet, he/she thinks of himself/herself alone in secretly rejecting this social order. When, however, frustration mounts in each individual, it takes only a small event to trigger an instantaneous and massive change of state, from *serie* to *groups en fusion*. As soon as each person in a serialized mass realizes that some others contest the established power and takes one step forward to openly express support, a chain reaction spreads through the atomized series and transforms it into a fluid group (*groups en fusion*) which instantly moves from the status of a subordinated passive object to that of a subject capable of action' (cf. Bertaux 1990, 155–56). Thus, collective actions construct the required space for transformation of structure into agency. According to Pizzorno, the direct participation in collective action is an essential component and 'connecting a process of formation for a collective identity' (1978, 293).

In the Marxian analysis, transformation in the collective identity has been viewed as transformation of class identities from that of 'class-in-itself' to 'class-for-itself'. An identity is constructed not solely on the basis of objective economic conditions but through the process of acquiring subjective consciousness about the objective conditions that transform a social entity into a self-conscious identity to bring transformation in the pre-existing social order. The social collectivities with a common economic position and conflicting economic interests vis-à-vis the others form the objective basis for a class-in-itself. This social class without a conscious identity is incapable of collective action as it lacks subjective consciousness. The class-in-itself acquires the collective identity of class-for-itself by getting mediated through class consciousness (Marx 1976). Significantly, in the Marxian analysis of class transformation, all pre-existing social entities such as caste, gender, race, ethnicity, etc., are subsumed under the class identity, and class formation and social transformation are largely conditioned by economic determinism.

Contemporary research on social identities, movements and transformation shows that collective actions, which bring solidarity and transform collective identity, are not always for the gratification of

Thus, though some social entities acquire a concrete essence through *habitus*, they also simultaneously undergo a process of construction. Though they are situationally represented by a singular term, they carry multiple possibilities of transformation and reconfiguration. These possibilities can be better understood through the interplay of the 'essential' character of identity at one end and its subjective 'construction' at the other.

Identity as Essential vs Identity as Construction

The process of formation of social 'we-ness' as a reflection of collective identity has remained deeply grounded in the classical sociological literature of Durkheim's 'collective conscience', Marx's 'class consciousness', Tönnies' 'Gemeinschaft', Cooley's 'primary groups', Redfield's 'little community' and so on. However, there have been diverse views on the formation of these identities. Identity studies have long inherited the debate as to whether individual and group identities are fixed, non-compromising and unchanging or whether these are flexible and amenable for change according to the need of the circumstances. The essentialists have seen collective identity to remain rooted in the notion of 'we-ness' of a group, stressing the similarities or shared attributes around which group members join together. To them, these attributes are the 'natural' or 'essential' characteristics of a group 'emerging from physiological traits and predispositions, geographical features, or the properties of structural locations'. The social constructionists, on the other hand, reject any category that sets forward essential or core features as the unique property of a collective's members. 'From this perspective, every collective becomes a social artifact—an entity molded, refabricated, and mobilized in accord with reigning cultural scripts and centers of power' (Cerulo 1997, 386–87).

To the constructionists, the relationship between culture and identity is intrinsic. As culture is specific to all social groups, so are the processes of construction and manifestation of identity. Hence, according to Hall (1996), 'identity is not a universal but a culture-specific discursive construction, this is formed continuously and it is a continually shifting description of us'. We can thus conceive of people as operating across and within multiple subject positions constituted by the intersections of varieties of identities. Hence, there is no automatic connection between various descriptions of identity as they can be articulated in different ways based on cultural specifications. This ascertains the formation and sustenance of multiple identities in society, which configure the weaving of the patterns of identity from the discourses of class, caste, ethnicity, nation, religion, region and language, race, gender, etc. Thus there is an element of plasticity in the formation of identity (Barker and Galasinski 2001). In fact, cultural and political significance lies in the plasticity of identity that depicts the shifting and changing character of identities and their transformation over time. Hence, identities tend to be subjective construction of mainly their objectively fixed phenomena (Hall 1996; cf. Stewart 2001). The inherent facets of shifting descriptions, multiple-subject position, plasticity of identity, etc., only underline the complex dynamics associated with construction of identity.

Though construction of identity has emerged to be an integral part of everyday social reality, many are of the view that social construction does not necessarily represent the true self. It may be deceptive and an expression of self-denial and revelation of falsehood.

Social Construction, Social Reality and Falsehood

The social construction of identity is not always based on an individual's choice and self-perception of reality itself. Levine (1999) elaborates that the idea that (social) reality is 'socially constructed' only reflects ambivalence towards reality; it denies social reality to be objectively grounded in a relationship with natural imperatives, understands individuals as social constructs and undermines them as a project on the basis of their constructed identities. Identity is a product of the way 'we' are seen by 'others' that does not reach down to the depths of our being (Levine 1999, 81–82).

It is further argued that as identity is dependent on how we are seen by others, it is not autonomous but contingent on context. Thus, the social construction of reality means the domination of the individual by his or her identities that have no reality at all, but only appearance (for others). 'That we exist only in the eyes of others, and that to exist in the eyes of others is to lose something vital about existence. There is in these both a profound need for and fear of being identified, which is to say, being known by "others"' (Levine 1999, 89–91). Hence, being for 'others' is an imposition and also 'a form of deprivation, though what we are deprived of is not clearly expressed'. This leads to the construction of a 'false self', which according to Winnicott (1965) hides the vital by becoming false to self and true to others. Since being for others is vital, having an identity can be anything more than the loss of (true) self (Levine 1999, 83; Winnicott 1965). The process of formation of identity in terms of 'others' has acquired added complexity in wake of perpetration of ICTs wherein the 'significant others' have gradually been replaced by 'significant elsewhere'. Hence, the false self acquires more fluidity and deception from reality (discussed further in the section on ICTs and identity).

Symbols, Identity, Solidarity and the 'Others'

Many identities are constructed around several cultural symbols. Many of these symbols, like totems, are socio-historically inherited. Most cultures and societies have their own variety of totems, for example, cow for the Hindus. Similarly, owl, lion, horse, fox, swan, etc., are totemic animals for other societies. New symbols are also created; for example, with the birth of a nation, its national flag, national anthem, etc., are created. Significantly, many of these symbols are socially, culturally and ecologically linked to life, similar to other symbols such as food, clothing and ornaments. Through symbols, one not only constructs solidarity among the members of one's own society but also identifies the others.

Postmodernist Critics on Identity

The social construction of identity takes shape within each category of generalized identities. However, such construction is not sui generis. It is rather widely shaped and reshaped by the dynamics of power and the dominant institutions of society. Hence, the postmodernists challenge the generalized description and the essentialists' perception of identity. Though the postmodernists widely accept the position of the constructionists, they find serious flaws in the constructionists' arguments as they simply list the process of identity construction; accept identity categories getting constructed through interactive efforts without highlighting essential variations within each collective identity such as women, class, race, caste, etc.; and underemphasize the role of power involved in the process of identity construction (e.g., Calhoun 1995, 199; cf. Cerulo 1997, 392–93; Connell 1987; Gilman 1985). According to the postmodernists, identities are not subjects of simple observation and reductionism, and there is a need for an analytical focus on public discourse as a source of power that privileges one identity over the other. Moreover, they also emphasize a need to deconstruct established identity categories and explore the full range of 'being'. They also question the model that equates discourse with truth, and aim to expose the ways in which discourse is objectified as truth and helps to sustain collective definitions, social arrangements and hierarchies of power (Cerulo 1997, 385). They specify 'changes in everyday life, social relations and the lived textures of identity', and believe 'in the deconstruction and reconstruction of the self as fluid, fragmented, discontinuous, decentred, dispersed, culturally eclectic, hybrid-like identities'. Hence, postmodern identity means

> life lived in the wake of collapse of modernist grand narratives of reasons, truth, progress and universal freedom, with a profound recognition that the enlightenment search for solid foundations and certitude was ultimately self-destructive. Identity in the post-traditional world of post modern, becomes principally performative—depthless, playful, ironic, just a plurality of selves, scripts, discourses and desires. (Elliott 2015, 9)

In the wake of penetration of new social, economic, political and technological forces, the state of flux has replaced the earlier forcing of stable group membership (Bococks 1993, 31), and identity is becoming relatively free-flouting, detached from the bases of social structure which used to constrain it. People are now relatively freer to pick and choose which of the various forms of 'you' on offer they want to be 'me' (Weeks 1990, 88; cf. Bradley 2016, 41). By taking a postmodernist stand, Hall (1990) further adds that 'instead of thinking of identity as an already accomplished fact ... we should think, instead, of identity as a production which is never complete, always is process, and always constituted within, not outside, representation'. According to him,

> cultural identity ... is a matter of becoming as well as 'being'. It belongs to the future as well as to the past ... But like everything which is historical they undergo constant transformation. Far from being constantly fixed in some essentialised past, they are subject to the continuous play of history, culture and power. (Hall 1990, 222–25)

However, since the latter half of the 1990s, there have been mounting criticisms of postmodern identities. The postmodern culture of 'anything goes' may have seemed liberating and intoxicating to some, but for others, it was simply another narrative about 'endings', with little of value to say about the novelty of identity transformation in the current age. It has also been pointed out that modernity is far from being over and the customary ways of organizing identities continue. According to Elliott (2015, 13),

> postmodernism had powerfully mixed transformations in culture and identity in equal measure. If there was pulsating desire and frenetic depthlessness to postmodern identity, there was also cultural dispersal, discord and disillusionment. In this, postmodernism made a fetish out of difference, thereby underwriting the plural, multiple and fragmented texture of human existence in an age of intensive computerization and high tech.

Social identity is constructed through the processes of interaction and daily engagement with both the local and wider society. The processes of identity construction get widely influenced by the economic, political, social and cultural institutional arrangements of society; get negotiated with historical and lived-in experiences of the people in society; and get interconnected with varieties of social collectivities. The processes of essentialization and construction of identity have experienced added complexities in the wake of its encountering with the forces of social movements, advancement of modernization, Westernization, globalization and penetration of ICTs and mass and social media, etc., on the one hand and changing convictions and aspirations of members of society on the other.

Social Movements and Transformation of Identities

Though social collectivities exist as essential categories, and they function as parts of a given social structure by exhibiting continuous and patterned interaction, they also get formed, transformed and rejuvenated as identities through their participation in collective actions. Collective actions, especially social movements, generate new collective identity or common identity, leading to the formation of a unified group out of scattered individuals, for example, transforming *serie* into *groups en fusion* (Sartre 1960), or this may lead to the transformation of an ordinary collectivity, that is, 'class-in-itself', into a self-conscious group for collective action, that is, 'class-for-itself' (Marx 1976), etc. Sartre calls *serie* the normal state of crowds, that is, a series of atomized individuals, each one seen as

Dynamics of Identity 23

economic interests but also for the realization of cherished subjective values, culture, and morality. In the context of new social movements, such as those for national liberation, environment, women's rights, human rights, etc., collective identities are founded on 'subjectivity' and 'idealism' to bring a drastic change in the fabric of social life (Bertaux 1990, 153). These new collective identities are voluntarily conceived 'to empower' members in defence of their identity (Melucci 1992, 1996). Hence Eyerman and Jamison 1990 candidly elaborate:

> By producing new knowledge, by reflecting on their own cognitive identity, by saying what they stand for, by challenging the dominant assumptions of the social, they develop new ideas those are fundamental to the process of human creativity. These help develop worldviews that restructure cognition, and re-cognize reality itself. (Eyerman and Jamison 1991, 161–66)

Morality, humanism and intersubjectivity, which have remained to be crucial concerns of new social movements since the 1960s, now encounter phenomenal challenge from sectarian and fundamentalist resurge of collective mobilization. With many of the old conflicts now getting institutionalized, new conflicts based on primordiality surfacing across the world, and social movements becoming a permanent component of political-interest mediation, collective mobilization of various forms contribute to the resurgence of varieties of identities in contemporary societies. Within these processes, while many of the predefined radical identities have transformed towards an institutionalized direction, some identities have also emerged with an ultra-radical image through coercive collective mobilization. The new world, along with the proliferation of environmentalist, human rights, gender, LGBT community, peasant, farmer, etc., identities, also encounters the inverted-image sectarian radical identities in the name of cultural/religious and other primordial collectivities. This inverted image has taken the form of social anti-movements which

> instead of promoting a social or a cultural identity, champions some abstract entity, essence or symbol, and speak in the name of a purity or homogeneity. Instead of building relationships with other actors, agreeing on the principles of debates and negotiations, they champion absolutes, and adopt do or die attitudes. And if they appear in an arena where social movements also exist, they try to destroy these movements, and fight against them. (Wieviorka 2005, 18)

The emergence of social anti-movements in many ways contributes to the formation of fundamentalist identities that are rooted in sectarianism widely guided by divisive forces and the idea of binaries. In the wake of globalization and socio-cultural decontextualization, not only has there been the proliferation of multiple identities, but there has also emerged the tendency of reinforcement of primordiality. While primordiality emphasizes on the essential dynamics of identity for keeping people rooted to their cultural heritage and history, at times and places, it is also used to introduce sectarianism—constructing an inverted image of identity by putting one group against the others by propagating love for one's own group's members and hate for the other groups' members.

Though identities are formed and transformed from within, they also get constructed, rejuvenated and transformed along with the broad processes of social transformation, modernization, colonization, globalization and so on. Now let us examine the changing facets of identities within these processes.

Social Transformation, Modernity, Colonization, Globalization and Identity: Changing Facets of Fluidity and Solidarity

Wider social transformation has always affected the process of formation and transformation of identity, as for Marx, the identity of class has undergone radical changes with the rise of capitalism; for Weber, status group with rationalization; and for Durkheim, collective conscience with increasing complexities in the social organization. Most of the pre-existing social identities of the Western world, and a fewer in other parts of the world, experienced new waves of transformation in the wake of Enlightenment and expansion of modernization in the 17th century, rise of the nationalism spirit in the 18th century, rise of fascism in the Western world and socialism in Eastern Europe and Asia in the 20th century, and rise of nationalism in colonized countries in the 20th century and thereafter. These faster changes and transformations in the social, economic and political fabric of society deeply impacted the process of construction and reconfiguration of social identities in these broad historical epochs. Since the latter part of the last century, especially with the decline of modern industrial society, the advancement of post-industrial society and the emergence of knowledge society, 'identity has become a dominant intellectual discourse for grasping the processes of larger and faster social change and transformation'. According to Elliott, these faster and wider changes, transformations and upheavals have brought a fundamental shift in the character of identities. These have transfigured them to become 'secularized, rationalized, administered, de-centered, dispersed, isolated, fragmented, fractured or split' (Elliott 2015, 1–2).

Since the 17th century, human societies have started to interconnect with each other through the forces of colonization, modernization, industrialization, Westernization and, of late, globalization. Owing to increasing interaction with cross-cultural economic, political and technological forces, a division is successfully constructed between the modern, Western and global identities at one end and local identities on the other. While the former identities are constructed to be universal, cosmopolitan, progressive, hegemonic and accommodative, the latter ones are perceived to be parochial, traditional and sectarian. Moreover, the former ones are designated as unstoppable penetration and expansion of superior processes for social, economic and political reproduction, consumption and distribution over the local inferior ones in the name of integration of the world with a common economy, polity and culture.

Each society is however marked by a distinctive variety of social interactivity and social solidarity. Conventionally, the local/traditional societies are marked by homogeneity, predominance of traditional social bondage and adherence to social solidarity based on informal and primordial informal affiliations. As these societies make their onward march from primitive to modern, from pre-industrial to industrial and from local to global, they dislocate many of the predominant identities by constructing several new ones out of the old ones. Such construction has contributed to both the consolidation and fragmentation of the pre-existing identities. This march, however, has not been automatic. In most cases, this has been imposed from above, and in the process, the native collectivities have lost their innocence.

Modernity: From Fuzziness to Counted Identities

Modernity was the first major colonial cultural and administrative intervention on the colonized society. It has constructed different varieties of identities out of the old ones through the application of its own tools of administration. In many places, it has given the pre-existing fuzzy communities the shape of colonial identities. According to Kaviraj (1995), modernity reconstructs new identities out of earlier ones by way of creating new forms of belonging. By introducing the modern English language, census, mapping, etc., modernity has transformed small, approximate and tentative forms of the social universe into the typical modern image of mapped and counted identities; specifically, it created identities of majorities and minorities. He further states, 'the majorities of the census, given the logic of modem politics, hold a permanent menace, and correspondingly subject the minorities to constant reminders of an equally permanent helplessness'. Such enumeration and modern mapping, in actual terms, converted the fuzzy communities—interconnected communities with 'a lack of clarity or objectification in terms of space and the geographical distribution of social groups, unclarity in terms of numbers, and about boundary between the self and the other'—to enumerated communities. This could effectively be seen either as a conspiracy of the colonial administration to divide the indigenous people or as 'an inevitable part of the modernist reconstitution of identity which colonial rulers used to their benefit'. This resulted in the altering of the traditional identities such as caste and religion by the forces of modernity. Modernity again submerged these enumerated identities of caste and religion in the identity of a nation. Regarding nation, Kaviraj elaborates that it is a new, constructed, willed and imagined type of identity, entirely produced by the modern imagination, which submerges all religious, caste, etc., identities (Kaviraj 1996). Such construction has contributed largely to the essentialization of primordial identities on the one hand and their reconfiguration into larger abstract entities on the other. It has made the process of identity construction layered and fragmented. In the contemporary world, the process of fragmentation of identity has furthered. Though there has been the process of consolidation of identities, it has been at different levels and in diverse forms.

ICTs, New and Social Media, Globalization and Identity

In recent years, the processes of globalization, initiation of new economic orders, revolution in communication technologies, and ushering of a knowledge society have promoted an unprecedented and ever faster movement of persons, goods and services, ideas and images, and animate and inanimate objects across the globe. The world now posits itself with a host of dichotomies that demonstrates its multi-centredness at one end and concentration of power and wealth at the other, and social decontextualization at one end and connectivity at the other. Hence, many social identities have apparently been disorganized at the roots and simultaneously experience new forms of isolation, reconstruction and rejuvenation.

It is now observed that in the decentred world of postmodernity, the core experience of everyday life—identity—has also been understood in terms of new structures of seduction, securitization, mediatization and virtualization. Now,

> culture in the form of de-centered and differential identity seemed increasingly out of step with our fast globalizing world—particularly the globalizing forces of media, communications and culture. It seemed difficult to track signs of cultural difference and identity diversity in a world increasingly dominated by News Corporation, CNN and Yahoo. (Elliott 2015, 14)

Scholars have also developed contradictory views on the contribution of these processes towards the articulation of self-planning, reflexivity and self-awareness of people in this emerging, fast-changing society.

Reflexivity and Individualization in Identity in Reflexive and Accelerated Modernity

This new order, in many ways, has transformed the logic of organizing societies; their organization of production, production relations and culture; the process of formation of social networks; and the process of construction of conventional, stable self-identify. In this globalized world with increased instability and fragmentation, most societies realize the existence of identity as half flow and half being. Here, 'for most individuals and social groups, reflexive self-planning has become impossible, except for the elite inhabiting the timeless space of flows of global network and their ancillary locales' (Castells 1997, 11).

Giddens (1991), however, finds the world to increasingly become commonplace and a single world having a unitary framework of experience. Though this world, to him, creates new forms of fragmentation and dispersal, making humanity become 'profoundly disembedded across the space', it is also creating conditions for self-identity to acquire self-reflexivity in the emerging world. To him, in the fast-moving world, while the social realities are getting de/reconstructed on a daily basis, many of the pre-existing identities are getting decontextualized or redefined in the new social and technological order; social existence is becoming atomized even within the intensive interactive world; old social bondage, solidarities and images are becoming fragile; and individual identity does no longer remain merely a state of self-representation. Locating self-identity within the interplay of local and global interactive processes, he, however, narrates that in the context of the postindustrial order, the self now becomes a reflexive project—'Reflexivity organizes self-planning ... (and) becomes a central feature of the structuring of the self-identity'.

The emerging life scenarios of people condition them to be the bearers of self-reflexive identity. Here, identity as a self-reflexive project creates and maintains the story of who we are and how we are. It is a person's own reflexive understanding of his/her biography. Self-identity has continuity—that is, it cannot easily be completely changed at will—but that continuity is only a product of the person's reflexive beliefs about his/her own biography (Giddens 1991, 53).

Similarly, for Beck (2009), under the conditions of reflexive or accelerated modernization, as tradition become less secure and reality is being taken for granted, the process of identity production has become increasingly open to choice, scrutiny and revision. Beck has termed it a process of individualization that doubts the importance of collective meaning and action and control on people in contemporary society. According to him, to live in a de-traditionalized world is to live in a society where life is no longer lived as fate or destiny. As the rise of reflexive modernization looks for justification, re-elaboration and reworking in social living, 'the integration of individualized individuals into the network of broader social relations necessarily arise in novel forms at both the micro and macro levels' (Beck 2009; cf. Elliott 2015, 14). Elliott and Lemert (2006) have taken it further to show that now there has emerged new individualism across the media-driven world that looks for continual self-actualization and instant self-reinvention which is taking place, among various other things, through the rise of plastic surgery and the instant identity makeovers of reality TV, compulsive consumerism, speed dating, therapy culture and so on. Now with the increasing desire for instant gratification and immediate results, developing habit of communication with others through social media across the planet in seconds, buying flashy consumer goods with the click of a mouse, and drifting in and out of relations with others without long-term commitments, the practice of identity has acquired a new height of individualism (cf. Elliott 2015, 15).

Identity through Generalized Elsewhere

The extensive usage of ICTs and new media such as mass email, Facebook, Skype, blogs, Twitter, WhatsApp, etc., has significantly contributed to the formation of Web-based epistemic virtual communities by challenging the established notions of identities that are founded on co-presence in the world (Cerulo 1997, 388). These have altogether changed the backdrop against which identity is constructed by reorganizing the sites of social interaction and reframing the generalized others and the 'generalized elsewhere and by weakening the connections between physical and social place'. This has also located the self in new hybrid arenas of action by bringing in new networks between public and private, signalling new types of performances and forming new collective configurations (Meyrowitz 1989, 309). The emerging social order has also produced new social boundaries, fluidity and fragmentations.

Solidarity and Fluidity in Identity

ICTs and globalization as the co-constituents of the information age are supposed to bring in a unitary framework of thought, action and culture by demolishing the pre-defined territoriality, bringing in common sets of institutions, and transgressing many of the pre-existing arrangements, thereby constructing a global collective identity of human beings with common thoughts, aspirations, appetite and morality. Though ICTs and globalization have been able to construct a powerful thin community of global corporate elite, a community of floating global *netizens*, and have been able to spread a market-driven consumerist culture, the process of formation of a mass global identity with common morality has remained a mirage. Rather, the ICTs-driven globalized world has brought a lot of fragmentations in the pre-existing collective self by uprooting predefined boundaries of social solidarity and injecting an increasing flow of instability, mobility and migration of people across the space. Hence, for many, collective identity has become a contested reality. It is observed that human societies now experience an increasingly unequal flow of people, information, money, images, risks, practices and emotions without clear beginning or end points. Within these emerging complexities, there have been the manifestations of fluid-like elements in society; and the society is becoming increasingly subject to shock waves of fluidity rather than solidarity, and public experience of self rather than reflections of collective identity (Urry 2000; cf. McDonald 2002).

In an emerging society, collective identities are often constructed on the basis of temporarily perceived articulated ideals and common interests. A significant number of these collectivities have contradictory interests and goals. Hence, it is inevitable that group memberships tend to be more fluid than solidified and are of varying strength. Thus, fluid and fuzzy memberships and the emerging fluidity of identity make the social order very weak. The increasing quantum of social mobility, interaction with the social world and fast exchange of information and ideas have provided people a significant space to exercise their choice for the assertion, invocation or transformation of existing identities or the articulation of alternative ones. Though ICTs and globalization have enabled people to choose an identity or identities at any particular point of time from a basket of multiple options, and many choose several options simultaneously to fulfil their need, these contribute more to the fuzziness or fluidity of identity than its solidarity. However, it is not an era of end of solidarity; rather, solidarity comes back through the neglected root of primordiality.

Globalization, ICTs and Resurgence of Primordial Identity

In a decontextualized and decentralized globalized world where people are made to be virtually 'elsewhere' and substantively only in a limited space, they tend to substantively become loners in the real world. People mostly get integrated with the larger formal society without having any intense and in-depth commitment. Though they tend to be members of many social groups, they also simultaneously want to remain grounded in the society through some roots. Hence, the primordial affiliation through linguistic, regional, caste, religion, ethnic, etc., identities comes in a big way in the world of such fluidly to provide such roots. Thus, along with the increasing demand for membership in clubs, alumni associations, religious cults, etc., rejuvenation of association with primordial groups has significantly increased for many. In this fluid world, for a vast section, primordial linkage has proved to be more stable than the socially constructed non-primordial ones.

ICTs, Globalization, Dominant Institutions and Identity

Economic globalization and ICTs have brought fundamental change in the nature of the state, multinational corporations and other dominant institutions of society. With the spread of economic neoliberalism, the relationships of these institutions with the people and society have taken new shapes. The functioning of these institutions has produced new forms of inequality, exclusion, domination and resistance in society. Against these backdrops in this emerging society, identities have been multifaceted and are formed diversely in terms of their relation with the power structure and dominant institutions in society. Castells (1997) has described these identities as follows:

- *Legitimizing Identity:* Introduced by the dominant institutions of society to extend and rationalize their domination vis-à-vis social actors.
- *Resistant Identity*: Generated by those actors that are in positions/conditions devaluated and/or stigmatized by the logic of domination, thus building trenches of resistance and survival on the basis of principles different from or opposed to those permeating the institutions of society.
- *Project Identity:* Constructed by social actors on the basis of whatever cultural materials are available to them to build a new identity that redefines their position in society, and by so doing, they seek the transformation of the whole structure.

These identities are, however, not fixed. According to Castells (1997), identities that start as resistance may reduce to project identity and may also, along the course of history, become dominant institutions of society, thus becoming legitimizing identities to rationalize their domination. In a network society, a large section of people who experience economic, cultural and political disfranchisement tend to be attracted to communal identity. They develop 'the commune of resistance' to defend their space and their places against the placeless logic of the space of flows characterizing social dominations in the information age (Castells 1997, 358). Castells has also talked about ludic identities where identities are flexible and are expressed diversely to respond to the situations.

Multiple Manifestations of Identity: Submission and Indifference

Though globalization has produced a good space for occupational and political choice through mobility and migration, the gap between the availability of choice and the capacity to exercise such choice has remained very large, especially for the marginalized sections of population whose life situation is conditioned by predominance of illiteracy, poverty, feudal domination and capacity and knowledge deprivation. Even though they have the potential for resistance against marginality, they seldom come out in the open for expressing their discontent. There may be the temporary arousal of assertiveness, either because of pressure from the community or motivation from political entrepreneurs, but they tend to withdraw or join back their world of passivity due to unforeseen fear or distrust in the idea of change or their empowerment in society. Many rejuvenated identities may end up becoming an 'entity of a beneficiary'—a dependent collectivity—rather than becoming an 'identity of a change agent'. However, a section of such identities may retain their autonomy or may become assertive, depending on their association with specific organizational, leadership or ideological resources.

Globalization and Reproduction of Marginal Identities in Urban Areas

In the wake of neoliberal globalization and the emerging domination of transnational corporate capital, the construction of marginal identity has taken a new shape globally, both in remote and rural areas and at fringe sites of urban areas. Marginalization relegates people to the margins of society, socially, culturally, economically and politically; deprives them of economic, social and cultural capitals; increases their livelihood insecurity, unemployment, poverty, social segregation and cultural de-recognition. Marginalization is reproduced through socialization and the functioning of the institutional arrangement of society, and is reinforced by globalization in varieties of ways.

Though globalization has been successful in promoting and sustaining the domination of the dominant sections of society, the social and economic position of the marginalized sections has widely remained unaltered. Globalization in fact has not only reinforced but has also produced varieties of marginal identities by changing the nature of economic activities and the patterns of engagement of labour force therein.

Sassen (1996) has pointed out that with globalization, cities have emerged to be sites for transinternationalization and valorization of corporate capital in real estate and telecommunications that yield speedy profits from financial services with intensification of work in these areas. In these cities, while the highly educated workforce is employed in service and get an increasingly higher income, the poor, migrants and women are employed as all varieties of manual, low-or-medium-skilled workers and earn a low income. Global cities now host, on the one hand, the upwardly mobile educated workers with transnational identity and, on the other, the disadvantaged workers whose 'self and identities are not necessarily embedded in the nation or the national community'. These cities now have emerged to be strategic and fragmented sites for the formation of dominant transnational identities with a rich, new transnational professional workforce on the one hand and poor migrant workers endeavouring to re-territorialize 'local sub-cultures' on the other. Within these global cities, immigration and ethnicity are constituted as 'otherness' by becoming de- and re-territorialized and excluded from the main stream of the society. These processes of construction of 'otherness' altogether cause 'unmooring of identities from what have been the traditional sources of identity, such as the nation or the village'. These developments promote new notions of community of membership of entitlement to secure the position of transnational elites, while the marginalized workers are relegated to be the 'others' through economic and cultural uprooting. According to Sassen (1996), these cities are now taking shape to be the sites for politics going beyond culture and identity even though there are partly likely to be embedded in it (211–20).

Globalization has also produced deconsolidation of identity for the highly mobile global elites from a different direction. In this context, Castells (1997) observed that with globalization, technological revolution, transformation of capitalism and the demise of statism, informationalism is disintegrating the existing mechanism of social control and political representation. With the exception of a small elite of globapolitans (half beings, half flows), people all over the world resent the loss of control over their lives. In a network society,

> [t]hus, on the one hand, the dominant, global elites inhabiting the space of flows tend to consist of identity-less individuals (citizens of the world); while, on the other hand, people resisting economic, cultural, and political disfranchisement tend to be attracted to communal identity. (Castells 1997)

Marginal Identities in Rural Areas

With the emergence of forces of consumerism, globalization, ICTs and social and mass media, a new economic and socio-cultural milieu is in the making in rural areas. This milieu aims not only to convert the rural gentry to be the consumer of global goods and services but also to replace traditional agriculture with agro industry, subsistence crops with cash crops, preservation with consumerism, local culture with global culture, nativity with migration, and indigenization with globalization. The lack of integration with this emerging milieu not only causes poverty, unemployment and frustration, but also self-destruction and suicide. While a section of upwardly mobile, economically well-off rural people get integrated with the emerging economic and socio-cultural milieu, many a time, it comes at the cost of loss of their own identity. A section of the poor rural peasants, artisans and workers being unable to cope up with the increasing livelihood insecurity, unemployment, poverty and social segregation are pushed to migrate to the urban areas, while another section slogs in the rural areas to bear the brunt of all deprivation. In both the cases, they only reproduce their marginal identity. Migration to the urban areas does not always bring to an end to marginality either. Rather, it becomes an extension of rural marginality in the urban areas as most of the poor rural migrants concentrate in slum areas and join the unorganized workforce for livelihood under exploitative terms and conditions of work. Within the globalized flow of culture, consumerism and work, they get uprooted from their own identities in both the urban and rural areas and emerge to be decontextualized as the 'marginal man' in the real sense of the term. The numerically dominant section of them is no longer known as agriculturalist in the rural areas but through new marginalised occupational categories that emerge in the rural areas. Their migrant counterparts in the urban areas are known through faceless socially demeaning collectivities as *modeshi, tapori, beldar, bhaiya, bai, coolie,* etc. Against these backdrops, large parts of the rural areas have also emerged as sites of fragmented identities and new politics of primordiality in many ways. In the social world of increasing mobility, migration, fragmentation and decontextualization, while the rural people are unable to locate these identities globally, they try to remain rooted in society through the route of primordial identity. Hence, rural politics is continuously shaped and reshaped through the reinforcement and rejuvenation of such identities.

Reconfiguring of Identities: Identity as an Expression of Itself and Identity as a Means to an End

The essential components of identity are designated to be the primordial or ascribed identities. People are said to acquire these identities by getting born in specific caste or ethnic, region, religious or linguistic groups. These may remain specific to culture as collective entities. Moreover, these are widely essentialized through specific cultural, geographical, linguistic, etc., traits. Though these entities remain widely fixed and unchanged and even un-invoked in the normal course of time, they also undergo a process of construction or rejuvenation to meet a situational need to become self-conscious identities. Along the line, there are the realities of construction, retention and transformation of identities out of achieved collectivity or solidarity. These processes have always acquired added complexity with the existence or the possibility of construction of multiple identities in society cross-cutting each other's mutual boundaries. Many wonder as to what keeps people attached to an identity if the very essence of identity is founded on fluidity or on multiple solidarities and they undergo frequent reconstruction situationally. Why are there tendencies for emphasizing one identity over the other?

The dynamics of essentialization and rejuvenation, and construction and transformation of identities are subject to objective and subjective considerations. Emphasis on an identity or reconfiguring of an identity with others is widely linked to the transitional duality of subjective morality and commitment to social values at one end and objective interest and achievement and quest for benefit(s) on the other. These identities are transitional because the definitions of neither morality and commitment nor of interest and achievement have remained fixed. Hence, identity exists and is formed both as an 'expression in itself' and as a 'means to an end'. As long as it is an expression in itself, it is predominantly passive in its assertion, even though it is widely visible through expressions in art, language, food habits/choices, cultural practices, music, rituals, social ceremonies, religious practices, etc. These expressions of identity as an end in itself are grounded not only in the traditionally inherited primordial facts of identity such as those of religion, linguistics groups, etc., but also in socially constructed identities that are formed by way of acquiring natural membership to various social groups, citizenship of a country, etc. Hence, identities exist or are formed parallelly, cross-cutting the boundaries of both the traditionally primordial and non-primordial groups, and both within and between these groups. The process of socialization, enculturation, education and social mooring and adherence to social norms, customs and values help sustain and reproduce the same for generations. Such identities are founded on the practice of cultural pluralism and tolerances and accommodation and inclusion. Even though there are elements of interests for the articulation of such identities, these are seldom expressed in terms of binaries against each other.

'Identity as a means to an end or for itself', on the other hand, is essentially assertive in its expressions, used as a means to gain identified interest(s). It is also simultaneously exclusive and forms a strong sense of binary—in-group and out-group—sentiments by forming its own boundary of inclusion and exclusion. This may rejuvenate primordial identities or construct new identities based on civic covers. Significantly, these assertions and boundary formation and maintenance usually take place to achieve certain desired social, economic and political goals.

It is observed by many that individuals and groups often use identities strategically to adapt to a variety of situations to produce and support effective self-gratification. Identity, according to Sahliyeh (1993), 'serves the practical needs and interests of the members of the community. The durability of [an] identity is contingent upon its ability to provide security, social status, and economic benefits for its members more than do other existing alternatives'. Eminov (2007) goes further to state that

> if more appealing alternatives for social and economic advancement are present outside one's group, then, individuals will take advantage of these alternatives and modify their identity, at least temporarily, to suit different conditions. Moreover, members of a given community have multiple identities, each activated upon appropriate circumstances.

Though both these identity definitions—identity as an expression of itself and identity as a means to an end, that is, for itself—are distinctive, they may not remain compartmentalized for ever. Very often, the former gets transformed into the latter, or vice versa. For example, many stigmatized and even dominant primordial identities remain operational as resources for economic and political mobilization and gain (Jesper 2010). Hence, they get transformed from emotional subjective manifestations to rational objective ones. However, the transformation of 'identity in itself' to 'identity for itself' is not automatic. The perceived and everyday experiences of threat, neglect, deprivation or exclusivity, or the prospect of achieving identified interests or gains contribute towards the articulation, transformation or invocation of specific identities for themselves. Even majoritarian and minoritarian religious identities may get transformed towards such direction. These also get largely mediated by various social entrepreneurs and their organizations and ideological underpinnings. Thus though identities are constructed in the name of morality and subjectivity, they are also constructed in the name of contentious politics (Tarrow 1997). Here, collective identities or solidarities are formed by constructing new or rejuvenating pre-existing social collectivities by framing an issue to be immediately contentious for the community and by constructing an imaginary world that is to be achieved 'here and now'. As identities are multiple and people have choices in a plural society, these social entrepreneurs very often articulate a common thread to connect social actors for achieving a defined goal by constructing a hegemonic common identity. At times, artificial exigencies are also created for articulation of such identities and their collective mobilizations. Hence, identity as a means becomes subject to instrumentality in society. However, the transformed identities may not sustain for long. This may be either dismantled or become dormant once the immediate goal of such identity articulation is achieved either in full or in parts, though the possibility of resurfacing of such transformation always remains a reality.

Changing Contours of Social Relationships, Self and Identity

Though historically all human societies have undergone change and development and experienced interconnectivity, in the contemporary society, the pace of change and development has been faster than ever, and the quantum of connectivity has been more extensive than ever. Hence, in the contemporary society, social realities are constructed, dismantled and reconstructed on a daily basis. The texture of social role relationships, depth of meaning and the nature of social solidarity, which provide essence for the formation and construction of identity, have emerged to be more fluid than consolidated. The element of fluidity has been extended further with the engulfing of society by the forces of globalization, ICTs, new and social media, mobility and migration of people, and movements of goods and services across the globe. Within these processes, there has been continuous fragmentation and rejuvenation of old identities on the one hand and the construction of new identities and reconfiguration of old identities to fulfil various cultural, economic and political purposes on the other. One of the important products of such processes has been growing individualism. How do we foresee the relationship between an individual and society within these processes? This question may be examined by elucidating the relationship between individual and collective identity first.

Individual and Collective Identity

In common parlance, a distinction is often made between individual/ personal and collective/social identity. The individual identity is marked by distinguishing characteristics or behavioural traits. This is depicted through one's status, performance of one's social role, expression of one's belief and value system, motives and goals. According to Brewer and Gardner (1996), unique traits are frequently emphasized as an important phenomenon to shape the 'individual self'. An individual self is achieved by differentiating a person from other persons as a unique constellation of traits or characteristics. It is argued that the unique constellation of traits distinguishes him/her from the rest in the given social context.

Interconnectivity between Individual and Collective Self

Psychologically, an individual self is linked to the ontology of 'who am I' reflecting an amount of distinctiveness. However, an individual makes sense of his/her existence in society through his/her association with some group or the other. Sociologically, all identities are socially grounded, and no individual is an independent or a discrete identity. He/she is made up of certain socio-cultural milieu, behavioural patterns and obviously specific historicity. Individual human beings are born in society as biological entities, and cultural traits and social conditions shape the individual identity to be a part of the collective identity—the 'we'. Following Weeks (1990) formulation, Bradley (2016) refers to 'individual identity' as the construction of an individual self evolving from the whole package of individualized experiences that every individual undergoes, and 'collective identity' to the way that we as individuals locate ourselves within the society we live in, how others see us and how we perceive others as locating us (Bradley 2016, 42). The summation of individual self-representations, in general, represents the collective self—the 'we'—prevailing over individual self—the 'I'. Hence, collective identities take shape in the form of 'we' placing 'I' in its backdrop (Coleman and Collins 2004, 2). The 'collective self' is achieved by inclusion in large social groups and contrasting the group to which one belongs—the in-group—with relevant out-groups (Brewer and Gardner 1996; cf. Sedikides and Brewer 1996).

In everyday reality, an individual is simultaneously a member of many social groups or identities. Moore (1988) points out that 'it is no longer easy to talk of the individual or of the self as an autonomous or a coherent unity, but instead we have come to understand that we are made up from and live our lives as a mass of contradictory fragments' (Moore 1998, 170; cf. Bradley 2016, 41). Hence, the relationship between the individual self and collective self is not of binary but of deep reciprocity.

Dyadic Self

We have discussed in the first section that identities are posited with differential probability of self-representation. Brewer and Gardner (1996) narrate that besides the individual and collective self, there is also the dyadic/relational self in society. The 'dyadic/relational self' is shaped by assimilating with significant others based on personalized bonds of attachment such as parent–child, teacher–student, husband–wife, friendship, etc., relationships. A deep scrutiny of these probabilities of self-representations suggests that though they are distinctive, they are interlinked with both the collective and the individual self wherein one may get precedence over the others based on circumstances.

Self and Society

The interrelationships between the self and society are depicted as self reflects society, that is, society shapes self which shapes social behaviours (Blumer 1969; Cooley 1902; Mead 1913). Stryker (1980), in his framework of identity, specifies a reciprocal relationship between a person and social structure—the 'self' and 'society'—wherein each one becomes a product and a producer in turn. According to him, 'identities are themselves tied to socially structured role relationships that have been internalized as parts of one's self'. A person may possess a number of identities related to his/ her structured role relationship as child, parent, worker, friend, spouse and so on in society. 'An identity is a "part" of one's self that is "called up" in the course of interacting with others based on the importance or need of a given situation or in many situations' (Stryker, 1980).

Though society has changed over the centuries, the basic interdependency between society and individual in shaping the identity of the people has remained fundamental till today. As E.H. Carr (1961) elaborates, as soon as we are born, the world starts working on us and transforming us from merely biological into social units with the interplay of language and environment. The primitive man in simple societies is less individual than the civilized man in advanced societies because of the conditions for less diversity in the former.

> In this sense increasing individualization is a necessary product of modern advanced society. However, the process of individualization is not an antithesis to the strength and cohesion in society. Civilized man like primitive man is moulded by society just as effectively as society is moulded by him. (Carr 1961)

According to Carr, the cult of individualism began with renaissance, and its rise is 'connected with the rise of capitalism, Protestantism, industrial revolution and the doctrine of laissez-faire'. He further states, 'the process of growth of individualism was a social process and not a revolt of individual against society or an emancipation of individual from social constraints'. Hence, what seems to him

> essential is to recognize in the great man an outstanding individual who is at once a product and an agent of the historical process, at once the representative and the creator of social forces which change the shape of the world and the thoughts of men. (Carr 1961, 55)

Multiplicity of Choice, Fluidity, Individualism and Reflexivity

In the contemporary world, the relationship between self and society is undergoing a phenomenal change. There is no denying the facts that the pre-existing institutional arrangements and processes of socialization, education, enculturation, etc., inject in the mind of the individual self a good deal of communitarian values and sentiments, morality and customs, and behavioural patterns and roles to shape him/her as a social product. He/she locates his/her 'self' within the essential primordial foundations of caste, race, religion, language, ethnicity or region. He/she simultaneously may become a part of construction of collective non-primordial selves in the form of environmentalist, humanist, citizen, nationalist, patriot, worker or professional of various sorts. Many of these collectivities may be contradictory in terms of their role, meaning and relevance in society. Notwithstanding these contradictions, individuals are part of multiple identities either by active choice or passive compulsion.

In the contemporary world, there has been growing importance on individual autonomy, creativity, responsibility and space for liberation, atomization and individualization. As human mind has emerged to be the site of power and creativity, a large part of social action is now circumscribed by individual choice, rationality, scientific spirit and innovation. Such actions and choices are not conditioned by biological or cultural determinism, but by the proactive empowering capability of the individual self that makes autonomous choices and takes autonomous actions. These individual selves become the conscious leaders and architects of their own destiny rather than become passive followers or the victims of own submission to collective pressure. They are part of individuation as pointed out by Castells (1977), growth of individualism as raised by Carr (1961), and individualism in accelerated modernity as suggested by Beck (2009). They are also simultaneously grounded, as asserted by Giddens (1991), in the reflexive project of self-planning to be central features of structuring of self-identity.

It is not an artificial binary between 'I' and 'we', between individual self and collective selves, but a reflection of the relationship between the producer, that is, society, and its product, that is, identity. These individual selves are not isolated but are linked to society and make conscious and independent choices.

Within the normal everyday discourse, an individual puts his/her 'self' first as a rational human being to maximize his/her interests or to excel in his/her areas of pursuit—economy, politics art, culture, music, etc. The individual self prevails over or becomes subsumed under the larger social self when the exigencies of society create new meanings of social existence. In particular, in emotionally surcharged situations, which demand collective intervention to protect the collectivity from threat or aggregation, or to promote its glory, the individual 'self' prevails over the collective self. Fluidity and solidarity, and individual and collective representations are shaped by social transition. Similarly, social transitions are also equally caused by individual and collective representations. In fact, society get backs what it produces out of social products. Hence, there is a cyclical relation between self-identity and social structure, as propagated by Stryker (1980): 'social structure (society) creates identities (self) that (re)create social structure that creates identities that (re)create....' (Stryker 1980, 53–79). Here, identity of the self acquires reflexive awareness. As Giddens (1991) points out, self-identity 'is what the individual is conscious "of" in the term self-consciousness'. It is not something that is given but something that is routinely created and sustained in reflexive activities by the individual. It is not a

> distinctive trait or even collection of a trait possessed by the individual. This includes the cognitive component of personhood ... what a person is understood to be certainly varies across cultures. The capacity to use 'I' in stiffing contexts, characteristics of every known culture, is the most elemental feature of reflexive conception of personhood. (Giddens 1991, 53)

This interrelationship between the product and the processes in the contemporary society is required to be seen in terms of the emerging scope and condition of reflexivity as created by the emergence of information/knowledge society that has made each individual the centre of power. Here, power is diffused and dispersed, yet interconnected, rejuvenated, critiqued, reframed and exercised on a daily basis. Individuals participate and respond to this exercise of power in terms of location of their self-identity in an interactive society. This identity of the self is not a simple description of an object or a phenomenon. It is located in a sense of purpose that swings between an 'end in itself' and 'a means to an end' at this stage of great social transformation. Hence, identity is now posited to represent its transformative essence in everyday discourse as discursive social category that resonates with resilience to be questioned and to question others.

2

Identity, Social Movements and Collective Mobilizations

Dynamics of Transformation and Reconfiguration

Social movements have always remained an integral part of social progression, and through their transformative zeal, they have always addressed collective concerns and transformed structured entities into self-conscious agencies for collective action and change. However, for a long time, social movements were negated as disruptive agencies and were considered to play a marginal role in creative social change and transformation. Though they have remained ever-present in the society, since the 1960s, social movements as collective social actors have started touching human lives, culture and existence in a fundamental way by creating new cognition, knowledge and identities in society. In fact, identity formation now occupies the core in the manifestation of social movements. Social movement theorists have developed a distinctive perspective, widely known as the identity/new social movement perspective, in comprehending the process of identity formation in social movements as against the pre-existing functional, Marxist, symbolic interactionist, functional and resource mobilization/political process perspectives on social movements.

A fast transitional society like India has been experiencing the manifestation of varieties of social movements and their subsequent transformations. All these have produced varieties of identities and interests in the Indian society, affecting the course of its social and political transformation. Against these backdrops, the central concern of this chapter is to examine the core constituents of social movements, process of formation of identity in social movements, meaning and implication of formation of identity in social movements, transformation of social movements and transformation of new identities therein. It also illustrates the changing trajectories of social movements in India and the place of identities therein. This chapter is based on conceptual understanding and in-depth empiricism.

Social Movements: Constructing Contestation and Ushering New Ideas and Identities

For a vast segment of population, their historical experiences of survival, well-being and mobility have remained circumscribed by man-made suppression, domination, coercion, exclusion, exploitation and marginalization on the one hand and contestations against these social products and processes on the other. While the systemic arrangements, through their established institutions and ideologies, provide legitimacy and reproduce these products and processes, these arrangements also produce the context for their contestations. These contestations primarily aim to usher a society founded on liberty, inclusion, equality, justice, peace and harmony for all. However, the process of formation of contestation is not automatic. It is constructed continuously through the generation of new thoughts, organized collective actions and identities that are intimidated by various forms of social movements.

Social movements occupy the core of social dynamics by integrating social tension, crisis, conflict, change and transformation with the process of progression of society. They produce social space for their emergence, challenging the existing values, norms and societal arrangements, and in the process, pave the way for the emergence of new culture and ideas, new identities and interests, new knowledge and new societal arrangements. At the heart of society, indeed, relentlessly burns the fire of social movements. As Touraine (1981) recognizes, 'They are not alien to the society, rather are the permanent expressions of the collective will'. Social movements are 'not exceptional or the dramatic events' but rather 'lie permanently at the heart of the social life'; moreover, 'they are not a marginal rejection of order, rather are the central forces fighting against the other to control the production of society by itself and the action of classes for the shaping of historicity' (Touraine 1981, 29).

Social movements speak the language of change for ushering a just, equal and inclusive society. They speak through turbulence, agitation, non-cooperation and, at times, violence. According to Melucci (1996), they express themselves as

> a sign; they are not merely an outcome of the crisis ... They signal a deep transformation in the logic and processes that guide complex societies ... Like the prophets, movements speak before: they ... are prophets of the present. They force the power out into the open and give it a shape and a face ... They speak a language that seems to be entirely of their own and they say something that transcends their peculiarity while speaking to us all. (9)

Social movements can speak a language of their own by organizing people and by inculcating collective identity for organized action. Hence, by constructing new collective identities, challenging the established social order, questioning the hegemony and developing a counter-hegemony against the dominant sections of society, the newly formulated and rejuvenated collective identities express themselves as the embodiment of a vast body of power. Through participation in social movements, these identities play historical roles that 'decide the course of the history and the structure of the society' (Touraine 1981, 2). People's participation in social movements brings qualitative change in the character of both the people and the movements. Neither the people remain as an ordinary collection of a collectivity nor is the movement simply a face of people's representation. Rather, both become expressions of new identity, solidarity and power. 'Power in movements grows when ordinary people join the forces in continuous confrontation. The higher the people's participation the more likely the movements are to spread and be sustained' (Tarrow 1995, 1).

Collective Actions and Identities

Social movements encompass not only organized cultural and political actions but also varieties of diffused forms of collective action (Melucci 1996a, 9). The contemporary world experiences the proliferation of collective actions in both the real and the virtual world. Many of such collective actions are organized while others are diffused and produce varieties of meanings, results and identities.

Collective actions get distinctive direction through their identification-specific collective identities. It is through such organized identification that a social movement distinguishes itself from a mob or a crowd or a routine initiative and gives shape to itself. In the context of social movements, the identities are not momentary, isolated or amorphous events. These are rather grounded in deep-down local and global concerns, and are intermediated by the ideals of globalism and humanism, by ideologies and worldview of change and transformation for an alternative world, and by organizations and leadership. These identities are rooted in reality with specific meaning and purpose for their sustenance in society. Collective actions in social movements often lead to the rejuvenation of pre-existing identities like those founded on primordiality such as those of caste, race, ethnicity, language, religion, etc., and also contribute to the formation of new collective identities based on common concerns for human rights, gender equality, sustainable development, ecology and environment, workers' rights, animal rights, rights of LGBT communities and so on, cutting across the boundaries of primordial bondage. In the context of social movements, many dynamics of primordiality and new collectivities get intertwined and acquire distinctiveness, simultaneously at times.

Social movements undergo change and transformation along with change in the dynamics of mobilization, organization, identity, etc., in the movements. Such transformations range widely from radical and revolutionary to institutional and reformative, from old to new, from political to cultural and vice versa. Significantly, the academic orientations to analyse such change and transformation have also changed over time, emphasizing on the relative significance of selected dimensions of social movements. For example, in the conventional analysis of the ideology and collectivity of social movements, organization, leadership, interest articulation, etc., have received prominent emphasis in the political process/resource mobilization perspective, whereas in the new social movement theory, identity formation, autonomy, cultural dynamics, etc., have acquired primacy over the rest. Again, the processes of collective mobilization and identity formation in social movements have also been perceived diversely and, at times, from contradictory points of view in these perspectives.

Collective Identities in Major Perspectives on Social Movements: From Subversion, Economic and Political Determinism to Cultural Autonomy and Space

Neither social movements nor the dynamics of identity therein were always seen positively by the state, public and social movement analysts. Under totalitarian regimes, the political attitude towards social movements and general public perception towards them was rather hostile until the mid-19th century across the globe. Social movements as an area of social investigation and theorization were relegated to the margins by the dominant intellectual discourse. The functionalists, who traditionally privileged stability over change, avoided including social movements in the arena of social analysis appropriately. They rather considered social movements and collective mobilization as a potential agency of disruptions to the social order. For example, in the USA, Haberle (1951) conceptualized social movements as potentially dangerous forms of non-institutionalized collective political behaviour that threaten the stability of the established social order. Similarly, the scholars who founded their formulation on the collective behaviour perspective, especially Turner and Killian (1957), Parsons (1969), Smelser (1963) and others, viewed social movements as non-institutionalized collective actions. For them, social movements are not guided by existing social norms but are formed to result undefined or unstructured situations. Social movements are understood by them in terms of a breakdown, due to structural changes, in the organs of either social control or normative integration (Cohen 1995, 671–72; cf. Eyerman and Jamison 1991, 14). While the functionalists see collective mobilizations in subversive terms, the Marxists see them in economic terms by emphasizing economic determinism. They have tended to reduce all varieties of collective mobilizations and social movements to class conflicts and have recognized social classes to be the sole agents of social change and transformation, and to be expressions of all identities. However, symbolic interactionists such as Blumer (1969, 99) have identified the desire for new life in collective actions in social movements. Though such positive depiction has paved the way for the emergence of rich theoretical perspectives on social movements subsequently, the significance of identity and the process of construction of identity in social movements received focused attention only after the consolidation of the new social movement perspective in Western Europe in the 1960s and thereafter. In between, social movements were also perceived in terms of articulation and fulfilment of common interests by the political process/resource mobilization perspectives.

Political Process/Resource Mobilization Perspective

Social movements have entered a new trajectory of theorization with American social scientists using dimensions of entrepreneurship and cost and benefit in the analysis of collective action in social movements since the early 1970s. However, they avoided giving identity a distinctive place in their discourse. They studied people's participation in social movements not in terms of formation of new meaning or identity but fulfilment of identified interests. They saw social movements as a political process of institutionalized protest or collective action that aimed to gain a share of political power by using various resources. They explained the occurrences of popular protest in terms of 'political opportunities' that emerge out of the involvement of the state with welfare activities and the increasing importance of parliamentary politics that accommodate collective mobilization and give legitimacy to petitions, demonstrations, strikes, mass meetings, etc., as a democratic process. They took the position that participants in social movements are guided by a rational calculation of the costs and benefits of their participatory action in collective mobilization (Tilly 1975), that social movements are manifested when the required resources are pumped into them by the rich for their benefits (Jenkins and Perrow 1977), and that social movements generate a 'demand' similar to an economic demand to which 'political entrepreneurs' respond by forming a counter-movement as business (McCarthy and Zald 1977).

A section of resource mobilization theorists emphasize that the acts of participation in social movements contribute to the construction of meanings and cognitive liberation of their members (McAdam 1982). Here, meanings are constructed through 'interpretative schemata that signifies and condenses the "world out there" by selectively punctuating and encoding objects, situations, events, experiences, and sequences of actions within one's present or past environments' (Snow and Benford 1992). A large part of this cognition and meaning is linked to 'framing and contentious politics' taking shape through the formation of social movements. According to Tarrow (1995, 3), 'social movements draw people into collective action through known repertoires of contention and by creating innovations around these contentions. The organizers exploit political opportunities, create new collective identities, bring people together in organisations and mobilise them against more powerful opponents....' The movements' entrepreneurs are also effectively engaged in 'naming grievances, connecting them to other grievances and constructing larger frames of meaning that will resonate with a population's cultural predispositions and communicate a uniform message to power holders and others' (Morris and Mueller 1992, 136–37). It is important that the resource mobilization theorists view the formation of meaning and social collectivity in social movements as a means to economic or political ends, rather than in subjective and cultural terms. For them, interest and objectivity are privileged over identity and subjectivity. The processes of creation of meaning and identity in social movements have received new perceptive attention in the understanding of the new social movement theorists.

New Social Movement/Identity Perspective

Against the backdrop of institutionalization of reformist and social democratic labour movements, emergence of nationalist movements, and development of industrial democracies, Fabian socialism and welfare state in Western Europe, social scientists therein, especially in France, since the mid-20th century have started conceiving social movements in terms of formulation of new collectivities or solidarities that accommodate new social and cultural concerns, and in terms of construction of new collective identities. They designated the whole gamut as the arrival of an era of new social movements. The arrival of the post-industrial information/ knowledge era has contributed further to the proliferation of new social movements. Going away from the economic determinism, identification of newness has been the major thrust to study social movements for them. Touraine (2006, 89–92) makes it very explicit:

> After World War II and even very recently—especially in the 1960s—many people, including myself tried to discover new forms of collective actions in a so called, at that time, post-industrial society and what we call now an information society ... I was convinced at the end of the twentieth century and beginning of the twenty-first century, the social and the political scene would be dominated by the growing role of these new and the cultural movements ... Many people were convinced that priority should be given to the formation of what I had myself called 'new social movements'.

Though the identity theorists locate identity within broad interactive social processes, they also simultaneously advocate the notion of autonomy of identity. Their focus has been on the theme of political autonomy against ideological determinism, personal autonomy and autonomy from localized determinism. The new social movement scholars explain social movements in terms of common concerns and meanings, and integrate the phenomena of culture, ideological and personal autonomy, and new social space in social movements (Eyerman and Jamison 1991, 17–18; Scott 1990).

According to them, though the realization of objectively defined economic goals has been a dimension of social movements, humanitarian concerns and subjectively articulated meaning have widely conditioned collective actions in social movements. The new social movements involve action as a matter of conscience and emotion, of responsibility and intention, of reflection and (com)passion. Such actions are basically founded on moral, global and individual consciousness (Hegedus 1990, 266). Furthermore, it is posited that there has been shifting focus in social movements from the empirical and the economic class position to the issue of values, culture, inter-subjectivity, morality and urge for the empowerment and formation of new collective identities. In essence, new social movements, as described by Touraine (1983), are now characterized by the realization of historicity, by self-conscious awareness and by the assertion of new collective identities. They have been recognized as the potential bearers of new social interests (Touraine 1981, 1983).

The birth of these movements has brought drastic change in the fabric of social life in the contemporary world orienting itself to culture and intersubjectivity (Bertanx 1990, 153). The social world now, according to Melucci, has in entirety become a cultural construct and 'social movements too seem to shift their focus from class, race, and other more traditional issues towards the cultural ground ...' (1996, 8–9).

With this shifting focus, social movements now provide public spaces for generating new actors and identities, new knowledge and ideas. According to Eyerman and Jamison (1991), 'By producing new knowledge, by reflecting on their own cognitive identity, by saying what they stand for, by challenging the dominant assumptions of the social order, social movements develop new ideas that are fundamental to the process of human creativity'. Moreover, they develop worldviews that restructure cognition, that recognize reality itself paving the way for a cognitive praxis and become an important source of new social images and transformation of societal identities (Eyerman and Jamison 1991, 161–66).

The new social movements are new not in terms of chronology but in terms of their association with and formation of new identities of humanitarian and cultural concerns. According to Melucci (1996), 'newness' of the new social movements is a relative concept, and it had a temporary function to indicate the comparative difference between the historical forms of class conflict and today's emergent form of collective action.

> The reality in which we live has in entirety become a cultural construct and our representations of it serve as filters for our relationship with the whole world ... Social movements too seem to shift their focus from class, race,

and other more traditional issues towards the cultural ground ... (Melucci 1996, 9)

Thus, social movements involve actions for 'doing'. 'The involvement in an action is a matter of conscience and emotion, of responsibility and intention, of reflection and (com)passion, it is basically moral, global and individual' (Bertanx 1990). In the world system, as pointed out by Wallerstein (2002), there always exist multiple identities and varieties of social movements—socialist, labour, women, nationalist, liberation, peasant, environmentalist, etc. Since the late 1960s, the new social movements are 'primarily triggered by the fact that the old movements— the social democrat, the communist and the nationalists had failed to address these issues' (Wallerstein 2002). The anti-systemic movements have 'overshadowed the ever-present other social movements which are now gaining significance. The performances and promise of these social movements are declining. The increasing failure of the state/political parties, labour movements/parties and socialism/Marxist parties as well as people's increasing refusal to be manipulated by them are now increasingly drawing people to be part of new social movements (Frank and Fuentes 2002, 177). Hence, Touraine (2005) points out that in the present moment the society is 'marked by the appearance new problems and new social movements which can no longer be explained by invoking another order of the phenomena—the laws of the capitalist development or the consequences of modernization ...' It is also a different intellectual moment that is 'causing the inability to the "traditional left" to understand social and the political events' of this era. 'Our most urgent need is to learn how to name and analyze the new social practices and the new forms of collective action which are shaping the societies of today and tomorrow' (Touraine 2005, 11–12, 25).

It is apparent that the identity/new social movement theorists significantly differ in their definition of the contexts, defining characteristics, genesis, basis for collective action, organization and outcome of social movements from those of the traditional collective behaviour and resource mobilization/political process theorists. To the traditional collective behaviour theorists, the social contexts on which social movements are staged are founded on political consensus and stability, and these are characterized by non-institutional orientation, and irrational, spontaneous and amorphous collective action with a host of negative attributes. To the resource mobilization theorists, elite fragmentation, realignment of political forces and emergence of new political opportunities have been the social contexts for the emergence of social movements.

To them, social movements are characterized by institutional orientation and rational instrumental actions which are planned and even manufactured sometimes. To the identity theorists, especially of the France School, on the other hand, the social contexts for the emergence of social movements have been delineated by new forms of conflict, on cultural, humanitarian and global concerns, which have seen the proliferation of new social movements. To them, these movements are characterized as anti-institutional but rational, moral, spontaneous and positive in orientation. As far as the genesis of social movements is concerned, the traditional collective behaviour perspective emphasizes on the social strain, the resource mobilization perspective on the changing availability of resources, and the identity perspective on the structural contradictions. For the traditional collective behaviour theorists, the organization of social movements evolved by following their life cycle; for the resource mobilization theorists, it was contingent upon goals, resources and external conditions; and for the identity theorists, it evolved from the grass roots with action as its structure. For the traditional theorists, the outcome of social movements is dependent on the leadership; for the resource mobilization theorists, on the relative permeability of the polity; and for the identity theorists, the outcome of social movements is a creation of space of autonomy and new identities (Hannigan 1985, 436). All social movements produce group solidarity and collective identity of their own variety. The new social movements are known for their anti-institutional appeal as they want to empower their members by making them non-hierarchical, and to transform human relations in a fundamental way by providing them autonomy and choices founded in humanitarian and global concerns for justice, equality and fraternity for all.

Each phase of history is marked not only by a specific form of economic foundation but also related forms of collective actions and distinctive varieties of social movements, notwithstanding a certain amount of overlapping. It has been widely observed globally that the 1920s was predominantly marked as the epoch of the communist movement, the 1930s and early 1940s by the expansion of the Nazi and other totalitarian movements, the mid-1940s and early 1950s by the anti-colonial movements, the 1960s and 1970s by the proliferation of the working class movement, the 1980s by the new social movements, the 1990s by the era of global movements, and the early part of the 21st century by the movements of movements and anti-globalization movements. According to Wieviorka (2005, 9), the former social movements and especially the working class movement of the 1970s though have not entirely disappeared, have remained either institutionalized incapable of raising to the level of historicity to challenge the overall control of the major orientations of collective life, or else has been radicalized to take the form of violence or of ideologies of rupture.

All these movements manifest distinctive varieties of identities and show diverse levels of anti-institutional zeal. This has been elaborated further in the following section.

Typology of Social Movements: Anti-Institutional Awareness and Identity Formation

Hannigan (1985), by analysing the work of Touraine and Castells, has identified four major types of social movements—social liberation, revolutionary, cultural and professional reform movements—to show that these movements are distinctive in terms of their relative association with the 'anti-institutional character' and the type of 'group identities' they have produced. The relative association of these types of movements with anti-institutional awareness and identity is given in Table 2.1.

In general, the anti-institutional awareness has been high both in the social liberation and revolutionary movements as these movements find the existing institutional arrangements to be oppressive and dysfunctional for the major sections of the population, and these movements advocate for structural change in the society. However, the social liberation

Table 2.1

Typology of Social Movements

		Emergent Group Identity	
		High	*Low*
Emergent Anti-institutional Awareness	High	Social Liberation Movement	Revolutionary Movement
	Low	Cultural Movement	Professional Reform Movement

Source: Hannigan (1985, 449–50).

movement has a high extent of group identity formation as the immediate social concerns overshadow many of the immediate social, economic and cultural differences among the movement participants for a larger cause. Though the revolutionary movement generates a high level of anti-institutional awareness, it constructs a low level of solidarity and a low level of intensity of group identity. This movement lacks a distinct cultural base upon which collective resocialization and identity can be mounted. The professional reform movement lacks both anti-institutional awareness and a sense of distinct identity. Identities get loosely defined and articulated in the professional reform movements as these have limited defined goods, advocate for selected reforms of the existing institutional arrangements and have least anti-institutional appeal. Moreover, the professional reform movements are predominantly institutional and are unable to overshadow the everyday sort of differences among its members. The cultural movement generates a low level of institutional awareness and develops a distinct sense of self-identity. These movements advocate for change in selected institutional arrangements of the society, and have a high level of collective identity formation as they unite members on the foundation of common culture. In general, all these social movements may further be categorized as radical and reformative based on their orientation to ideology, organization, change and transformation, and nature of collective mobilization (SinghaRoy 1992). These are also marked by the raise of distinctive varieties of identity formation.

Transformation of Social Movements and Construction of Identity

Social movements are not static; rather, they get transformed with the transformation of society and transformation in the ideology, organization, leadership, interest articulation, orientation towards change and patterns of collective mobilization of social movements. Change in these components of social movements brings forth fundamental change in the identity of the groups involved in social movements.

Every social movement has a life cycle and gets transformed through various stages such as radical to routinized or institutionalized or vice versa. There have been numerous episodes of proliferation of radical or non-institutionalized social movements and the subsequent process of their institutionalization. Many 'radical movements' that resorted to non-institutionalized large-scale collective mobilization, initiated and guided by a radical ideology for rapid structural change in society, have transformed into 'reformative movements', taking recourse to institutionalized mass mobilization initiated by recognized bodies for a gradual change in the selected institutional arrangement of society guided by a reformative/modified ideology of social change. While the lifespan of radical movements, especially their extensive period of action and collective mobilization, has been short, the lifespan of institutionalized social movements has been longer. The institutionalized social movements have tried to get old institutions, norms, values and customs selectively redefined in a new context. Many social movements have internally transformed from revolutionary to institutionalized or reformative, or have been co-opted and integrated with the political system, depending on the social, cultural and political surroundings of the society concerned (SinghaRoy 1992, 27).

Both the processes of transformation of social movements, that is, from 'radical' to 'reformative' and vice versa, directly affect not only the processes of formation and rejuvenation of new collective identity but also the articulation of new areas of collective action. In fast transitional societies, collective mobilizations have emerged as an integral part of social progression wherein social movements and new collective identity formation work simultaneously both as processes and products. Here, collective mobilization and institutionalization are not contradictory but complementary to each other; this paves the way for persistent and renewed efforts towards a just society. T. K. Oommen (1994) points out that the processes of mobilization and institutionalization do co-exist, that 'institutionalization provides new possibilities of mobilization', and that 'mobilization is not displaced by institutionalization but goes hand-in-hand to a large extent and often the latter process accentuates the former' (Oommen 1994, 251–53).

Sustained mobilizations, whether radical or institutionalized, have always functioned to produce a politically conscious and socially aware community of social actors. In many ways, these help redefine the social context and generate social awareness of a higher level among the social movement participants. The resurged minds question many of the oppressive and discriminatory social institutions, practices and norms which are otherwise described as normal. These have brought at times a high level of conscientization and fragmentation in the pre-existing identities by fostering multiple identities and new social movements. This formation has been widely facilitated and many a time altered by the arrival of new economic and technological forces in society whereby possibilities of connectivity of local identities with global ones has become an everyday reality.

ICTs, Fluidity in Identity and Social Anti-Movements

Now in the wake of the fast expansion of ICTs, shaping up of networks and knowledge society, and the increasing quantum of migration and occupational mobility across the globe, the processes of proliferation of new varieties of social movements and construction of new collective identities therein have taken new shapes. Unprecedented flow of information, usage of social media such as email, SMS, Facebook, Twitter, blogs, etc. contribute to the formation, renewal, consolidation and fragmentation of identities in the cyberspace on a daily basis. These add to the shaping up of interconnected social movements and collective identities, at times without boundaries of immediate geographical and societal concerns. Now the social space for social movements has become a distinct area of the system and no longer coincides either with the traditional forms of organization or solidarity or with the conventional channels of political representation. Again, the 'notion of movement itself, which originally stood for an entity acting against the political and governmental system, has now been rendered inadequate as a description of the reality of reticular and defused forms of collective action' (Melucci 1996).

The epistemic communities that are formed in the cyberspace predominantly remain grounded in informal networks for the expressions of various forms of protest (della Porta and Diani 1999, 16) and construct their identity on the basis of temporarily perceived articulated ideals and interests independent of geographical boundaries. Their members become part of multiple organizations and switch over from one collective identity to another. By getting associated with loosely constructed multiple identities, they acquire added complexity in the process of construction of new and essentialization of pre-existing primordial identities. Within these complexities, the fluid and fuzzy membership and the emerging fluidity of identity have emerged to be a reality in the emerging culture of forming solidarity through social movements. Now with the increasing manifestation of autonomy, emerging fluidity of identity and formation of multiple identities in a culture of collective action, contemporary social movements increasingly experience shockwaves of fluidarity (McDonald 2002). Notwithstanding the proliferation of such fluidity in the changing world, collective mobilization is now getting institutionalized, and social movements are becoming a permanent component of political interest mediation, and legitimate factors in contemporary societies. All these are leading to the conspicuous formation of the 'movement society' wherein the emergence and sustenance of plurality of social movements is taking long-term and permanent positions in society on diverse issues and interests (Rucht and Neidhardt 2002). The globalized world now observes the proliferation of varieties of social movements at a global scale, and the most prominent face of such movements has been the alter-globalization movement, social anti-movements, movement of social movements and grass-roots resistance of various sorts. In the process of manifestation of these movements, the process of construction of pre-existing identities is undergoing a profound process of socio-cultural de-contextualization.

Wieviorka (2005) points out that 'the era of new social movements is behind us now. It corresponded to a transitional phase between the working class movement of yesterday and the global movements of today, between industrial society and the societies which we now refer to as network societies rather than industrial societies.' The very idea of society has been challenged. While on the one hand, there has been proliferation of multiple identity movements paving the way for the emergence of global movements, on the other hand, there have been visible assertions of identity leading to 'withdrawal into communities, or to be set in a context of sectarianism, nationalism—even terrorism' (Wieviorka 2005, 89). With the multiplicity of social movements in the movement society, social movements are to encounter their inverted image—the social anti-movements which, instead of promoting a social or a cultural identity, are

> champions of some abstract entity, essence or symbol, and speak in the name of a purity or homogeneity. Again instead of building relationships with other actors, agreeing on the principles of debates and negotiations, they champion absolutes, and adopt do or die attitudes. And if they appear in an arena where social movements also exist, they try to destroy these movements, and fight against them. (Wieviorka 2005, 18)

Social movements in the contemporary world have become as much a global phenomenon as much a local one, and so are the contexts for the construction of collective identities. Most of the transitional societies have remained hotbeds for the manifestation of social movements on diverse issues, and their transformation. These societies have also provided the contexts for developing interconnectivity among these social movements, and most conspicuously, proliferation and transformation of new collective identities through these movements. Against the backdrop of the broad processes of such proliferation and transformation of social movements, the following sections of this chapter will discuss the changing trajectory of social movements in India and the processes of formation of new identities therein.

Changing Trajectory of Social Movements in India and Identities

Societies in India have experienced the proliferation of varieties of social movements over time and space. Notwithstanding the historical legacies of old social movements, new varieties of social movements have surfaced in India, cross-cutting the boundaries of predefined social issues and collectivities. Besides the manifestation of the anti-colonial movement since the late 19th and early 20th century, India has also bore witness to a varieties of rural revolts in the form of tribal and peasant movements, including the Moplah rebellion in the 1920s, Chauri Chaura in Bihar in 1922, Bardoli in Gujarat in 1925, peasant agitation of Oudh in the 1920s, All India Kisan Sabha in the 1930s and 1940s, Tebhaga movement in 1946–47, Telangana movement in 1946–52, workers' movements in the 1950s, 1960s and early 1970s, and women's, students', ethnic, regional, caste, environment, human rights, LGBT community rights, and several other movements since the mid-1970s and thereafter. Along with the continuity of these movements in one form or the other, contemporary India has also experienced the proliferation of anti-globalization movements, and movements of movements of various forms. Significantly, many of the sites of old social movements are now experiencing the manifestation of new social movements, and many old social movements are also experiencing a transformation towards new social movements. For example, Andhra Pradesh, which has witnessed the proliferation of radical peasant movements, that is, the Telangana movements (1948–52), has also seen the proliferation of separate Telangana statehood movements since the late 1950s; Naxalite movements since 1972 and sustained agrarian conflict spearheaded by the CPI(ML) (also called Peoples' War Group) and various other Naxalite outfits; mobilization for the protection of the citizens' civil rights by Andhra Pradesh Civil Liberties Committee (APCLC), Organization for the Protection of Democratic Rights, citizens' forums, etc.; mobilization of Scheduled Tribes by Thudum Debba (a militant organization of the Scheduled Tribes), mobilization of Madiga (a group of Scheduled Castes) by Madiga Reservation Porata Samithi (MRPS) and mobilization of cultivators by Rythu Seva Samithi, Jala Sadhana Samithi (demanding irrigation facilities for peasants); the Anti-Arrack Movement in the late 1980s and 1990s to mobilize women against production and consumption of liquor and also for women's liberty, political participation and social development; and so on.

Identity, Social Movements and Collective Mobilizations 59

Similarly, in West Bengal, there had been radical peasant movements such as the Tebhaga movement (1946–47) for a two-thirds share of the produced crops for the share croppers instead of one-half and Naxalbari Movement (1967–71) for the implementation of the 'land to the tiller' policy by overthrowing the state through guerrilla warfare. The state has also witnessed the state-sponsored Operation Barga Movement (1977 until the late 1990s) to provide tenurial security, 75% of the produced crops and institutional support to the sharecroppers (the Bargadars), Gorkhaland movements since the 1980s for separate statehood for the hill people of the Darjeeling district, Kamtapur movement since the 1980s for a separate state for the Rajbanshi people of the northern part of West Bengal, resurgence of Naxalite extremism in the southern part of West Bengal since the early 2000s, movements against acquisition of agricultural land in Singur and Nandigram, tribal villagers' resistance against police oppression in the Lalgarh area of the Midnapore district, and several other grass-roots mobilizations.

Many such movements are also manifested in several parts of the country against displacement; globalization; corruption; oppression based on caste, class, gender and ethnicity; and for right to information, environmental protection, human rights, regional autonomy and many such issues. Significantly, most of these social movements have retained their continuity and their legacy through sustained collective mobilizations. As the root causes of the conflicts—poverty, unemployment, livelihood insecurity, social exclusion, cultural indignation, discrimination, etc.—are yet to be eradicated, collective mobilizations and protests against such ills have remained an inseparable part of social progression in India. Significantly, in addition to being organized by distinctive organizations, guided by distinctive ideology for mobilization, projected by specific types of demands, and marked by specific response from the state, all these movements are also represented by distinctive collectivities and construction of their own varieties of identities. Some of these facets of a few social movements as historically experienced in Independent India are shown in Table 2.2.

Social movements in India have produced and reconfigured varieties of identities from caste, linguistic and regional to peasant, farmer, rural worker, environmentalist, agriculturalist, spiritual (religious/cult follower), LGBT, social activist, etc. As far as the essential backgrounds of these identities are concerned, they are predominantly represented by various regional, religious, ethnic groups especially the SC, ST, OBC, women and linguistic communities who have transformed into agencies of change

Table 2.2
Major Facets of Social Movements in Independent India

Name of Movement	Nature of Organization, Ideology and Mobilization	Type of Demands	Nature of State's Response	Social Collectivities Involved and Identities Formed
Tebhaga movements 1946–47	Radical	Land to the tillers and higher share of produce	Strong opposition	Predominantly represented by SCs, STs, OBCs and women for fostering class-based peasant identity
Telangana movements 1948–52	Radical	Abolition of forced labour, tenancy and land right, etc.	Strong opposition	Predominantly represented by SCs, STs, OBCs and women for fostering class-based peasant identity
Telangana statehood movement 1960s onwards	Partly institutionalized and partly radical	Separate statehood	Opposition, co-option and negotiation	Predominantly represented by SCs, STs, OBCs and women; articled regional, linguistic and cultural identities
Naxalite movements 1967–71	Radical	Land rights, throwing out the state, etc.	Strong opposition	Predominantly represented by SCs, STs and women; fostered class-based peasant identity
Farmers' movements 1980s and 1990s	Partly institutionalized and partly radical	Higher price of agricultural produce, fertilizer subsidy, loan weaver, tax exemption, fair price, free electricity, etc.	Opposition and accommodation	Predominantly represented by dominant OBCs and caste groups from the middle layer of caste hierarchy; fostered farmer and rural identities

Regional/Ethnic Movements: Chhattisgarh movement in Madhya Pradesh, Jharkhand in Bihar, Gorkhaland and Kamtapur in West Bengal, Telangana in Andhra Pradesh, Vidarbha in Maharashtra, Bodoland in Assam, and Bundelkhand in Uttar Pradesh	Partly institutionalized and partly radical	Formation of a separate state within the Indian Union based on linguistic, cultural and geographical specificities. Explicitly cultural and economic but implicitly political	Opposition, negotiation, accommodation	Predominantly represented by SCs, STs, OBCs and linguistic communities for fostering ethnic and regional identities
People's War, Extremist Movements: People's War/Maoist movement in Andhra Pradesh, West Bengal, Odisha, Bihar, Jharkhand, Chhattisgarh, Madhya Pradesh, Maharashtra, Uttar Pradesh since 1980	Radical and partly disguised	Land and forest rights for the poor, land distribution, and withering away the state	Opposition	Predominantly represented by SCs, STs, OBCs and women; fostered class identity
Pro-Mandal Commission Movement 1990s	Institutionalized	Reservation in education and jobs in the government institutions for the OBCs	Accommodative	Predominantly represented by OBCs; fostered primordial identity
Anti-Mandal Commission Movement 1990s	Institutionalized	Opposing the demand for reservation for the OBCs	Opposition	Predominantly represented by upper castes; fostered primordial identity
Environmental Movements: Chipko, Save Bhagirathi and Stop Tehri Project in Uttarakhand, Silent Valley in Kerala, Narmada Bachao Andolan in Madhya Pradesh and Gujarat, Appiko Movement in Karnataka, Movements against missiles base in Baliapal, Odisha; Vedanta Alumina Ltd in Niyamgiri hills of Odisha; Jaitapur Nuclear Power Project in Maharashtra; nuclear plant in Koodankulam, Tamil Nadu and Kerala; etc.	Institutionalized	Protection of land, water and forest and the rights of the local people	Opposition and negotiation	Led by middle-class intellectuals; followed by localities from cross-sections of population; formed a pro-conservation environmentalist identity

(Table 2.2 continued)

(Table 2.2 continued)

Name of Movement	Nature of Organization, Ideology and Mobilization	Type of Demands	Nature of State's Response	Social Collectivities Involved and Identities Formed
Civil Liberty Movement 1980	Partly institutionalized and partly radical	Protection of citizenship rights of the citizens	Critical, integration and negotiation	Predominantly represented by people from all walks of life; formed civic and political identity
Anti-Arrack Movement 1985	Partly radical and partly institutionalized	Imposition of ban of alcohol	Encouragement and integration	Predominantly represented by women from STs, SCs, OBCs and also from upper-caste groups; fostered strong gendered identity
Madiga Reservation Porata Samithi 1995	Mostly institutionalized	Categorization of Scheduled Castes in terms of the level of economic and educational development	Integration, co-option	Caste-based, predominantly represented by SCs; fostered primordial identity
Mala Reservation Movement 1995	Mostly institutionalized	Preservation of their caste identity and self-respect	Integration, co-option	Caste-based, predominantly represented by SCs; fostered primordial identity
Agriculturalists' movements against land acquisition in Lucknow and Noida, Uttar Pradesh 2008–09	Mostly institutionalized	No acquisition of agricultural land for non-agricultural purposes	Negotiation and co-option	Represented by people from all primordial groups; loosely fostered land owner identity.
Agriculturalists' movements in Singur and Nandigram, West Bengal 2007–10	Partly institutionalized and only radical	No acquisition of agricultural land for non agricultural purposes	Steep opposition	Represented by agriculturalists from all primordial groups; loosely fostered agriculturalist and rural identities

Neo-religious Cults: Art of Living Foundation, Sathya Sai Baba, Baba Ramdev, etc.	Institutionalized	Spiritual and moral uplift	Accommodative and encouragement	Represented by people from all walks of life, though predominantly represented by the middle class; loosely fostered spiritual and moral identities within own cult
Civil liberty and human rights movements	Institutionalized but critical to dominant sections and state apparatus; sustained mobilization	Establishing rule of law; humane treatment to all including prisoners and extremists; livelihood security	Critical, integration and negotiation	Represented by the middle class, intellectuals and social activists from all groups; fostered transnational and civil identities
Women's Movements: Movement for women's reservation, violence against women, declining female sex ratio, rape and sexual violence	Institutionalized	Providing 33% reservation for women in Parliament and in state legislature; establishing gender parity by enacting laws, creating enabling mechanisms for women empowerment	Civic and political encouragement, negotiation and integration	Represented by women from cross-sections of society, though predominantly represented by middle strata; fostered a strong woman identity
Gujjar movement in Rajasthan, 2012, and Jat movement in Haryana, 2016, to change caste status	Violent	Change in the Caste status from OBC to ST and the General to OBC respectively	Opposition and negotiation	Represented by these caste groups for fostering strong primordial identities
Movements by LGBT communities	Mostly institutionalized	Forming Federation among social movements on the issue of social and human rights	Accommodative	Represented by social activists and intellectuals against MNC, Stat
National and Global Networking: National Alliance of People's Movements, India Social Forum	Mostly institutionalized	Forming network for development and human rights.	Accommodative	Represented by social activist and intellectuals and the LGBT community

Source: Author's own.

through collective mobilizations of various sorts, for example, institutionalized and radical or a combination of both. Significantly, while the radical mobilizations and, to some extent, the combinations of radical and institutionalized mobilizations have surpassed, transcended and transfigured essential primordial grounding of these identities, the institutionalized mobilizations have tended to reinforce these primordial identities. The processes of fostering class-based peasant, farmer, rural, linguistic, cultural and regional identities reflect the transcending and transfiguring of these primordial identities. However, some violent mobilizations also enforce primordial identities, as has been observed in the case of the Gujjar movement for reservation in 2012 and 2016 in Madhya Pradesh and Jat movement for reservation in Haryana, Rajasthan and NCR Delhi in 2016–17.

All processes of identity formation are linked to interest articulation that can be known by the types of demands asserted through these movements. The interests have been both implicit and explicit in economic, political and cultural terms. Strong interest articulation and sustained mobilization not only transcend the difference among the primordial groups but also transfigure them to be the reflexive identities in society.

Social movements in contemporary India intersect with the phenomenal shift in the economic structure of the Indian society and erosion of the bases of traditional economic resources, thereby increasing occupational diversifications and dilution of the conventional modes of social mobility, socio-cultural de-contextualization and the resurgence of multiple identities and interests in society. Furthermore, the regular political interventions of secular democratic and primordial forces at the grass-roots level have opened up the possibilities of formation of new collective identities and multiple collective mobilizations of the same sets of people with diverse economic, social, cultural and political issues and interests. These have helped in sustaining the culture of collective mobilizations and rearticulation of caste, religious, regional, ethnic, gender, etc. identities. The sustenance of social movements is positively linked to sustained social, economic and political deprivation of large sections of population in India. Their stagnation and immobility, livelihood insecurity, poverty, unemployment, social isolation and political powerlessness provide the basis for their sustained collective mobilization in society on one issue or the other. In recent years, the fast social and economic transitions of the Indian society have generated a big momentum for social mobility. However, the quantum of upward social mobility has been faster for those segments of the population that have better access to economic, political and other social resources, while spatial and horizon social mobility has circumscribed the marginalized sections of people having too little alteration in their pre-existing condition of marginality to break the barriers of marginality. Significantly, this mobility and growing interconnectedness with the wider world has helped them to get associated with multiple collective mobilizations and question the bases of legitimacy of their marginalization in society.

As the largest section of population has remained deprived of the basic necessities of social and human development, opportunities of upward social mobility and integration with the larger society on civic terms, they rearticulate their old primordial identities in a new context to become stakeholders in the larger society, its mobility and development. These have redefined the paradigm of legitimacy of conflict, protest and collective mobilization and processes of identity articulation and assertion in this transitional society. Hence, social movements in contemporary India have emerged to be hotspots for consolidation of caste, class, ethnic, tribal, religious, religious cult, regional, peasant, woman, etc. identities along with farmer, agriculturalist, human and animal rights, LGBT, environmentalist, etc. identities that intersect frequently with politically mediated primordial and cultural considerations.

In the changing trajectory, the state has provided the liberal democratic space to accommodate cultures of protest, resistance and collective mobilizations wherein many of the radical mobilizations have transformed to become institutionalized and co-opted, and have sustained themselves being institutionalized and reformative. Moreover, majority of the radical mobilizations have transformed into established political parties, and in the process of continuous political mobilization, the difference between the state and the political parties has been minimized in many places. Within such formations, despite the trend for routinization, many of the social movements emerging out of daily resistance have retained their radical zeal for wider change in society and many identities are being reconfigured with primordial ones.

Imbalanced Mobility, Institutionalization of Social Movements and Construction of Multiple Identities

The imbalanced and assorted forms of mobility have induced social conflict and extensive mobilization at the grass-roots level on various interrelated issues, and have paved the way for the construction of several new identities and rejuvenation of old identities. For example, an agriculturalist simultaneously joins caste-based pro-reservation, environmental, anti-liquor, literacy and human rights movements and acquires varieties of identities. Society now experiences the proliferation of multiple identities and multiple assertions of these identities. These identity formations are not isolated but are linked to their historical experiences of neglect and deprivation, and to the emerging processes of political and cultural assertions in society. Being part of such multiple identities, the social actors move like a pendulum between these mobilizations, shifting quickly from one end to the other by cross-cutting the boundaries of several social identities. They emerge to be highly flexible to retain the significance of their pre-existing gender, caste, ethnic, religious and regional identities on the one hand and to articulate their social, economic and political interests on the other. The process of fluidification of identities has been largely accentuated through their simultaneous association with multiple organizations, ideologies and concerns.

In the context of routinization of social movements and proliferation of multiple mobilizations, identities are frequently rearticulated and asserted on the basis of primordial considerations and are also reconfigured from among the primordial categories as class, subaltern groups, environmentalists, human rights and civil society activists, women and so on, as warranted by the dynamics of collective mobilization. Institutionalized mobilization has provided the required space for not only the sustenance of a social movement culture but also the articulation and sustenance of the multiple identities that look for liberation from the coercive bases of dependency and domination (SinghaRoy 2004). Herein, many of these identities have also been encapsulated as a project to attain specific political and economic goals. However, these identities have not remained conditioned from the outside but are rather associated with multiple institutionalized movements. These rejuvenated identities not only question the bases of legitimacy of pre-existing arrangements but also assert for a share in the social, economic and political spheres in the established orders.

In the contemporary society, the scope of such interconnectivity of localized mobilizations has widened and is sustained with fast expansion of the forces of globalization, ICTs, education, social media and mass communication. Significantly, the emerging scenario of interconnectivity is embedded deeply in society with an increasing quantum of socio-cultural de-contextualization, migration and imbalanced mobility of people across the space. Hence, the processes of expansion of ICTs and globalization,

Identity, Social Movements and Collective Mobilizations **67**

mobility and migration, and socio-cultural decontextualization of vast sections of people have profoundly diffused the pre-existing modes of organizing collective mobilization and formation of new collective identities, as social identities now get regularly reconstructed, reconfigured and adjusted with varieties of social situations and mobilizations in the interconnected world. These interconnected identities have now become highly mobilized and flexible, wherein solidification and fluidarity of collective identity go hand in hand and the dynamics of 'identity' and 'interest', 'morality' and 'rationality', 'primordiality' and 'modernity', and 'autonomy' and 'dependence' function as combinations of these composite social processes by becoming dichotomous forces in one context and complementary in another. These identities have given birth to a social movement society—an interconnected collectivity regularly mobilized on the principle of fragmentation at one end and unification on the other, and which is in a process of continuous renewal and rejuvenation.

Conclusion

The new social movement scholars have largely identified cognition, empowerment, collective subjectivity, morality, etc. to be the key components of identity formation in the context of new social movements. They have also emphasized on the non-violent, non-hierarchical, non-coercive, cross-class, cross-ideology, cross-age (Hegedus 1990, 263) and autonomous character of social movements (Scott 1990, 18–20). Within the institutionalized process of collective mobilization, the social movement actors by becoming cross-class, cross-ideology and cross-organization, and by exercising their autonomy, stand for fluidly in their identity. Besides remaining non-violent and non-hierarchical, these actors also predominantly remain non-committed to a fixed identity.

Significantly, the elements of morality, intersubjectivity, meaning, cultural and political empowerment, etc., which were considered to be the essential foundation of collective identity in new social movements, have always retained their place in the class- and interest-based collective mobilizations. In contemporary India, many economic and political interests are still loosely defined in cultural terms, and class-based old social movements tend to get fragmented and transformed into identity-based new social movements. Therefore, the possibility of coexistence of primordial and non-primordial identities and old and new social movements has remained an empirical reality. Frequent performance to or rejuvenation of primordial identities for the enhancement of economic interest only validates such reality. In India, there has always been a hide and seek game between the relative significance of primordial identities in social movements. Though social liberation or revolutionary social movements often tend to minimize the significance of these primordial identities, and these identities may temporarily go behind the scenes while responding to the exigencies of society, they again reappear when the movements get transformed into reformative ones. This is like a play of ebb and flow of tides in social movements wherein the swelling flow of tides of liberation or revolutionary movements submerges the rocks and rubbles of primordial grass-roots differences for the time being. However, once this flow of tides in the social movements recedes, the rocks and rubbles of the everyday primordial realities get resurfaced again for use in collective mobilization.

In essence, the elements of emotion and intersubjectivity in collective identity formation do not always prevail over rationality of thought and action. Consequently, in such social fluidity, identities are not always privileged over material interests. In the process of such transition, there is a need to recognize identity as relational, contingent and socially constructed, as opposed to a non-problematic resource to be mobilized, and to affirm that identities are not durable or encompassing attributes of persons or collective actors as such (Bevington and Dison 2005, 287–89; McAdam, Tarrow, and Tilly 2001, 133). Hence, the observation of Castells (1983) is very relevant, who points out that in a social structure, there are institutionalized forms of domination and also potential forms of challenges 'coming from new actors in history and society' as 'society is structured around conflicting positions which define alternative values and interests'. Here, social movements as collective actions consciously aim at the transformation of the social interests and values embedded in the forms and functions of a historically given society and 'a movement develops not only in relationship to its own society, but also in relationship to a world-wide social system' (Castells 1983, i–xvi).

In contemporary India, the essence of formation of collective identities in social movements is linked to the formation of multiple social realities that economically twist between agrarianism industrialism and post-industrialism; culturally between tradition and modernization, globalization and localization, secularization and communalization; politically between democratic liberation and feudal domination; and substantively between prosperity and poverty, knowledge and ignorance. These composite processes help generate and reshape new collective identities and rejuvenate old identities in new contexts. A vast body of collective mobilizations are staged and collective identities are articulated on the basis of the objective realities of economic exploitation, political subordination, ethnic and caste segregation, gender inequality, destruction of environment, violation of human rights, etc. Many of the historical experiences of social conflicts and collective mobilizations have remained associated with the process of articulation of new collective identities and their transformation. As the objective realities have largely remained unaltered for many, the culture of collective mobilizations continues to construct and reconstruct politically conscious communities to rejuvenate the process of formation of multiple social identities. These self-conscious identities constantly question the structure of their domination in society through everyday forms of collective mobilization. The struggles of poor peasants, SCs, STs, women, ethnic minority groups, grass-roots environmentalists and human rights activists are related as much to the issues of their livelihood security as to the issue of their identity that questions the established structure of their domination in society. In the emerging contexts, the rearticulated collectivities and social identities are no longer the emergent responses to the exigencies of society; rather, they have emerged as the valid processes of the emerging social order that strategically use multidimensional identities to create social spaces for their collective assertion. Significantly, though the issues involved in these collective assertions are old, the actors involved in the actions and the strategies of their actions are new.

3
Peasant, Caste, Class and Identity
Contesting Marginality

Peasant societies in contemporary India are undergoing a process of fast transition. This transition is taking place along with indigenous processes, declining land–man ratio, the emerging phenomenon of their landlessness/semi-landlessness, preponderance of marginal holding, and un/underemployment in agriculture on the one hand and the fast penetration of exogenous forces like those of mass media and education, ICTs and urban connectivity, road and transport facilities, state and civil society–sponsored developmental initiatives and sustained political mobilization of rural people on the other. Though this transition has brought in new scope and conditions for peasants' occupational diversification and horizontal mobility, arousal of their new economic, social and political aspirations, it has not been able to do away with their marginalized identity in large parts of the Indian society. Thus, collective mobilizations of peasants continue to play a significant role, in one form or the other, to reorient the identities of peasants and their association with the identities of class, caste and ethnicity in society. Against these backdrops, the central thrust of this chapter is to delineate the major facets of marginalization of peasants in the Indian society, the emerging intertwining between peasant, caste and class identities in contemporary India, patterns of their participation in collective mobilizations in the context of their sustained marginalization in society, and the processes of reconfiguration of their identities in the context of transformation of peasant movements in the interconnected world. The chapter is based on both the macro- and micro-level empirical data obtained from secondary sources.

Conceptualizing Marginalization, Peasants and Peasant Identities in India

Understanding Marginalization

Marginalization, as a complex process of relegating specific group(s) of people to a lower or the outer edge of the society, operates as a process, a social product, a social function and also as a cause. It has been widely used to describe the processes of social exclusion of groups or sections of population from the recognized key domains of society and their non-participation in and non-integration with several key activities therein. It results in their isolation, stigmatization, non-recognition, subordination and deprivation in society. It is predominantly imposed from above, sustained from within through a normalization process and reproduced collectively in society. These processes are socially, culturally, economically and politically interlinked to remain legitimized through the interrelated dynamics of denials and deprivations, hierarchy and domination, legitimacy and reproduction, and insecurities and protest. The sustenance of marginality gives birth to marginalized identities in society with a host of social ramifications.

Denials and Deprivations as Operational Dynamics of Marginalization

The process of marginalization *economically* denies a section of society ownership, control and even access to productive resources; pushes them to concentrate on the underclass occupational activities; victimizes them through underemployment and seasonal employment; and converts them to cheap labour through uprooting, transition and migration. It *socially* denies them equal status and reinforces their lower status through the practice of caste, race, gender and ethnic hierarchical order. *Politically*, they are denied meaningful access to the formal power structure and participation in the decision-making processes, pushed to emerge as the underdogs, and remain un/under-represented and disempowered in society. *Culturally*, they are deprived of cultural capital by having little access to the opportunities of education, training and other capacity-building facilities, and are relegated to become 'part society with part culture' (Redfield 1959), 'outsider from within', alienated and disintegrated. They emerge to become immigrants or migrants and 'marginal man' due to compulsion and are segregated through linguistic, dress, cultural, etc., barriers. *Spatially*, they are pushed to live in geographically fringe, remote and neglected areas, especially at the outskirts of the village in rural areas and in slums and shanties in urban areas. Hence, they are conditioned to live without even the basic amenities of life and without social, physical, health, food, shelter, etc., securities.

Hierarchy, Domination and Insecurities for Sustenance of Marginalization

Marginalization produces an artificial structure of hierarchy by converting natural differences into a hierarchical order of inequality. Through the practice of segregation on the basis of gender, caste, race, ethnicity, etc., it reinforces the cultural hierarchy, shapes the process of stigmatization and de-recognition of the contribution made by weak and disadvantaged people in society, devaluates the work done by them, and discourages the dominant group (if they want to stay dominant) to share their powers and opportunities with the subordinate strata (Dickie-Clark 1966). Marginalization sets in motion several varieties of insecurities by dislodging the disadvantaged people from their habitats, pushing them to work in insecure and most hazardous working conditions to earn a livelihood, and constraining them to accept jobs without basic minimum economic returns, social security, legal protection, etc. These objective situations very often deprive these people of the required space for upward mobility and push them to construct a sense of subjective insecurity as members of an ethnic minority in a majoritarian society.

Dimension of Legitimacy and Reproduction

Marginality gets legitimized and reproduced through the institutional and normative arrangements and varieties of social practices. It reproduces hierarchy to sustain the hegemony of the dominant group through socialization, education, politicization and enculturation. It culturally conditions the marginalized people to accept the discriminatory social practices as normal by constructing a culture of submission in them. It also simultaneously reproduces the hegemony of the dominant section of society over the marginalized.

Protests as Products of Marginalization

Sustained marginalization promotes deviant, nonconformist social behaviour of the deprived, converts them into passive dropouts or active critics of society and constructs a marginal identity by way of narrowing social distances within the marginalized groups, intensifying a consciousness of identity and generating community solidarity based on the experiences of deprivation, discrimination and exploitation (Gist and Wright 1973). It also helps breed radicalism, violence and social disruption, provides a firm foundation for radical political views (Germani 1980) and constructs strong resistant and new varieties of collective identity and urge for protest. This may push the deprived to get concentrated in a community of primordial identity by developing a feeling of the community of exclusion of the excluded by the excluded (Castells 1997).

These dynamics of marginalization operate through both the relational and cumulative frames of reference. Marginalization is *horizontally relational* with reference to the economic, social, cultural and political undercurrents of society. Further, it is *vertically cumulative* with add-on impacts of the historically experienced and inherited facets of denials, deprivations, insecurity, domination, segregation, and legitimization and reproduction of marginality. The process of articulation of identities and protest of the marginalized are also shaped by the interactivity of these relational and cumulative dynamics (for details, see SinghaRoy 2010).

Conceptualizing Peasants

Though in general parlance and for a section of the academia, peasants are interchangeably used to mean farmers or agriculturalists, they represent a district social category. In the sociological and social anthropological literature, peasants have widely been described economically as small producers working for their own consumption (Redfield 1956) and as subsistence cultivators (Firth 1946) who produce predominantly for fulfilling the needs of their own family rather than to make a profit (Chayanov 1966). They are described *culturally* as 'unsystematic, concrete tradition of many, unreflective, unsophisticated and the non-literati constituting the mosaic of the "little tradition"' (Redfield 1956), the 'incomplete' and a 'part society with part cultures' (Redfield 1959). *Politically*, they are found to occupy an 'underdog position and are subjected to domination by outsiders' (Shanin 1984), and are unorganized and deprived of the knowledge required for organized collective action (Wolf 1984, 264–65). *Historically*, peasants have always borne the brunt of extreme forms of subordination and oppression in society. However, specific socio-economic conditions of their existence have largely shaped the roles of the peasantry in social change and transformation.

Interestingly, peasants are described to have dichotomous social identities. On the one hand, they have been described as an undifferentiated, conservative and awkward social category devoid of the potential for social movements of wider social concern and revolution; on the other hand, they have been described as a progressive and autonomous social group capable of concrete class actions. In the context of 18th-century France, for example, Karl Marx described peasants as a social category devoid of revolutionary potential. Their community members were isolated from one another. Even though they were a community, it was 'formed by the simple addition of homologous magnitudes, much as potatoes in a sack form a sack of potatoes' (Marx 1974, 231). To Lenin, however, the peasantry in late 19th- and early 20th-century Russia was differentiated by unequal patterns of landholding, income and contact with the market. They were also described to have revolutionary potential (Lenin 1972, 497–98). Notwithstanding the dichotomous perceptions, the peasantry has played crucial roles in several great revolutions, social movements and in daily grass-roots struggles.

Peasants in Political Action

Historically, peasants have demonstrated the potential for protest, revolt and revolution, and have participated in all varieties of collective political actions. Scrutinizing data from all over the world, Shanin (1984) has categorized peasants' political action as independent class action, guided political action, fully spontaneous action, amorphous political action and passive resistance that was practised under the leadership of Gandhi during India's freedom movement (251–63). However, peasants' participation in collective political mobilizations is not mechanical. Rather, it is dependent on the changing nature of the economic foundation of the society, what Marxists call the historical stages of participation in a revolution (Alavi 1965, 243), on the structure of power and class alignments in the society (Moore 1966), and on mobilization techniques, leadership and ideologies of the movements that could earn the trust of the peasants. Historical evidence shows that while peasants have often constituted a 'break in the middle- and working-class revolutions in the West, they have played a crucial role in anti-colonial movements in the developing world. The starving peasant, outside the class system, is the first among the exploited here to discover that only violence pays' (Fanon 1971, 47).

According to Hobsbawm (1972, 13), 'though "peasantness" of the peasantry can be described by "subalternity, poverty, exploitation and oppression," they are also capable of resisting attack and developing counter attack'. Antonio Gramsci (1998) observed the peasantry in the context of Italy as a part of a larger socio-political order and not as a discrete entity. Though they lack unity and collective consciousness and participate in their own subordination by subscribing to hegemonic values constructed by the ruling class, they can develop subaltern consciousness to break their subordination through an alliance between workers (Gramsci 1998). In the Indian context, peasants as subaltern groups maintain an autonomous domain of politics in their own way to contest the structure of subordination through spontaneous mobilizations, as reflected in their uprisings and insurgencies, unrest in looting *hats* (local village markets) and also in organized peasant movements (Guha 1982, 4–6).

Peasant resistance is also reflected in a covert form through 'hidden transcripts' as described by James Scott (1985). To him, subordinates in the structures of domination of society have a fairly extensive social existence which is outside the immediate control of the dominant. Behind the scenes, they are likely to create and defend a social space in which offstage dissent to the official transcript of power relations may be voiced. Every subordinate group creates, out of this ordeal, a 'hidden transcript' that represents a critique of power as spoken behind the back of the dominant (Scott 1990, 4–15).

All through the history, peasants have represented themselves through distinctive identities either by their everyday existence and participation in verities of social movements or though their hidden transcript. In the emerging globalized world, though the peasantry no more represent the largest segment of humanity, they in many ways represent the largest segment of the marginalized people on earth, and their marginalization is reproduced and sustained within the broad economic, cultural, social, economic and political arrangements of society. In India, peasants have remained circumscribed to be marginalized. However, in recent years, with the fast social transition, the nature of construction of identity of peasants and their intersectionality with their inherited caste and ethnic identities has acquired added significance and complexity.

Peasants, Castes and Tribes in India

Peasants in India are a socially and economically marginalized, culturally subjugated and politically disempowered social group that is attached to land to eke out a subsistence living. They represent a vast mass of landless agricultural labourers, sharecroppers, tenants, poor artisans and small and marginal cultivators. In the localized vocabulary, peasants are also known as

- *kisan, krishak, rythu, chashi*, etc. (more or less indicating cultivators who cultivate land with their own labour);
- *adhiar* and *bhagchashi* (sharecropper and tenant); and
- *majdoor, majur, coolie, pait, krishi, shramik*, etc. (agricultural labourers).

A section of peasants also combine part-time activities of fishing, cattle raising, smithy, pottery, small shop keeping, bee keeping, etc. activities with agricultural activities. Though in a rural society, peasants are linked to farmers, there are both qualitative and quantitative differences between them from social, economic, political and numerical considerations. While the peasants are numerically vast in size, they are socially, economically and politically subjugated and dominated. On the other hand, while the farmers are numerically smaller is size, they are economically, politically and socially dominant. In the localized vocabulary, the farmers stand for *Bada Kisan, Zamindar, Jotedar, Bhuswami, Malik* and many such indigenous categories (notwithstanding the declining significance of many such categories in the wake of land reforms) who essentially own large sizes of land, employ modern technology (tractors, threshers, deep tube wells, chemical fertilizers, high-yield-variety seeds, etc.) and predominantly employ agricultural labourers, sharecroppers and tenants for the cultivation of their land. They mostly engage themselves in a supervisory role in agriculture even though a section of them may be self-employed in agriculture. They primarily produce for the market. They are economically affluent, enterprising, and mobile, and are linked to the market. They are politically influential, represent the dominant section of the rural society and experience a good deal of upward social mobility. Socially, they predominantly belong to the upper and middle strata of the caste hierarchy and have a higher level of access to education, mass media and the formal power structure of society. Being self-employed and employers, they get a higher recognition and status in society.

Peasants in India, on the other hand, own a very small or marginal size of land or use such land as small and marginal cultivators, sharecroppers or tenants, or are engaged in others' land as labourers. They seldom have the capacity to employ modern techniques of cultivation; to get access to market, good education and powerful social networks; or to experience upward mobility and get connected with political authorities and the formal institutional arrangement of the state. They traditionally occupy a subjugated position in society. In the localized cultural terms, their work participation is devaluated, and they are often termed as belonging to uncivilized, rustic, primitive, etc., segments of society, these terms openly indicating their demeaning, marginalized and inferior status in society. Peasants are thus widely depicted through cultural connotations that invariably represent their marginalized status in society.

Furthermore, in India and especially within the broad fold of the Hindu social order, peasants predominantly belong to the outcastes represented by the *Antaja*s and the *Sudra*s belonging to the social categories of untouchables and others practising unclean ascribed occupations and extramural manual activities of various sorts. Within the conventional cultural framework of the *Varna* system, they are provided with a stigmatized existence and are considered to be impure and are kept away from varieties of social and cultural interactions with the higher *Varna*s, namely, the *Brahmin*s, *Kshatriya*s, and *Vaishya*s. The so-called 'outcastes' of the *Varna* hierarchy in the real sense of the term form the core of the peasantry in rural India. They have a close social interface with the socially deprived categories of STs, SCs, OBCs, religious minorities, women and rural poor. The age-old association between this lowest social status and low economic position has always provided a basis for their socio-economic marginalization and political disempowerment in society.

Peasant societies in India, however, have neither remained isolated entities nor homogenous in character. Fast economic transition, implementation of state policies of land reforms and varieties of developmental initiatives, penetration of the forces of globalization, spread of communication networks and road and transport systems, adoption of new technologies and introduction of commercial crop cultivation and the practice of democracy at the grass-roots level have altered many of the predefined notions of these societies. Along with occupational diversification, a vast segment of peasants have emerged to be the part-time or seasonal milkman, rickshaw or cart pullers, construction workers, petty shop keepers, etc., in rural areas. Moreover, many of them now migrate seasonally to urban areas and have emerged to be connected with the wider world for economic pursuits. Herein, a section of them have also become politically active by getting associated with ideologies and organizations of various political parties, and have been persistently part of varieties of collective mobilizations and social movements such as nationalist, tribe, Dalit, peasant, environmental, anti-displacement, etc., movements. However, despite such transition, the historically inherited marginalized status has remained attached to the peasantry in India, and this has provided the basis for their sustained mobilization in society on one issue or the other.

Indian history is replete with several vehement radical peasant movements and their sustained political mobilization for routinized collective action There has also been a shift from radicalization to institutionalization in the patterns of peasant mobilization in the country. This shift been marked by peasants' participation in collective mobilizations for land rights, land distribution, higher wages for work, implementation of development schemes, reservation policy or statehood, and exercising their adult franchise for Panchayat (local self-government at the village level), state assembly and parliamentary elections. As developmental initiatives of the state and the broad processes of agrarian transformation have been unable to break the foundations of their relational and cumulative marginalization in society, peasants' participation in collective mobilizations, whether radical or institutionalized, has remained to be an integral part of agrarian dynamics across the country. They have always articulated the strategy of resistance and collective protests and have become part of varieties of social movements to break the circle of their marginalization in society. Hence, the patterns of peasants' participation in collective mobilizations are linked to the very nature of agrarian transformation in India and their economic status therein.

Peasantry and Agrarian Transformation in Independent India: Reflection on Economic Status

Independent India inherited an extremely stratified agrarian society from the British which was characterized by an exploitative intermediary system of land tenure, innumerable subinfeudation in landholding, tenurial insecurity, rack renting and extra economic coercion of peasants. In this agrarian society, peasants were experiencing sharp downward mobility from the category of small cultivators to tenants or sharecroppers and further to agricultural labourers who form the core of the peasantry. Such mobility was accompanied by their unbearable state of unemployment, poverty, feudal domination, inhuman treatment and deep-rooted social and political exclusion in society. From the early parts of the 20th century, organized peasant movements such as the Champaran movement (1917), Kheda Satyagraha (1918), Bardoli Satyagraha (1928), etc., manifested in many parts of the country to protest against the oppressive anti-peasant measures of the British. There was also large-scale participation of peasants in the civil disobedience movement for India's independence. These movements were mostly non-violent in nature. On the eve of India's independence, radical peasant movements such as those of Tebhaga (1946–47) in Bengal and Telangana (1947–48) in Telangana also surfaced, with demands for 'land to the tillers', *tebhaga* (two-third instead of one-half) share of agricultural produce for the sharecroppers, human dignity and abolition of forced and bonded labour, etc. These movements compelled the state to look into the state policy on land and the status of peasants in the Indian society very seriously. Immediately after Independence, several progressive land reform legislations were introduced by all the provincial governments in India to abolish the intermediaries, provide tenurial security to the tenants, distribute the surplus vested lands among the poor and consolidate landholding. However, due to the unquestioned domination of the landed class, lack of political will of the state and lack of awareness and organization of peasants, except for the abolition of the Zamindari, etc., systems, land reforms were not sincerely implemented in most parts of the country. The productivity of land remained unaltered and the condition of peasants deteriorated heavily. Hunger and starvation to death became so rampant that India emerged to be a major food-borrowing country in the 1960s. Peasants were hit the hardest. Radical peasant movements, especially the Naxalite movements of West Bengal, raged like wildfire in many parts of rural India. The Government of India again formulated national guidelines for land reforms in 1971 to radicalize the land reform programme. Though the extent of implementation of these land reforms has not yet been the same all over India, over the decades, the intermediary system of land-holding has been abolished, the size of big landholdings has declined, the proportion of landless households has declined and the proportion of semi-marginal and marginal landowning households has increased across the country. Land reforms have also caused large-scale eviction of sharecroppers and their sharp downward mobility. Within these processes, peasants have been effectively concentrated to the categories of small and marginal cultivators, landless and semi-landless landowners, sharecroppers and agricultural labourers. The changing patterns of landholding and the location of peasants within these processes are shown in Table 3.1.

As shown in Table 3.1, in 1961–62, around 60.6% of rural households belonged to the category of marginal cultivators owning up to one hectare of land. In 1991–92, the proportion of marginal cultivators increased to around 62.8%, and in 2012–13, to above 75%. There has also been a significant increase in the area occupied by these categories of landowners from 7.59% to 15.06 % and further to around 30% of the total cultivable area during this period. On the other hand, the proportion of semi-medium cultivators declined from 12.86% to 5.1%, medium cultivators from 9.07% to 1.93% and large cultivators from 2.85% to 0.24% of rural households during the period between 1961–62 and 2012–13. There has been a corresponding decline in the area of the land occupied by medium and large landowners from 31.23% and 28.24%, respectively, during 1961–62 to 18.83% and 0.24% during 2012–13.

There, however, has been a marginal increase in the quantum of landholding among the semi-medium category of land owners from

Table 3.1

Percentage Distribution of Rural Households by the Size of Landholding and Covered Area in 1961–62, 1991–92 and 2012–13 in India

Categories of Households	1961–62	1991–92	2012–13
Marginal (0–1.00)	60.06 (7.59)	62.8 (15.6)	75.42 (29.75)
Small (1.01–2.00)	15.16 (12.40)	17.8 (18.7)	10.00 (23.54)
Semi-medium (2.01–4.00)	12.86 (20.54)	12.0 (24.1)	5.01 (22.07)
Medium (4.01–10.00)	9.07 (31.23)	6.1 (26.4)	1.93 (18.83)
Large (10.00+)	2.85 (28.24)	1.3 (15.2)	0.24 (5.81)
Total	100 (100)	100 (100)	100 (100)

Source: NSS, 1961–62, 1992 and 2013.

Note: Figures in parentheses show the percentage distribution of the area owned by each category.

20.54% to 22.07% during the period under reference despite a decline in the proportion of this category of agrarian households in rural areas. Very significantly, the quantum of land occupied by the small cultivators has substantially increased from 12.40% to around 23.54% during this period even though the proportion of small cultivators has decreased from 15.16% to 10%. A holistic scenario suggests that in 1961–62, less than 25% of rural upper-strata households (semi-medium, medium and large) had occupied around 80% of the land, while around 75% of lower category landowning households (marginal and small) occupied less than 20% of the land. In contemporary India (i.e., 2012–13), a total of 7.18% rural households (semi-medium, medium and large) occupy 47.54% of the rural land, and 85.42% of marginal and small households occupy 43.29% of the rural land. The increase in the semi-medium, small and a section of marginal ownership, however, has not always been caused by land reforms and land distribution but also by division and subdivision in land ownership of the joint family system, and large scale malafide land transfer in the 1960s and 1970s for avoiding the land ceiling acts. Thus, an increased concentration of rural households in these categories is not an indicator of increase in the category of cultivating peasants, as in substantive terms, the land–man ratio has drastically decreased in the country. This has also impacted the patterns of work participation in agriculture.

Declining Land–Man Ratio

Notwithstanding such land transfer and unequal state of landholding per household in the country, landholding has declined from 1.78 hectare in 1961–62 to 0.73 hectare in 2002–03 and further to 0.59 hectare in 2012–13. As far as the per capita landholding is concerned, it has sharply declined from 0.48 hectare per person in 1951 to 0.12 hectare per person in 2013. The phenomenon of increasing decline in per household and per capita landholding over the last half century is shown in Tables 3.2 and 3.3.

Table 3.2

Availability of Per Household Land in 1961–62, 2002–3 and 2012–13 at All India Level

	1961–62	2002–2003	2012–13
Average area owned per household (ha)	1.780	0.725	0.592

Source: NSSO, 1961–62, 2003 and 2013.

Table 3.3
Availability of Per Capita Land in India in 1951, 1981, 2001 and 2013

Year	Cultivable Land Including Forests	Total Cultivable Land Excluding Forests
1951	9.89	0.48
1981	0.50	0.20
2001	0.33	0.15
2013	–	0.12

Source: Census 1951, 1981, 2001 and NSSO 2013.

Peasants and Changing Patterns of Work Participation

Peasants predominantly belonging to the categories of landless, semi-landless, marginal and small landowning cultivators altogether form 92% of rural households of India. (The phenomena of landless and semi-landless are discussed in relation to the caste and tribal composition of peasants in the next section of this chapter.) In terms of the average size of landholding and the average size of the household with four to five family members, none can sustain their livelihood on the meagre income from the land. Hence, they engage themselves in wage earning both inside and outside agriculture as labourers. Significantly, with the declining economic condition, there has been declining work participation as cultivators and increasing work participation as agricultural labourers and marginal workers among peasants.

Over the decades, as shown in Table 3.4, the proportion of cultivators has sharply declined from 49.9% in 1951 to 31.7% in 2001 and further to 24.65% in 2011. On the other hand, work participation as agricultural labourers has increased from 19.5% in 1951 to 30% in 2011 and as non-agricultural workers from 30.6% in 1951 to 45.4% in 2011. These data

Table 3.4
Changing Work Participation Patterns of Peasants in Agriculture since 1951

Year	Cultivators	Agricultural	Non-agricultural
1951	49.9	19.5	30.6
2001	31.7	30.08	37.5
2011	24.65	30	45.4

Source: Census 1951, 2001 and 2011.

Table 3.5
Percentage of Main and Marginal Workers among Total Workers, India, 1981–2011

	Percentage of Main Workers			Percentage of Marginal Workers		
Year	Total	Rural	Urban	Total	Rural	Urban
1981	91.0	89.4	97.4	9.0	10.6	2.6
1991	91.0	89.3	97.8	9.0	10.7	2.2
2001	77.8	73.9	90.8	22.2	26.1	9.2
2011	75.2	70.5	87.6	24.8	29.5	12.4

Source: Census 1981, 1991, 2001 and 2011.

show that a section of peasants are working more as agricultural labourers than as cultivators because of the meagre size of landholding and that a large section of them are also shifting very fast towards the non-agricultural sector for employment. This shift can also be attributed to the fact that full employment is not available for a large section of these peasants in rural areas and they remain underemployed. This is aptly reflected in the quantum of increase of the category of marginal workers in rural India.

Table 3.5 explicitly shows that the quantum of work participation of peasants as main workers has substantially declined in India, while their work participation as marginal workers (who get less than 180 days of work in a year) has phenomenally increased, especially in rural areas. In 1981, only 10.6% of the total workers in rural India were marginal workers, but in 2001, this figure phenomenally increased to 26.1% and again in 2011, it increased to 29.5%. Marginal work participation is a function of underemployment and economic and livelihood insecurity that have shaped the life stories of peasants even in contemporary India.

Peasant, Caste and Tribe: Reflection on Their Interface and Status

As mentioned in the first section of this chapter, peasants predominantly belong to lower caste and ethnic backgrounds. Despite land reforms, the close association between the social and the agrarian hierarchy has remained largely unaltered, especially for peasants. This is illustrated with the emerging patterns of landholding among the STs, SCs and OBCs in rural India, as shown in Table 3.6.

Table 3.6

Landholding by Caste/Ethnic Backgrounds

Size Class of Land Possessed (ha)	Percentage Distribution of Agricultural Households by Social Group				
	STs	SCs	OBCs	Others	All
<0.01	9.4	28.0	52.2	10.4	100.0
0.01–0.40	9.7	22.4	44.6	23.3	100.0
0.41–1.00	15.7	15.9	45.2	23.2	100.0
1.01–2.00	17.6	10.9	45.5	26.0	100.0
2.01–4.00	13.8	7.7	47.2	31.3	100.0
4.01–10.00	8.0	6.2	44.4	41.4	100.0
10.00+	3.2	2.9	52.8	41.1	100.0
All sizes	13.4	16.3	45.4	24.9	100.0

Source: NSSO (2013).

Table 3.6 shows that the landless, semi-landless and marginal cultivators are largely represented by the STs, SCs and OBCs who traditionally occupy a lower social position in the Indian society. Of the total rural households owning less than 0.01 hectare of land (majority of them are landless), 9.4% belong to the STs, 28% to the SCs, 52% to the OBCs and only 10% to the other social categories. Similarly, of the total rural households owning land with sizes in the range 0.01–0.40 hectare and 0.41–1.00 hectare, 9.7% and 15.7%, respectively, belong to the STs, 22% and 15.9% to the SCs, 44.6% and 45.2% to the OBCs and 23.35% and 23.2% to the other social categories. As far as landholding with sizes of 1.01–2.00 hectare and 2.01–4.00 hectare are concerned, 17.06% and 13.8%, respectively, belong to the STs, 10.09% and 7.7% to the SCs, 45.5% and 47.2% to the OBCs and 26% and 31.3% to the other social categories. Of the households holding 4.00–10.00 hectare and above 10 hectare, 8% and 3.2%, respectively, belong to the STs, 6.2% and 2.9% to the SCs, 44.4% and 52.8% to the OBCs and 41.4% and 41.1% to the other social categories. Though the OBCs are more advantageously placed than the SCs and STs, only a small section among them have greater access to landed resources. It is very explicit that as the landholding size increases, the representation of lower castes and tribal groups decreases, thus showing a higher degree of concentration of peasants among the STs, SCs and OBCs. This is further reflected in their average sizes of landholding and in the pattern of their work participation.

Table 3.7
Landholding and Employment among SCs, STs, OBCs and Others in Rural Areas

Social Category	Average Size of Per Household Landholding	Landless and Semi-landless (0–0.04 ha)	Nature of Employment		
			Self-employed	Labour	Others
ST	0.77	34.51	45.7	45.3	8.9
SC	0.30	56.9	34.2	56.0	9.8
OBC	0.75	38.2	56.2	32.7	11.0
Others	100.00	31.1	61.4	23.7	15.3
All			51.7	36.7	11.6

Source: NSSO (2013).

Table 3.7 shows that in comparison to other social groups, the STs have a relatively higher average size of landholding with per household landholding at 0.77 hectare. In comparison to all other categories, they have a less proportion of households with 34.51% belonging to the category of landless and semi-landless households. However, in comparison to the OBCs and others, they have more people working as labourers. As high as 45.3% of them are employed as labourers to earn their livelihood, and 45% of them are self-employed on land. Higher landholding is seldom an indicator of higher economic status for the STs as a vast section of them traditionally possess rocky and forest lands. They lack the appropriate technology to bring all such land under cultivation. The SCs, on the other hand, have the least average size of per household landholding at 0.30 hectare. They have a high proportion of landless and semi-landless households with 56.9% of them belonging to these categories. Only 34.2% of them work as self-employed, while 56% work as labourers. The OBCs have an average size of landholding of 0.75 hectare, and 38.2% of these households are either landless or semi-landless. More than 56% of the OBC households are self-employed, while 32.7% are wage employed as labourers. For the other social categories, the average size of landholding is 1 hectare; 31.1% of their households belong to the category of landless and semi-landless, and as high as 61.4% of these households are self-employed while only 23.7% of them are employed as labourers. In fact, higher incidence of rural workers participating as labourers depict a high degree of economic uncertainty and poverty among these households. The incidence of poverty is highest among the STs at more than 47.3% followed by the SCs at around 37% households below the poverty line.

Though peasants are attached to land, the meagre size of their landholding neither provides them livelihood security nor the scope of upward mobility. In general, in the peasant society, a lower status in the caste hierarchy is positively linked to a lower amount of landholding, landlessness and semi-landlessness. The positive correlation between lower social status, low access to land and effective productive resources, and higher degree of work participation as wage labourers and sustained livelihood insecurity has remained a historical and contemporary reality of peasants in India. Despite such insecure relations to land, their attachment to agriculture is widely conditioned by the lack of potential alternative choices of livelihood security. A vast section of them are compelled to remain engaged in cultivation mostly by compulsion than by choice. In general parlance, their engagement with manual agricultural activities is culturally considered to be demeaning and stigmatized, and their contribution to society remains non-rewarding and unrecognized. Culturally, they are considered *chasa* (uncivilized), *voranga* (non-intelligent), rustic, etc., in many parts of the country. Hence, besides remaining economically weak and exploited, they also culturally remain non-integrated in society. Consequent upon such non-integration, they are subjected to social and political domination by the dominant section of society. Hence, their voices mostly remain unrepresented in wider society. Such deprivation, disempowerment and denigration have been reproduced in society for generations, thereby constructing their distinctive marginalized identity in the Indian society. Such a situation has always provided the basis for the protest and mobilization of the peasantry in India for varieties of collective actions.

Transformation of Peasant Movements and Formation of New Identities

India has a long history of peasant movements. While many of these were organized by established organizations or charismatic leaders, many have also emerged from the lower strata of society. In fact, sustained poverty, unemployment, traditional coercive bondage, virtual lack of mobility and choice, extortion by the market, state and many leaders, subjugation by the traditional structure of domination and formation of new identities of peasants at the grass-roots level have provided the basis for their sustained mobilization in society.

In contrast to the observations of a few scholars that the structural features of the Indian society, which are dominated by caste, religion, and ethnicity, ensured that the peasantry played a passive rather than a revolutionary role in the country (Moore 1966), peasants in India have actively participated in all verities of collective actions.

Peasants in India have revolted on many occasions against their oppression through various means. They were mobilized to take part in various protests against the oppressive feudal order and the anti-peasant measures of the British. As the nationalist movement emerged, they took part in the Champaran movement (1917), Kheda Satyagraha (1918) and Bardoli Satyagraha (1928) in the civil disobedience movement for India's independence through non-violent means (Alavi 1965, 242–43). Tribal peasants also participated in the tribal movement against their oppression by land owners, outsiders, government officials, money lenders and other such categories.

The Radical Movements

As pointed out in the previous section, India experienced vehement peasant movements just before and after the departure of the British from the Indian subcontinent. The Tebhaga movement took place in Bengal in 1946–47; it was organized under the auspices of Bengal Kisan Sabha, a provincial wing of All India Kisan Sabha spearheaded by Communists for the implementation of the demands for a two-third share of agricultural produce for sharecroppers as against the traditional one-half and 'land to the tillers'. Peasants asserted their rights by forcefully cutting and stacking paddy in their own courtyard against the will of the landlords, resisted the combined force of the police and landlords and unitedly fought the armed forces with traditional weapons. The movement saw an unprecedented participation by SC, ST, OBC and women peasants. Women, in fact, came to the forefront of the struggle to resist the police and protect their family from attacks of the landlords. This movement spread rapidly across West Bengal, and in Khanpur village of Dinajpur district, which was the epicentre of this movement, police firing killed 14 peasants in one day. Though the peasants tried to develop strong resistance against the combined force of the police and landlords, it collapsed shortly in the face of strong repressive measures such as killing, torture and public flogging by the police and administration on the one hand and lack of coordination among the peasantry and the collapse of their leadership on the other (SinghaRoy 1992, 2013).

The peasant movement in Telangana also took place around the same time. Through armed struggle in 1946–52, the peasantry of the Telangana region of Andhra Pradesh engaged themselves in a prolonged struggle against the feudal land tenure system and its exploitative practices, such as land grabbing, illegal taxing, forced and bonded labour, extra-economic coercion, rack renting, indebtedness and daily humiliation. Under the leadership of the Left-dominated Andhra Maha Sabha, the peasantry took part in a guerrilla armed struggle to overthrow the Nizam (the princely ruler) of Hyderabad. The organized collective action by the SC, ST, OBC and women peasants became the driving force behind this movement. The Government of India initiated military action against the Nizam in 1947 and overthrew him, resulting in the region's merger with the Indian Union. The state subsequently initiated military action against the peasant movement activists in September 1948. The Communists adopted the path of protracted struggle. Several hundreds of peasant rebels were killed while facing the army of the Nizam and of India. However, after the Nizam was overthrown by the Indian Army in 1951, the Politburo of the Communist Party of India called off the struggle and opted for parliamentary democracy to espouse the cause of the peasantry (Dhanagare 1983; SinghaRoy 2004, 2013).

India again experienced the manifestation of radical peasant movements in late 1969 in the Naxalbari area of West Bengal against the backdrop of non-implementation of land reform laws, large-scale eviction of sharecroppers from their land, poverty, unemployment, continuation of feudal coercion and livelihood insecurity of peasants. The peasants of Naxalbari, under the leadership of the Darjeeling District Committee of West Bengal of the Communist Party of India, started taking possession of surplus vested lands, arming themselves with conventional weapons such as bows and arrows and spears, and set up a parallel administration to look after villages. They also declared a few 'liberated areas'. Although the state objected to such actions by initiating police action, the movement spread like wildfire across the state and in many other parts of India and propagated the seizure of state power through guerrilla warfare within the Marxist–Leninist and Maoist ideological frameworks. In addition to peasants, many urban intellectuals and students from reputed educational institutions in the country participated in this struggle. The Communist Party of India (Marxist–Leninist) was formed in 1969 to spearhead the movement across the country. However, this movement was unable to sustain itself in the face of strong state action that killed hundreds and arrested thousands on the one hand and lack of popular support for this movement on the other. This movement, however, continues to reappear in rural India through Naxalite extremism, widely known as the Maoist

Movement, as more than a dozen of Naxalite outfits are active in contemporary India under different names, covering more than one-third of the country's territory, mostly in the backward areas (SinghaRoy 1992, 2004).

Though these peasant movements took place in different places and at different points of time, ideologically and also in terms of orientation towards change and forms of mobilization, they were radical in nature and constructed a radical identity of peasants. The solidarity of their collective identity was reflected through their collective act of forceful occupation of land, cutting of standing paddy, harvesting of paddy in their own courtyard against the will of the landowners, attacking the police and administration, participating in guerrilla warfare, sheltering injured radical activists, developing self-defence against the police, maintaining a channel of communication with underground activists, etc. The Telangana and Naxalite movements were explicit in their radical attempt to overthrow the state.

Drive towards Institutionalization

Since the late 1970s, India, however, has been experiencing the intertwining between radical and reformative peasant movements. With the Communists coming into power in West Bengal, Kerala and Tripura, and emerging as a viable political force in the country for taking up the issues of peasants, many radical peasant leaders have shunned radicalism and joined parliamentary politics. Along with such changes, the process of institutionalization of peasant movements has taken place in many parts of the country. Besides participating in institutionalized collective mobilizations on the issues of speedy distribution of surplus vested land, tenurial security of sharecroppers, higher wages for agricultural labourers, the peasants are now also participating in collective mobilizations on the issues of road, education, electricity in rural areas, protection of environment, prohibition of liquor, reservation and reorientation of the reservation policy, displacement implementation of development initiatives, etc. They have emerged to be a driving force of democracy in grass-roots politics and mobilization. In many places, they have been the elected members of Panchayats.

Peasant movements have acquired new dimensions in India since the late 1990s with the participation of peasants in anti-land acquisition movements spearheaded by local agriculturalists. Those were in fact anti-globalization movements at the grass-roots level in one form or the other. Though these movements have taken place in many parts of the country, they have acquired a new social and political collective identity in West Bengal through the large-scale participation of peasants in agriculturalists' agitation against forceful acquisition of land by the state for private industrial houses in Singur and for a special economic zone in Nandigram. Small and marginal cultivators, who were again the driving force of these movements, came to the forefront of these agitations by apprehending immediate loss of their land and livelihood. As urbanization, rural–urban connectivity, migration and a plethora of development initiatives were unable to bring a substantive alteration in the life and livelihood of peasants, their attachment to land has remained the ultimate source of their economic and social security. They have also always remained rooted to the society, culture and history of their surroundings through their possession of land, despite it being very meagre in size. Dispossession of land without any immediate sustainable support brought in them a deep sense of threat to their last source of livelihood, food security and cultural and social rootedness. As their perceived threat started getting political collective articulation at the grass-roots level, they found in the All India Trinamool Congress, the then main opposition party in the three-decade United Left Front–ruled state of West Bengal, a big potential to lead the movement. These movements got huge support from most sections of rural population and from unban intellectuals. Continuous mass mobilization and protest and opposition by agriculturalists compelled the state to postpone its land acquisition plan in Nandigram and Tata Motors to suspend its automobile manufacturing unit from Singur and shift its plant to Gujarat. These movements were a game changer in West Bengal politics as through these movements the Trinamool Congress started gaining a stronghold among the peasants, and in the next Assembly elections of 2006, it dislodged the 35-year-old United Left Front government from power. Through political and legal battle, the peasants also got their land back by developing an alliance with established political parties. These movements were in essence institutionalized in nature.

Similarly, peasants in other states have also participated in various environmental movements and in movements against listed industrial projects, such as agriculturalists' movements against land acquisition in Lucknow and Noida in Uttar Pradesh, the Gujjar movement to change the caste status in Rajasthan, etc.

The contemporary collective mobilizations of the peasantry have been characterized by their frequent participation in political meetings, processions, strikes, demonstrations, voting and campaigns, making legal petitions, collective persuasions, etc. These mobilizations of peasants have widely emerged to be reformative and institutionalized when organized by recognized political parties and civil society organizations for varieties of routinized collective actions. In India, a section of peasants have retained their association with radical Maoist movements that are covertly active in many backward and forest areas in the country. However, a large section of these peasants have also transformed their mobilization to be reformative and institutionalized in essence. A section has also started participating in the democratic electioneering processes. In the process of such transition, in general, the radical identity of peasants has taken the shape of a reformative one that is looking for changes within the institutionalized arrangement of the society. The trends of such changes are shown in Table 3.8.

Table 3.8

Changing Trends of Collective Mobilizations and Construction of Peasant Identities

	Radical Peasant Movements	Reformative Peasant Movements
a)	Mobilizations aimed to construct class identities to direct against identified class enemies—big landowners, usurers, police and administration.	Mobilizations construct and rejuvenate varieties of identities varying from geographical (i.e., rural) to gender, caste, tribe, environmentalist displaced person, etc. Though these mobilizations are directed against the state, the immediate 'others' have remained diffused.
b)	Peasant identities were solidified for aggressive and hostile mobilizations, against old arrangements, norms and values. Such mobilizations were without immediate limit.	Peasant identities are reformulated on diverse issues and interests, and these are calculated and their aggressiveness and hostilities are kept within given limits and directions. Mobilizations of peasants have also been for re-informing selected old norms and values and inculcating new ones.
c)	Political identities of peasants were constructed under the auspices of a single ideological and organizational (at times, secret organizational) pursuit wherein the leadership came from outside.	Political identities of peasants are nurtured under diverse ideological and organizational (mostly, recognized organizational) pursuits wherein the leadership is grown even from within.
d)	Constructed identities were mostly closed in nature by ideology and organization. Diverse views were not encouraged, and all diversified identities were subsumed under the class identities.	Constructed identities experience a good deal of openness and autonomy as peasants become simultaneously members of more than one ideology and organization.

(Table 3.8 continued)

(Table 3.8 continued)

Radical Peasant Movements	Reformative Peasant Movements
e) Constructed identities aimed to bring in far-reaching structural changes, and peasants acquired the identity of 'change agents'.	Constructed identities mostly propagate for structural stability and reformative initiatives within the given structure; and peasants acquires the identity of 'beneficiaries'.
f) Peasant identity was constructed mostly on localized issues; primordialities were overcome in addressing common interests as most of them had a common history of struggle.	Peasant identities are not necessarily constructed on localized considerations as they are subjected to inter-penetration of diverse political and ideological forces; primordial ties are asserted to essentialize identities.

Source: Author's own.

From Class Orientation to Multidimensional Identities

The processes of construction of peasant identities through these two phases—radical and reformative—may be exemplified with cases from West Bengal and Andhra Pradesh. Both in West Bengal and Andhra Pradesh, radical peasant movements constructed a 'class identity' of the peasants by categorizing them as the rural 'proletariat' taking cognizance of their common economic plights and social deprivations and directing their collective action against the identified class enemy of the landowners, money lenders and the state apparatus. The euphoria of class action overshadowed the economic, social, cultural and gender differences among the peasants.

However, once the radical phase of the movement was over, many of these differences resurfaced, asserting their inherited primordial and cultural distinctiveness. Importantly, despite such attempts of rearticulating their identities through primordiality, the Left political parties have been mobilizing peasants to construct class identities by articulating the issues of poverty, unemployment, landless livelihood, tenurial insecurity, land ceiling, land distribution, etc. The United Left Front government of West Bengal that came into power in 1977 emphasized on 'classness' of peasant identity and speedy implementation of land reforms, rural development, etc., programmes. However, due to the persisting livelihood insecurity of rural peasants, increasing meagre size of landholding and declining land–man ratio on the one hand and gradual expansion of non-agricultural avenues of employment in rural Bengal on the other, an important segment of poor peasants now look for alternative non-agricultural avenues of employment. In West Bengal, land reform is no more a 'hot' political issue.

With increased interactivity with the outside world and expansion of non-agricultural activities in rural areas, peasants now have emerged to be part cultivators, part labourers, part sharecroppers, part milkmen, part rickshaw pullers, part petty shop owners, part contract labourers, part migrants and part natives. The democratic practices and civil society activism at the grass-roots level have helped them to articulate their identities beyond their conventional identity of a poor peasant in the rural society. They are now tied up in multiple employee relations with varieties of employers who are devoid of traditional dependency relations on the land owners. Such a situation has helped construct a new identity and outlook for peasants that look for an alliance and sustained interactivity with the wider world.

Though peasants' association with land is inseparable, as it is through land they remain linked to their culture, environment and society and get a good sense of social and livelihood security, they also want to improve their life in society by getting training for themselves, education for their children, new technology for their land and road and communication facilities for their society. They also want to get associated with the exercise of power at the grass-roots level. Hence, they articulate new identities and get associated with new verities of mobilizations. In Singur in West Bengal, they took recourse to an agriculturalist identity that was more inclusive than the class identity. It was a cultural identity used for a larger economic and political purpose. They become part of established political parties with diverse political pursuits to demand for implementation of development schemes for employment and generation of regular earnings, healthcare, education, shelter, good roads and other facilities. In the process of such mobilizations, they have become exposed to the wider world through contact with mass media, ICTs, and migration and commutation to urban areas. As their social, cultural, economic and political marginalization continue, they rejuvenate their identities in diverse areas by participating in all varieties of collective mobilizations, including those initiated in the name of caste and religion. For example, in the northern part of West Bengal, alongside their political mobilizations under the auspices of political parties like Revolutionary Socialist Party (RSP), Communist Party of India (CPI), Communist Party of India (Marxist) [CPI(M)], Indian National Congress, All India Trinamool Congress (TMC), Bharatiya Janata Party (BJP) and various other political parties for developmental and secular agenda, they are also being mobilized for caste, religion and regional agenda. In recent years, a section of Rajbanshi peasants are mobilized in the Kamtapur movement that emphasizes the need of a separate state for Rajbanshi people. Muslim peasants have got associated with the activities of the Indian Muslim League, while a small section of Hindu peasants have got associated with the Vishwa Hindu Parishad and the BJP. Interestingly, a section of tribal peasants have got associated with the activities of Christian missionaries in rural areas. Peasant identities now intersect with the political identities of established political parties and frequently criss-cross their association with various religious and caste organizations. Participation in multiple mobilizations by peasants is in fact linked to their multiple marginality in society that involves the art of gaining immediate economic benefits on the one hand and the art of resistance against domination and uncertainty of all forms on the other.

Similarly, in Telangana and Andhra Pradesh, grass-roots mobilization has been multidimensional. Besides the political parties in power initiating the grass-roots mobilization through institutionalized means to keep their support base intact, a large chunk of mobilization is initiated by radical Naxalite groups such as CPI (ML) (People's War) (now CPI Maoist) and various other Naxalite outfits, political parties such as Telugu Desam Party, Indian National Congress, BJP, Communist Party of India and the Telangana Rashtra Samithi (TRS), and several civil society organizations. These mobilizations have got both radical and institutionalized facets. The civil society has emerged to be an important player in this process even though radicalism has substantially declined. All these have given the peasantry sufficient space to articulate their identities by associating themselves with varieties of collective bodies. They simultaneously become peasants, civil society activists, caste and tribal group members, etc. Continuous and multidirectional grass-roots mobilizations have paved the way for articulation of multiple identities of peasants.

Innovation of New Identities and Their Fragmentation

The Left movements, especially the radical ones, have played a crucial role in West Bengal, Telangana and Andhra Pradesh for inculcating a secular identity for the peasantry, that is, a class identity through collective mobilizations. These mobilizations helped in reducing the dependency of the peasantry on landowners–cum–money lenders and demolishing the pre-existing structure of primordial dependency and subordination of the former by the latter. However, the lifespan of radical mobilizations is short. The Left political parties have initiated sustained mobilizations of peasants by invoking their class identity for parliamentary democratic practices. In the process of participating in the democratic practices, these parties have not only undergone ideological revisionism but have also made class alliances with other social groups for getting electoral advantage. These modified class-based collective mobilizations have been unable to secure social and economic security for peasants in the countryside. Peasants look for avenues for their livelihood security and mobility and space for the expression of their accumulated discontent. As mobilizations have become multidimensional and multiple actors and organizations are involved in these mobilizations, peasants take part in multiple mobilizations and construct multiple identities through participation in these mobilizations. The sustained mobilizations have now given birth to varieties of local movements by rejuvenating multiple identities in the form of caste, gender, tribe, religion, region, etc., identities from among the peasantry. The process of formation of these new collective identities frequently and explicitly transcends the pre-defined process of class identity formation.

The new identities are in their own ways autonomous of the organizational, ideological and pre-defined boundaries of collectivities as propagated in the class discourse. Though these identities have defined boundaries of inclusion and exclusion—and also at times use the organizational linkages and ideologies of the wider society as guiding principles for their actions—these are not always imposed on them from outside by external agencies. Rather, the peasantry articulate their issues through their everyday experiences of marginalization, and new identities are formed from within in the process of responding to the emerging challenges they regularly face. Sustained mobilizations have made the peasantry aware of the various bases of their oppression and subordination in society, be it caste, class, gender, ethnicity or regionalism. Hence, they accordingly articulate the acts of their resistance both individually and collectively, if needed by reconstructing parallel and at times alternative identities. Here, linkages with external agencies come at a later stage through increasing interactivity with the larger world around. Now through their everyday experiences of struggle and prolonged participation in collective action, the peasantry have been trained to defend their identity and to articulate the strategy of their resistance against domination. These everyday life experiences of resistance form the basis of the praxis of the peasantry against domination whereby they have also got alternative choices to express their resistance against domination.

The Emerging Multiple Identities and Criss-crossing Alliances

Through sustained mobilization, peasants now have become part of local–regional–national connectivity through organization and ideology for a change. Over a period of time, through the process of mobilization and conscientization, a thin layer of peasant leaders are grown from within; however, the peasantry still get their leadership from the middle strata of society who are relatively more connected with the outside world. As class solidarity has got fragmented at one end and the caste, ethic, regional, gender, human rights, etc., solidarities are reformulated at the other, new sorts of social, emotional and economic alliances are in the making for the peasantry. These alliances are cross-class, cross-ethnic, multifaceted and multidirectional. While peasants forge their primordial identity, they privilege their linguistic and ethnic alliances over the pre-existing class identities. Many a time, their economic, social, etc., needs condition them to have association with other primordial groups. Similarly, in the political arena, they form and become part of alliances with various other groups for the practise of democracy at the grass-roots level. Hence, their multiple identities are not formulated in terms of binaries; rather, these are linked to their sustained multiple marginalities in society that are sustained and reproduced historically in India.

The process of marginalization of peasants has remained relational and cumulative. Their social denials due to their lower caste and ethnic backgrounds is reinforced by their economic, cultural and political denials and deprivations, hierarchy and domination, and their reproduction and sustenance. Peasants have always tried to resist and protest against their marginalization. Being the marginalized people in an interconnected world, they now articulate and take recourse to multiple marginalized identities to resist their continued denials, deprivations, domination and subordination in society. Collective protests have been an integral part of such resistance and everyday action in the peasant society. However, in the process of formation of multiple protests, peasants as a social category have acquired a fluid shape that gets consolidated at one end and diffused at the other in the process of articulating their response against their marginality. In the process, they innovate and accommodate new ideas, strategies of actions, and develop new alliances with emerging social forces.

4

Environment, Development and Indigenous People's Identity

Annihilation, Reconciliation and Resistance in Australia*

The indigenous people of Australia, who have distinctive ways of practising and sustaining their life and livelihood, and articulating their traditional identity, have experienced the worst forms of segregation, neglect and torture in society for centuries that have not only taken away their traditional sources of livelihood but also devaluated their identity in the society. For long, they were kept away from the mainstream of the society by the state and its developmental concerns. They are, however, now in the process of engaging themselves with the developmental and reconciliatory initiatives of the state that has initiated host of measures for the integration of indigenous people with the fabric of a plural society. Within this process, they find themselves at a crossroads in their efforts to protect their intrinsic relations with land, nature and culture, on the one hand, and engage with the reconciliatory and developmental dynamics of the state, on the other. In many ways, these engagements and efforts have contributed to the reconstruction of varied forms of indigenous identities

---

*This is a revised version of the paper published in the *Cosmopolitan Civil Society Journal*. I am deeply grateful to Professor James Goodman for his keen interest, regular guidance and wholehearted support in enabling me to undertake this research at the Civil Society Research Centre, University of Technology, Sydney as Endeavour Fellow. I am also grateful to Professor Heather Goodall, Dr Heidi Norman, University of Technology, Sydney, and Professor Stuart Rosewarne, University of Sydney for their profound encouragement and insights. I am extremely thankful to the respondents for kindly allowing me to conduct my field work and agreeing to give me time for discussion with them.

at the grass-roots level. This chapter examines the processes of articulation and rejuvenation of these identities that negotiate with culture, environment, sustainable livelihood and developmental needs of the community, on the one hand, and produce their protests and movements to redefine their relationship with the state and society, on the other. Locating these movements within wider socio-historical contexts, this chapter focuses on the processes of reformulation of indigenous identities in the Australian society that have at places juxtaposed the pro-conservation indigenous perception on cultural and environmental sustainabilities while others have taken the shape of pro-development indigenous identity.

Indigenous Life, Culture and Identity

The life and culture of indigenous people across the globe have largely been characterized by their intrinsic relationships with land, nature and environment. These relationships are further grounded on the ideals of solidarity of their identity, the quest for their autonomy, and the struggle for the preservation of these relationships, and their identity and autonomy. Specifically, large parts of struggle of the indigenous people have remained centred around the protest against their dispossession from traditional land and livelihood, culture and environment, and historical colonization and marginalization in the wider society. For them, collective resistance has remained an integral part of their identity against historical and contemporaneous oppression by the colonial and post-colonial powers who have encroached on their lives and autonomy with the attempt of 'civilizing', 'modernizing', 'mainstreaming', 'developing', 'educating' and 'globalizing' their specific ways of life, institutions and culture. But these initiatives in many ways have resulted in the destruction of the symbiotic relationship between the indigenous people and their environment, causing their economic deprivations, environmental dispossessions, cultural isolation, political subordination, physical annihilation and forced assimilation with a prescribed way of life. As against these backdrops, the engagement of the state, market and civil society with the affairs of the indigenous people has in many places resulted in the reconfiguration and transformation of the identity of indigenous people and the proliferation of their organized social movements against the alleged domination of the state and larger society.

The issues of indigenous identity, the autonomy of indigenous people and their culture have been a part of global concern in the contemporary world. In view of these concerns, the Australian state since the mid-1990s has initiated several measures for the implementation of international obligations, developed elaborate national policies for the accommodation and reconciliation of the indigenous people and has been able to create a thin layer of middle class among them. However, large sections of these people are not yet fully integrated with the state and its developmental reconciliatory initiatives. This has made the indigenous peoples' struggle multidimensional, and the process of rejuvenation and formation of their identity has been very delicate. Herein, the view that indigenous social movements have predominantly constructed and rejuvenated indigenous identity, which has remained mostly fixed to the realm of contestation and protest against the state, its coercive apparatus and the dominant sections of society, would be critically examined. Hence, the major questions are as follows: What has been the nature of formation of indigenous identity in the context of indigenous movements in Australia that engage with the issues of culture, nature and development? Has there been any uniformity in the process of such formation? What has been the nature of transformation of such identity? Towards this endeavour, the following three cases have been selected for investigation: (a) indigenous people's resistance against the Sandon Point Housing Project in Thirroul, Wollongong, (b) initiatives to undertake sand mining and commercial use of traditional land for community development and agitation against these initiatives in the Worrimi Land Council, and (c) engagement with the protection of land and welfare initiatives in the Gandangara Land Council in NSW, Australia. The fieldwork for this study was conducted during March–September 2010.

Historical Trajectory and the Indigenous People of Australia: Few Milestones

Through the process of colonization of Australian aboriginal and Torres Strait by the British imperial power in 1788, the British settlers had started grabbing the land and autonomy of these people and robbing them of their inherited linkages with nature, their culture and their livelihood, despite their resistance.

Dispossession of Land, Language, Culture and Childhood

The process of colonization and dispossession had continued unabated all through the 18th, 19th and mid-20th centuries. It is estimated that at the time of arrival of the European settlers in the late 18th century, there were more than 300 indigenous clans, described as nations, 250–300 spoken languages and over 700 dialects. Each group had its own territory linked to their own stories and dreamings, and each of the clans had a spiritual connection with a specific piece of land. The story lines and dreaming still continue with each of the surviving groups of the indigenous people. Demographers estimate that prior to the arrival of the British settlers in 1788, there were approximately 315,000–750,000 indigenous people across Australia, while in 1900, this number declined to approximately 93,000 (Australian Bureau of Statistics 2002).

The colonial state initiated and followed a policy of annihilation, exclusion and forced assimilation of aboriginal people until the 1960s. These policies also saw the practice of confining the indigenous people to the reserves and forceful removal of aboriginal children from their parents with a view to establish the political and cultural supremacy of the Europeans over the Australian natives. The *Report of the National Enquiry into the Separation of the Australian Aboriginal and Torres Strait Islander Children from their Families: Bring Them Home* (1997) reveals that one of every three to one of every ten aboriginal children in Australia was made part of this forceful removal. This report also concluded that the Australian authorities committed genocide by removing indigenous children from their families. The practice of child removal continued until 1969. It produced a hugely traumatized and neglected category of aboriginal people known as the 'stolen generation' who are the victims of and witnesses to the blemish chapter of British colonial history in Australia. Besides, the state-sponsored initiatives also dispossessed the indigenous people of their land, autonomy and human dignity.

Farming of solidarity among indigenous people: Though these initiatives generated discontent among the indigenous people, they seldom took the form of organized social movements until the mid-20th century, coinciding with the American Civil Rights Movement in the United States. The indigenous people's movements for land rights and their cultural and political autonomy have passed through several stages since colonization. The internal pressure came into the frontage in the late 1950s through the formation of various leagues and networks, coalitions, public meetings, campaigns, strikes, deputation of protests, filing of legal petitions and other such activities. Solidarity among the indigenous groups also started taking shape through the merger of several groups.

Consolidation of Land Claim

Land occupies the core of indigenous life, culture, economy and identity. It is through land that the indigenous people of Australia are linked to their ancestors, dreams and story lines, and geographical and cultural autonomy. Before colonization, the indigenous people collectively possessed the entire land of Australia and shaped its intrinsic relations with nature and culture. As their movement started getting consolidating, the aboriginal leaders started demanding for land not only as theirs by right but also as the basis of livelihood, as an aspiration to the preservation of a distinctive aboriginal way of life (Marlen 2005, 484). The indigenous people's movements became visible at the regional and national levels and started getting concrete shape since the early 1960s against the backdrop of indigenous people's mobilization in Australia, on the one hand, and the United Nations' resolutions related to the self-determination of the indigenous people, on the other. The Australian state granted the indigenous people the voting rights in 1962 and, subsequently, they were included in the census through a referendum in 1967 (Marlen 2005).

Since the mid-1960s, the collective mobilization of the indigenous people started getting intensified, leading to the enactment of various land-related laws, for example, the Aboriginal Lands Trust Act of South Australia 1966 and the Aboriginal Lands Act 1970. These laws created new enthusiasm among the indigenous people for their autonomy. However, the indigenous people's movements received a setback in 1971 when in the famous Gove Land Rights case, an Australian court ruled that Australia had been *terra nullius* before the British settlement, and that no concept of the native title existed in Australian law. However, this judgment has never dampened the morale of the indigenous activities. Subsequent to this judgement, Australia witnessed a significant proliferation of indigenous people's movement across the country for land reclamation. In the process of organizing collective actions, the indigenous people also received support from a good body of sympathizers and activists, including several prominent and distinguished white advocates, professionals, churches, trade union groups, academics, left parties, environmental groups, feminists, students and many other liberal groups. These created a positive atmosphere for the land rights movement of the indigenous people. Significantly, on 26 January (Australia Day) 1972, a group of young Aborigines made history in the aboriginal movements in Australia by erecting an 'Aboriginal Tent Embassy' on the lawns of the Parliament House in Canberra demanding the Northern Territory (NT) as a State to be predominantly represented by the indigenous people, the granting of all land and mining rights for indigenous people and rights for the preservation of their sacred sites, and compensation money to the indigenous people for lands across Australia that could not be returned (for details, see Goodall 1996). When the Whitlam government come into power in 1972, it replaced the hitherto existing government 'policy of assimilation' with the 'policy of aboriginal self-determination', which had a provision for aboriginal-controlled organization, limited land rights for the aboriginal people. This government also instituted for the first time the Department of Aboriginal Affairs to look into the issues of the indigenous people of Australia. The Aboriginal Land Rights (Northern Territory) Act 1976 was enacted to facilitate land claims followed by the NSW Aboriginal Land Rights Acts in 1983. (For the indigenous struggle for land rights in NSW, see Norman 2007.)

The rejuvenated indigenous movements that had occupied significant public space in the 1970s and 1980s got a big push forward by the judgment of the famous *Mabo V. Queensland* case in 1993, which declared that the previous legal concept of Australia being a *terra nullius* is invalid and that the native title of the indigenous people is recognizable under the common law. The paradigmatic shift in this judgement was followed by the enactment of the Native Title Act 1993 and the Australian High Court decision in 1996 that recognized the indigenous rights over pastoral leases. All these led to the setting-up of the Indigenous Land Corporation (ILC) and, subsequently, the (state and local) land councils as statutory bodies to assist indigenous people with land acquisition and management and to achieve economic, environmental, social and cultural benefits for them.

Bring Them Back Home: Condemnation of Blemish Chapter and Apology to Indigenous People

With the indigenous land rights getting recognition, indigenous identities started getting rejuvenated in the late 1990s. With sustained mobilization and pressure, the Royal Commission into Aboriginal Deaths in Custody was formed in 1991 to investigate the disproportionate number of deaths of indigenous prisoners in custody, and the Human Rights and Equal Opportunity Commission (HREOC) was formed to enquire into the practices of removing aboriginal children from their parents. The HREOC report, widely known as the Brining Them Home report of the National Enquiry into the Separation of the Australian Aboriginal and Torres Strait Islander Children from their Families, was tabled in the Parliament in May 1997.

The indigenous people's movements achieved another milestone in 1999 with the acceptance of the Reconciliation Motion by the Australian Parliament which named the mistreatment of the indigenous people by the British colonizers as the 'blemish chapter'. On 28 May 2000, the Council for Aboriginal Reconciliation (CAR) hosted the People's Walk for Reconciliation, where more than 250,000 people walked over the Sydney Harbor Bridge on foot, following a major public event called Corroboree 2000. In its final report, the CAR 2002 states: 'Reconciliation has begun to enter the hearts and minds of the Australian people creating one of the most determined and vibrant people's movements ever seen in the history of the nation'[1] (Haebich 2001).

One of the recommendations of the HREOC was that a formal apology be made by the Australian Parliament for the forcible removal of aboriginal children from their parents. Following huge public pressure, on 13 February 2008, the Australian government under the prime ministership of Kevin Rudd presented an apology to indigenous Australians as a motion voted on by the House:

> Today we honour the Indigenous peoples of this land, the oldest continuing cultures in human history.
> We reflect on their past mistreatment.
> We reflect in particular on the mistreatment of those who were Stolen Generations – this blemished chapter in our nation's history.
> ...
> We apologise for the laws and policies of successive Parliaments and governments that have inflicted profound grief, suffering and loss on these our fellow Australians.
> We apologise especially for the removal of Aboriginal and Torres Strait Islander children from their families, their communities and their country.
> ...
> To the mothers and the fathers, the brothers and the sisters, for the breaking up of families and communities, we say sorry.
> And for the indignity and degradation thus inflicted on a proud people and a proud culture, we say sorry.
> We the Parliament of Australia respectfully request that this apology be received in the spirit in which it is offered as part of the healing of the nation.

Recent acrimony: A large section of the indigenous people of Australia, however, is yet to be reconciled with Australian nationalism. United protests as the Aboriginal Day of Mourning is observed on the occasion of Australia Day on January 26 every year by the indigenous people since

---

[1] See http://www.austlii.edu.au/au/orgs/car/m2000/quickguidewalk.htm.

1938. The days of mourning were also observed on Cook Bicentennial in 1970 and on the Bicentennial of the First Fleet in 1988. The indigenous people have also provided a united voice of opposition and protest against the federal government's intervention in the NT (Northern Territory National Emergency Response Bill 2007) to the declared crisis of child abuse in NT aboriginal communities. The act suspended one of Australia's primary anti-discrimination laws, the 1975 Racial Discrimination Act. The intervention, among other things, suspended the permit system, removed customary law and cultural practice considerations from bail applications and sentencing within criminal proceedings, abolished the Community Development Employment Projects and deployed federal police force in the NT. Many experts are of the opinion that 'Australian measures are extreme in the way they "impair basic freedoms" and "stigmatize or at least are perceived by indigenous people to be stigmatizing," as well as the way they were enacted without any consultation or consent from aboriginal people themselves'.[2] Lee Rhiannon, a Green NSW Senator, in an interview with me on 16 May 2010 expressed that:

> [T]he Northern Territory Intervention is a black mark on the government. It was done without consultation with the indigenous people. Army has been deployed, a legitimate government has been suspended and there have imposition of several policies on them. This is very unfortunate and need to be stopped ...

A similar concern has also been expressed against Queensland's Wild River law. Although according to the Queensland government,

> The pristine rivers of Cape York are among the last of their kind on Earth, and must be preserved at all costs, to the indigenous people it is an encroachment on their traditional practice and that they should be trusted to keep the rivers as pristine as they have done for thousands of years.[3]

Meanwhile, on 27 August 2010, the UN Committee on the Elimination of Racial Discrimination (CERD) requested that the Australian government take urgent action to ensure that the Northern Territory Intervention complies with Australia's obligations under the Convention on the Elimination of All Forms of Racial Discrimination. Though the committee has welcomed a number of recent positive developments in Australia, including the National Apology to the Stolen Generations, the endorsement

---

[2] See http://www.ethicaltraveler.org/2010.
[3] See www.apo.org.au/audio/wild-rivers-act-debate.

of the UN Declaration on the Rights of Indigenous Peoples, the commitment to 'close the gap' in indigenous health inequality and Australia's closer engagement with a number of UN human rights instruments and mechanisms, it has raised serious concerns about a range of Australian laws, policies and practices, including the Northern Territory Intervention, the suspension of the Racial Discrimination Act, the treatment of refugees and asylum seekers, and the impact of Australia's counter-terror laws.[4]

However, despite these acrimonies, a visible shift has been marked in the reconciliatory approach of the Australian state towards the indigenous people. The policy of accommodation and reconciliation that has been introduced in the wake of the proliferation of self-conscious indigenous movements since the early 1970s has opened up new possibilities and challenges in re-establishing the linkages between the indigenous culture and environment. Have these measures for reconciliation been able to provide equal status to the indigenous people in the Australian society? We shall discuss this in the following section.

The Indigenous People Today

Population and Language

While historically indigenous people have the victim positions in Australian society, within the contemporaneous social dynamics, they have also emerged to be disadvantaged both in the absolute and relative terms. Though over the past 20 years, the indigenous population has been doubled from 227,593 in 1986 to 562,861 in 2009, currently they form only 2.7% of the total population of 22,586,212 of Australia (Australian Bureau of Statistics 2010). In the process of colonization, the indigenous people of Australia have lost control over their language and culture. Only 12% of them can speak in their own language, and only 1% of them practise own indigenous faith.

Health

Though the population of young people is higher among the indigenous than the non-indigenous groups as a whole, the proportion of elderly

---

[4] See http://www.hrlrc.org.au.

people is substantially lower among the indigenous people, with only 3% of the indigenous and 13% of the non-indigenous people belonging to the age group of 65 years and above which is a reflection of the low health, low education and low economic status of the indigenous people of Australia.

The indigenous people have a substantially higher proportion of teenage mothers among them with 20% as against 4% among the non-indigenous people. The infant mortality and maternal mortality rates among them are 9.7% and 21.56%, respectively, while for the non-indigenous people these are 4.3% and 7.9%, respectively. They have lower life expectancy with 59.4 years for males and 64.8 years for females as against the 78.7 years for males and 82.6 years for females, respectively, among the non-indigenous people. Twenty-seven per cent of them live in crowded housing in comparison to only 6% of the non-indigenous people. More than 9% of the indigenous people are homeless as against 2.5% of the non-indigenous people.

Formal Education and Employment

The proportion of learners completing year 12 education among the indigenous people is 22% as against 47% among the non-indigenous people. The learner groups attending university level or technical education are only 6% among the indigenous people as against 25% among the non-indigenous population. Similarly, the proportion of employed population belonging to the age group of 15 years and above is 46% among the indigenous, in comparison to 62% among the non-indigenous people. Again, 16% of them are unemployed and 46% are not in the labour force, in comparison to only 5% and 35% respectively among the non-indigenous people. The most common occupation among the indigenous worker is that of labourer as compared to the professional nature of employment among the non-indigenous groups. The mean gross individual income per week for the indigenous people is and $278, while for the non-indigenous people it is $473.They are also a politically deprived lot.

The 'professionals' have the highest median gross weekly income while 'labourers' have the lowest. It is again that the indigenous people in an average earned 28% less as professional and 16% less as labourers than their non-indigenous counterparts. Of all the indigenous workers 93% are employees, 6% work in their own business and 1% are family workers. Seventy-four per cent of them are employed in the private sector, and 26% work in the public sector. Over half (57%) work on full-time, as high as 39% of them work as part-time indicating a high degree of employment insecurity among the indigenous workers.

Assets

The low status of indigenous people in employment and work participation results in their low access and control over crucial assets such as housing, motor vehicles and communication technologies. According to the 2006 Census, 63% of the indigenous households are renting their home and 24% own their home with a mortgage, while only 12% own their home outright. More indigenous households (approximately double) live in the rental accommodation than the non-indigenous households. Seventy-seven per cent of indigenous households have a registered motor vehicle as compared with 90% of non-indigenous households. Indigenous people also have less access to advanced technologies than non-indigenous people. Forty-three per cent of indigenous households are reported to have Internet access in comparison with 64% of non-indigenous households. It is but natural that the indigenous households living in remote areas have less Internet access (13%) than their people living in the major cities (53%).

Political Participation

Even though they got the right to vote in 1960, indigenous people had no elected representative in the Lower House of the Parliament until the 2010 Parliamentary Election (Australian Bureau of Statistics 2006).

Significantly, a national political identity of the indigenous people is in the making. Though several regional political outfits have made their presence felt in the regional political dynamics of Australia, their national presence had long been missing. In 2010, with the resurgence of indigenous people's movements, the First Nation Political Party was formed by merging with the Ecological, Social Justice Aboriginal Party.

Marginalization and Continuing Protests

In all conventional indicators, the indigenous people have remained marginalized and disadvantaged in Australian society. All of the negative markers for disenfranchised populations—imprisonment, domestic violence and alcoholism—are much higher for indigenous peoples. Indigenous adults are six times more likely to be arrested and 13 times more likely to be jailed than other Australians, and an indigenous teenager is 28 times more likely to be in jail than other Australians (The Christian Science Monitor 2010). The *Report of the Royal Commission into Aboriginal Deaths in Custody (1991)* stated that *aboriginal* disadvantage is directly associated with their dispossession and forced removal from their traditional lands. Such dispossessions have destroyed the balance between nature and indigenous culture and their relationship between dreaming stories and the spirit of 'country' on the one hand but have also produced waves of discontents among the indigenous people against the Australian state.[5]

This balance, as the indigenous people say, is yet to be restored. The indigenous people in general wish to preserve the balance between people, culture, land and resources, the relationship between dreaming stories and the spirit of 'country'. Within these complex processes, there have been state-driven initiatives for reconciliation and development, and the response of this indigenous people towards such initiatives have been diverse.

Development, Conservation and Indigenous Movements

Developmental and reconciliatory initiatives as initiated by the state for the indigenous people have always remained contested as these initiatives try to integrate divergent values, ideologies, expectations and experiences. There have been contradictory views on these initiatives as they are viewed by certain sections as a possible potential to break the barriers of marginalization, while by others as a threat to break the link of the indigenous people with their culture, land, environment, and dreaming and story line. Significantly, the indigenous views on conservation and development at the grass-roots level also represent an increasing eclecticity, causing contradictory perceptions not only between the state and the indigenous activists but also at times among the indigenous people themselves.

---

[5] See http://www.culturalsurvival.org.

In the wake of the emergent need of a section of indigenous people for development, integration and reconciliation with the wider society on the one hand and the innate desire of another section to preserve their linkages with cultural heritage, nature and livelihood on the other, the indigenous people's movement in Australia now moves through a changing trajectory. Along the process, there has been a reconstruction of their identity at the grass-roots level in terms of both their historical experiences and the contemporary realities of their lives. The following case studies will reflect on some aspects of these movements and reconstructions.

Sandon Point

Sandon Point, also known as the McCauley's Beach, comprises 61 hectares of open, scenic space between the coastal villages of Thirroul and Bulli in the northern suburbs of Wollongong, on the east coast of NSW, Australia. The indigenous people claim that it has been their traditional place of worship, storytelling, and tool making, and it relates to their 'dreaming' and is a burial site dating back 6,000 years. In 1998, a human skull-bone was exposed on the sand dune. The local indigenous people believe it to be ceremonial burial remains of aboriginal cleaver man—Kuradiji—a man with special spiritual status. This land was once public land zoned for mining and industrial use. It had been sought by the community to be returned to public since 1980. This area emerged as a bone of contention between developers and the state on one side and the indigenous people on the other when it was sold to a Sydney-based property developer, Stockland, in 1995 for a proposed 1- to 20-stage luxurious housing project of 1,200 dwellings units.

The indigenous people started their agitation in early 2000 in the wake of Wollongong City Council's finalization and approval of this project. Though spontaneous protest and agitation compelled the developers to suspend the development work in the identified site, with a report of archaeological survey in February 2001, the Wollongong City Council (WCC) and, subsequently, the Land and Environment Court allowed the development to resume for Stages 2–6.

The protesters felt that the archaeological surveyors were biased as they had consulted only one Wodi Wodi Elder, while the other traditional owner groups representing Korewal, Illawarra, Jerrungarugh and Shoalhaven were ignored and that the surveyor had not collected sufficient materials by digging appropriate places on the site for a proper conclusion, and the agitation was intensified.

Under the leadership of Uncle Dootch Kanedy, a community elder and elected chairperson of Illawarra Local Aboriginal Land Council, and the overwhelming support of the indigenous people, the Sandon Point Aboriginal Tent Embassy (SPATE) was established in December 2001 by igniting a secret fire and erecting a tent on the site of construction to stake their inherited claim and keep a 24×7 vigil on this area. Meanwhile, to muster support from all over Australia, the sacred fire was carried from Sandon Point Aboriginal Tent Embassy to Canberra, Victoria, Cockatoo and Wombarra and was brought back as a symbol of indigenous unity, resistance and cultural autonomy. Over an elaborate ritual, Yurin elder Uncle Guboo Ted Thomasre named the Sandon Point as *Kuradji* (community elder) to reassert the indigenous claim. The Illawara Local Land Council also declared the whole Sandon Point area as a place of significance for aboriginal culture and heritage.

As the developers stated fencing off the area on 14 February 2002, the community formed a human chain to prevent vehicle movement for construction in the area. Police arrested of large number of protesters. On a legal petition of Uncle Dootch Kanedy though, the NSW Land and Environment Court put an injunction on the development activities on the site. After a few months, the court upheld the development approval of Wollongong City Council with some conditions, resulting in the resumption of construction activities in late 2002. However, the speed of the construction was slowed down in view of the sustained agitation.

The protesters also approached the NSW government in, but in vain. In December 2006, the NSW Minister for Planning approved the development plan at Sandon Point, ignoring the significance of aboriginal heritage on the disputed site. The movement activists also approached the judiciary. Though the NSW Land and Environmental Court in early 2007, considering the issue of flood and ecological disaster, declared the development concept of Stockland in Sandon point to be null and void, following an appeal by the NSW Minister for Planning, the Supreme Court of Australia overturned the decision. Significantly, in May 2007 with the persisting appeal by the protestors, the Government of Australia declared Sandon Point an aboriginal area that is to be protected under National Park and the Wild Life Act 1974; and the development work get suspended again. However, the Minister of Planning, as the ultimate authority on developmental planning, approved Stockland's project application in October 2009. The indigenous activists again moved to the Land and

Environment Court in November 2009, raising the issues of environmental hazards and disaster. However, in July 2010, the Environment Court declined the appeal of the protestors. The protestors appealed in the Supreme Court against the decision of the Environmental Court. Meanwhile, on 8 April 2011, the developer Stockland had been fined $1,500 by Wollongong City Council on the complaint of the SPATE that recent heavy rains which triggered a flood crises in the south of the region had also caused a buildup of storm water at the McCauley's beach residential site. This action has widely vindicated the environmental concern raised by the protesters, but was ignored by the state on several counts (*Sunday Morning Herald* 2011).

The phenomena of turning and twisting invited a host of confrontations between the NSW government and the developers on the one hand and the indigenous people on the other. All through the struggle, the protestors strongly felt that in a white-dominated Australian society, it is very difficult for the indigenous people to get their collective concern and voice recognized, as they are being marginalized. To them, the government is guided by the interest of the developers and not by respect for the indigenous culture and heritage. Such a feeling is resonated in the voice of Roy Dootch Kennedy, the chairman of SPATE:

> We are marginalized as we are only a tiny minority in Australia ... and our voice is not heard them (the government ... They have given this land to the developers to earn money. They are not the native Australians; they are not linked to the land ... its ecosystem, its cultural heritage. They are linked to the land through extraction of natural resources to earn profit for them ... The government in Australia is run by the miners, developers, international companies who have little respect for the land heritage and culture of the indigenous people ... They are killing the aborigines like animal. They have destroyed our land, our nature our cultural heritage and we have lost control on our life. We are fighting with our own people to protect our heritage ...

The mobilization now questions the propriety of the state in damaging the indigenous people's linkage between nature and their culture:

> They call us savages, but they keep on committing genocide ... Why have you robbed of my heritage? Why should we continue to be robbed? Why our mother earth is to be sacrificed? What have you done and what are you doing to our land? All cultures in this earth have respect for their own land, why should we be deprived of such respect? We want them to stop disrespecting our culture and stop harming our land ... our culture. They

should repair all the damage they have done to our mother earth, our cultural heritage ... They don't understand and don't want to understand the way we speak and the way we do we think and the way we live with nature. What they have done to us, they can't repeat the same to our children. Through this protest we want to create a space to move freely ...

Through this movement, the indigenous people want to preserve and rebuild their linkage to culture and environment:

We need to establish the significance of indigenous people in the community in Australia. You are to recognize the cultural linkages of the indigenous people with the story telling, craft and tool making values that connect them to their country ... While taking about assimilation you are to take care of indigenous values as well and you are to connect the country through their cultural heritage, language. You have to believe in the adaptive nature of indigenous culture.

The protesters are confident of the strength of their unity and are optimistic about the outcome of their movement, despite a few setbacks:

We have lost in the court but there is the win this loss. It strongly indicates that the aborigines can't get justice in Australia since the law and the state machinery is operated by the non-aboriginal. The journey does not end here. We are neither going to bow down my head, nor throw our hand in the air saying that we have lost. The journey begins now. We are united—all aborigines of Australia are with us in the struggle for our land, culture and environment. (Roy Dootch Kennedy, interviewed, 1 August 2010)

Many of the white participants also echo the sentiments of Kennedy:

We give lip service to the issue of the aboriginal issue. We have a very limited view on the aboriginal interest in Australia. The land belongs to them. Evan if the sacred site is out of the boundary of the development project, we should have respected their sentiment ... Belief is not guided by an artificial boundary ... We have played our innings ... We have developed the country by destroying their culture, nature and everything. Let us allow them to have their say in the development (Sandon Point Resident, interviewed, 1 August 2010)

The Sandon Point activists have developed a common voice and identity through their collective action by resorting to indigenous symbols, rituals and comprehensive collective action. They not only develop response against developers and the state initiatives but also proactively develop networks of local indigenous people with the wider society in their efforts to preserve their relation to nature, culture and environment.

Sand Mining through the Worimi Local Aboriginal Land Council (WLALC)

The Aboriginal Land Council in Australia has emerged out of long-drawn struggle of the aboriginal people to protect their interests and aspirations related to land rights.

> [It is] committed to ensuring a better future for Aboriginal people by working for the return of culturally significant and economically viable land, pursuing cultural, social and economic independence for its people and being politically pro-active and voicing the position of Aboriginal people on issues that affect them. (Marlen 2005)

The Worimi Aboriginal Land Council is made up of several indigenous people—the Buraigal, the Gamipingal and the Garawerrigal—and is recognized as one of the most vibrant and active land councils of NSW. It has been successful in acquiring a vast track of land by getting 153 plots of conservation land against 155 applications. Besides land claim, it has also initiated business ventures in a pleasure park to attract tourist. However, in 2003, Worimi became bankrupt due to alleged corruption and mismanagement of land and resources that invited an enquiry in 2004 into the loss of $720,000 of the land council (*Sydney Morning Herald* 2004).

However, despite the previous experience of failure, the Worrimi Land Council has initiated a sand dune touring company and a large-scale sand mining programme from the traditional sand dune. Though it has got support from majority of the indigenous communities and members of the land council, a section of the indigenous community elders, environmentalist and local administrators have opposed the economic expansion plan, especially the sand mining activities.

According to the pro-development members of the land council, 'the project is expected to generate about 60 operational and contract jobs and a handsome revenue and that the income that would generate out of these scheme would be used for the housing, health, employment and environmental sustainability programs for the Aboriginal community'. However, the pro-conservationists allege that these initiatives are pushed forward by the vested interests undemocratically, unmindful of the significance of indigenous art, craft, and heritage and sentiments of the majority of the indigenous people. There have also been claims and counter-claims on the status of actual occupiers of Worimai land.

Aunty Carol Ridgeway-Bissett, a community elder who claims to be the actual traditional occupier of the land, has strongly opposed the mining project with the fear that the sand mining would not protect the traditional spiritual and cultural sanctity of this land. She has organized protests against mining and gets regular support from the locals and the environmentalists. She has also asserts that:

> Sand dune is a part of our culture, our heritage. The sand dunes are the ancient landscape of my ancestors it is full of the bones and artifacts of my people. We get blessings from them from these sand dunes. We would protect it ... Who knows how much and how many have already been crushed and destroyed by the mining.

Again, to her:

> [T]o promote their own interest the miners conduct biased archaeological studies without consulting the actual owners of the land. These development and mining activities are anti-indigenous people, their culture and heritage ... Land Rights Act has not handed over land to the people who have link to the land. The Local Land Council and not to the actual owner of the land ... The Land council in connivance with the developers is destroying the aboriginal cultural heritage ... (Aunty Carol Ridgeway-Bissett, interviewed, 3 September 2010)

Aunty Carol Ridgeway-Bissett is in the process of preparing an alternative archeological report. She is lobbing extensively with the NSW politicians, using new media, appealing to federal ministers, and organizing rallies to stop sand mining and commercial ventures of the land council. Environmentalists are also critical on the sand mining and echo the voice of the indigenous people. The director of Total Environment Centre, Jeff Angel, is of the view that the coastal sand mining had run its course and ought to stop. 'There has been enough devastation ... Dune systems are dynamic and always moving. Interfering with them is something that ought to be approached with caution'.

However, Andrew Smith, the chairperson of Worrimi Land Council is a pro-development activist. He wants to use the available indigenous resources for the economic and social benefits of these people. He is personally enterprising, and wants to take risks and learn from the experience. Andrew Mathews says:

Environment, Development and Indigenous People's Identity 115

> They (the Government) have given back our land. We feel good. However, we have also got lots of liability. We are to give tax ... We have huge expenditure ... So we are to generate revenue by using our land undertaking culture heritage programme through the developers and through extraction of sand from the sand dune. This money we use for education, for health, for fellowship and training programme of the indigenous unemployed youth and also for the community awareness on environmental sustain ability programme ...

Only 30% of the revenue generated from sand extraction comes to the local land council, the remaining 70% goes to the state land council and the developers. Sand extraction from the sand dune, to him, also has an immediate practical purpose:

> The sand extraction is done not for this little money alone, but also to protect the indigenous community from the disaster of ever expanding sand dune. The moving sand dome will engulf us very fast if we don't stop it ...

Andrew Mathew is also an assimilationist. Though he is very critical of the injustice that was historically meted out to the indigenous people of Australia, he is in favour of rebuilding the indigenous society and culture by bringing a synthesis between indigenous traditional values and ways of life of contemporary Australian society and culture. He looks for a respectable assimilation of the indigenous people in Australian society. To him:

> Assimilation however should not be the way the Australia tried to assimilate the aboriginals. They introduced a genocide killing millions of aborigines ... The aboriginal people have been dispossessed of their cultural heritage ... They are alienated from the mainstream society ...
>
> Assimilation of indigenous culture with the ... Australian culture is going to happen sooner or later ... We are so assimilated now that we don't live the way we lived thousand years ago. We don't wear lap-laps and live in the dunes. We live in houses, at the end of the day we slip in the bad, and eat in the McDonalds, drive cars and watch TV ...
>
> Despite all these changes we the indigenous people are still there with our own cultural heritage and our connection to the land and the country. We are struggling to get back our country of dreaming, our autonomy and independence. We want to preserve our culture and our linkage with nature and environment. However it should be done by removing the community from the Australian society ... (Andrew Smith, interviewed, 25 August 2010)

Gandangara Local Aboriginal Land Council, Liverpool

The Gandangara Local Aboriginal Land Council covers nine local government area councils including Parramatta, Penrith, Fairfield, Auburn, Bankstown, Holroyd, Sutherland, Campbell town and Liverpool. It is located in the traditional area of the Cabrogal clan, the Darugnation and is considered to be a model land council that has acquired distinction for several of its activities. It excelled in providing employment and training to the indigenous unemployed youth, education, health and old age care and housing services, undertaking indigenous land care (e.g., Mount Annan botanical gardens), construction and maintenance of the memorial to the stolen generation and strengthening aboriginal cultural awareness among the aboriginal youth. The land council has taken initiatives to exploit the potential community land resources to extract benefits for its members. In March 2009, the Gandangara members passed a resolution for the land use and an elaborate business plan. The commercial housing project is a part of this plan is that supported by all the members of the community.

The members have developed a missionary zeal to initiate welfare and development activities. They meet regularly with the community elders, stolen generation members, young job seekers and others for taking proactive initiatives and resolving several problems, and to rebuild a new future for the indigenous community through welfarism. In a larger context, they have initiated a social movement to reconstruct their identity through developmental process. Indeed, assimilation and integration has emerged to be the dominant perspective for them, even though they are not devoid of criticality of the colonial oppression and dispossession. Such views are widely reflected in the formulation of several activists of the land council like that of Karol Brown. Karol Brown is an aboriginal assimilationist. She says:

> My father is Irish and my mom was an aborigine, so I have a mix heritage. I have the best of both cultures with me. My mom told me to take best from both and I look the both. My first husband was black and second husband was a white and I have two beautiful children from these two partners. They represent both world of Australia...the Aborigines and the White. We have best of both the culture ... *Abba—Gabba...*

However, the indigenous people face several problems in the white-dominated Australia. To her,

> Being minority we face problem. In the growing up process the children loss confidence. We are forgetting our culture, language, songs, and music ... These have started only getting antique value but not in real life ... We train the children to know our culture; we also let them know the other culture as well as to protect the indigenous cultural heritage. The aboriginal people should maintain their own culture and be developed by their own rights ...
>
> This is unfortunate that a huge number of in the youth from the mix parentage are unable to speak the indigenous language. They are not aware of the significance of indigenous culture in our developmental activities ... Because of mixed parentage, and the long practice of child removal from the indigenous community, knowledge about cultural heritage is declining among the aboriginal people also declined especially among the youth ... Australian society got too much technology, too much consumerism and too much of comforts. Many *of indigenous are forgetting their culture because of the pressure of these technologies, consumer culture, comforts* ...

To remain rooted in one's own culture despite getting historically uprooted in a multicultural context is understandably a very difficult task. Cultural protectionism can't be devoid of development process of community. What are the strategies? The land council has initiated organized initiatives for cultural change and also for economic development:

> We have also activities related to day care of the community elders. In the day care centre we keep them engaged with the activities like indigenous painting and drawing and making of indigenous craft and tools. We have also a health care centre that takes care of their health related issues of the aboriginal people especially for the elderly one who come here not only for health care service, but also to share each other experiences ...
>
> We are trying to change the culture. We are going to bring back the culture through education and training. I give counseling to the indigenous children; train them not only to be aware and proud of indigenous culture but also to take best of both traditional indigenous games, traditional story telling ...
>
> We have land development, land caring activities. We have identified a housing project that is supported by the community... This housing is opening for all- indigenous and non-indigenous. The profit is supposed to help us for employment generation, age care, health and education programme. The land is carefully selected and there is no problem.

Within these developmental activities, indigenous culture is carefully preserved by bringing harmony. She says:

It is big thing that we have got the land rights now in the hype of all these development the youth tend to forget their own culture. The indigenous people are to educate themselves about their cultural heritage. We need harmony between indigenous culture and development. We teach the young generation to be honest to you by a becoming respectful both the culture. This approach will bring lot of harmony in society. (Karol Brown, interviewed, 12 August 2010, 17 August 2010)

Within this urge for harmony, there is also the voice of discontent which is existential, but historically rooted. Forceful removal of children has brought traumatic experiences not only for the victims but also to their parents. The mother of a victim of the stolen generation, who works with the Gandangara Land Council, has a horrific experience. She was united with her son after 40 years of forceful removal. She says:

You can't simply explain what the torture is ... It is emotional, psychological and physical ... Hundreds of thousand mothers in Australian lost their children. I am mother; I also lost my child who was taken away from the ground of race. That was a new baby. I was kept in church in Brisbane to serve the Priests and others ... They have destroyed everything ... our culture, nature, our lives.

Though her life is circumscribed by bitter experience, she looks for reconciliation for harmonious coexistence in Australian society. She finds a hope in the unity and activities of the land council. To her:

It is a time to rebuild ... that is however is not an easy process. All victims of stolen, the children and the parents are to be given land compensation and these to be managed by the Local Land Council to maintain the eco system. It is through this land that we will build connection between nature and our indigenous culture. (Mother of a stolen generation member)

Conclusion: Co-option, Contestation and Indigenous People's Identity

It has been pointed out by scholars that despite hostility, 'throughout their history since 1788 aborigines have sought a "composition" with white society in which their links with the land and the essence of the "Aboriginal way" can be maintained'. The creation of a symbol has also been talked about where the two streams of people, black and white, which are forming Australian society, each with its own origin and character but influencing each other, yet preserving even into the ocean itself, its own identity and its distinctive contribution to the character and life-sustaining capacity of the Bay as a whole. (Coombs 1991)

Though there are possibilities, there are also challenges towards to construction of such symbol.

One of the prominent challenges is that there are perceptive cultural differences in the understanding of each others' culture. 'Aboriginal people see their relationship with the Australian nation as requiring recognition of their status as its original resident and as different to—as superior to—the position of all others.' Although the Western view of rights talks of each individual's right to be treated equally with all others, aboriginal people see their 'first-people' status as demanding different treatment from that given to all others because 'western legal systems have provided inadequate protection for the group rights of indigenous people.' It is in respect of such views that Aboriginal people have had the greatest difficulty in having their message understood by other Australians (Bennett 1999, 10).

Besides these differences, the indigenous people have remained disadvantaged in Australian society. Indeed they are not merely 'disadvantaged Australians' or a 'minority' group; they are the First Nation Peoples of this country who are yet to be formally recognized. 'They have been the victims of poverty and inequality caused by historic treatment and the persistence of systemic discrimination' (Calma 2007, 19). The issues of their discrimination and marginalization now have got articulated for grass-roots collective action and their empowerment in Australian society through an awakening and politicization of social questions that challenge the parochialism and institutions of authority (Clark 2008, 249).

Though the awakening created awareness and tried to unite them under one flag, aboriginal communities in Australia remain intensely, and proudly, local (Behrendt 1995, 27). Despite such localization, indigenous identity and social movements encounter a host of tensions in contemporary Australia, which are caused not only by colonization but also by the processes of modernization, economic development and the state policy of assimilation and reconciliation. To Sarah Maddison (2009), the aboriginal people today encounter the challenge

> as they grapple with the often-uncomfortable intersection of their fractured (but not abandoned) traditional and cultural life, the legacies of colonization,

and their own diversity across the continent. These intersections of history, culture, experience and identity have produced an extraordinarily complex political culture. These complexities have produced tensions between autonomy and dependency; sovereignty and citizenship; tradition and development; individualism and collectivism; indigeneity and hybridity; unity and regionalism; community and kin; men, women and customary law; elders and the next generation; and mourning and reconciliation. (Maddison 2009, XXIV)

Despite these challenges, there has emerged the possibility of creating a common symbol by widening the understanding of indigenous people's linkage between their life, culture and nature. Rowley's (1973) observation holds the key when he says: 'Aborigines always assumed, that Man is no more than part of nature' (Rowley 1973, 194). Thus there is innate logic of indigenous grass-roots protests, assertion and initiative which are circumscribed both by the tensions within the indigenous society on the one hand and their symbiotic relations with nature on the other. In sum their common symbol, culture, livelihood, collective mobilization and protests are intrinsically linked to nature.

Logic of Grass-roots Protests and Their Divergence

The culture of social protests has emerged to be a vital link between the indigenous people and their linkage to nature, state and civil society. These have been sustained and institutionalized in Australian society through the functioning of the local land council, the development initiatives of the state and the formulation of linkages of the indigenous social movement organizations with the trade unions, environmentalist, and students' and many other groups. Through these mobilizations, the indigenous people have developed diverse orientations towards their own culture, nature, environment and state; have developed a variety of support bases for their collective action; have followed different strategies of collective action; have articulated a distinctive solidarity through their everyday struggle and have acquired specific identities; and have received varied state and civil society responses towards their mobilizations over the decades. These variations in orientations, actions and attitudes have implicit associations with the kind of issues addressed by this mobilization in particular at the one end and the frame work of assimilation as propagated by the Australian state on the other.

In the Sandon Point, the indigenous people have united themselves to preserve their culture, nature and environment. In the process, they have developed conflicting attitudes towards the developers and the state by forming solidarity among themselves that rejuvenates their identity in terms of their traditional cultural heritage and its association to nature. Significantly, through these protests, not only does their association with nature and culture get reinforced ideationally, they also get their relationship rejuvenated with fellow indigenous people and get integrated with the wider network of civil society represented by environmentalists, students, trade unionists, feminists and others from across Australia, cutting the boundary of localized resistance. In the process of articulating their organising protests, these indigenous people have articulated in them a strong identity of resistance against the domination of the state apparatus and the developers who have devaluated their culture, ways of life and injected hardship in their livelihood. However, the strategies of resistance have remained circumscribed within the democratic space. Significantly, the attitude of the state towards this mobilization has remained predominantly oppositional, even though the space for reviewing the appeal and applying legal remedies has been made available within the framework of the state.

The local land councils of Australia provide the framework for assimilation of the Australian aborigines within the state and wider society. Though the indigenous people are invariably critical of the European invasion to their native land, culture and environment, and the perilous treatment, humiliation and torture inflected on them in by the 'settlers,' they want to give the process of assimilation a chance, though not by choice but by compulsion. However, their approach and perception towards the state initiatives are highly eclectic.

Despite a section of the indigenous viewing developmental initiatives as destructive to nature and indigenous cultural heritage, the dominant section of the Worrimi Local Land Council aims to commercially exploit their cultural heritage, nature, land and other assets to generate income. They look for a synthesis between conservation and welfare-induced development, 'selected assimilation' and integration with the state, self-determination of indigenous people without compromising the space for development. Though they are critical of the past injustice and white domination, they are in the process of creating a space for their engagement with the reconciliatory process. Thus, among them there are riffles in the process of reconstruction of indigenous identity that moves like an pendulum between the legitimizing and resistant identity even though the tendency has been towards a 'legitimizing identity with criticality'. On the other hand, the conservationist has rejuvenated indigenous identity which is predominantly locally resistant in nature. However, at a wider level, they recognize the state apparatus and look for legal intervention. Significantly though, the state is indifferent towards oppositional perspective of the conservationist; it is accommodative of the pro-development activists' view and action. Thus in the process of mobilization, while the pro-development/pro-assimilationists have emerged to be integrated with the state apparatus, the conservationist are in the process of getting linked with wider civil society networks.

The Grandangara Local Land Council is essentially pro-development in its approach even though it is critical of the state for the historical injustice metted out to them. They are simultaneously protective of their cultural heritage and in favour of commercial use of the land as well as selectively conservationist in relation to the environment as they use the development initiative to bring about changes in the economic, health and educational status and lifestyle of the indigenous people. They are united among themselves and have also developed the tendency of being a 'legitimizing identity with criticality.' They are in the process of getting integrated with the state apparatus for development and welfare of the community. The state is accommodative of the aspirations and the activities of these indigenous people.

In brief, indigenous movements in Australia are in the fast process of transition at the grass-roots level causing diverse orientation towards indigenous cultural heritage, nature and environment, inculcating and attracting specific support base, initiating distinct collective action, constructing varieties of collective action, solidarity and collective identity, forming specific attitude towards the state and inviting distinctive state response. The distinctive forms of indigenous protests, identities and state responses are given in Table 4.1.

The indigenous people's linkage to land culture and environment is intrinsic and locally circumscribed, as are their protests against historical and contemporary oppression. While within the developmental and reconciliatory dynamics there has been resistance against the development initiatives that threatens these linkages, there has also been a legitimizing process through the cooption of indigenous people's initiatives within the welfare domain of the state.

The resistance and the legitimizing processes have created tensions not only between indigenous people on one hand and the state and developers on the other but also within the indigenous society itself. The

Table 4.1

Diversity in the Orientation to Culture and Nature, and Support Bases, Nature of Collective Action, Attitude towards the State, the Attitude of the State towards the Indigenous Peoples' Protest, Solidarity and Collective Identity Formation in the Indigenous People's Movements in Australia

Cases	Orientation to Indigenous Culture	Orientation to Nature/Environ	Support Base	Nature of Collective Action	Attitude Towards State	Attitude of State Towards Protests	Nature of Indigenous Solidarity	Nature of Identity
Sandon Point	Protective	Pro-conservation	Indigenous people, environmentalists, students, trade unions, feminists, etc.	Agitation, symbolic rituals, legal petition, blockade, Tent Embassy	Conflicting	Oppositional	Total solidarity	Resistant
Worrimi Land Council	Selectively protective	Selective conservation	Sections of indigenous people, environmentalists, students	Agitation, legal action	Partly conflicting partly integration	Accommodating	Part solidarity	Predominantly legitimizing
Gandangara Land Council	Selectively protective	Selective conservation	Indigenous people	Collective development initiatives	Integrating	Accommodating	Total solidarity	Legitimizing

Source: Author's own.

pro-preservation/pro-conservation activists across the investigated areas, guided by their sensitivity and moral value towards cultural heritage, land and environment, rejuvenate their indigenous identity to resist the initiative of the state, developing agencies and of local land council alike. They propagate for autonomy and self- determination in terms of indigenous cultural heritage, protocol, and pre-colonial historicity.

Significantly, the policy of reconciliation as propagated by the Australian state since the 1990s has provided space for the integration and cooption of many conflicts and initiatives of the indigenous people in Australian society. The new institutional state mechanism like the local land council, by proving space for democratic development at the grass-roots level and solidarity among the indigenous people for their collective assertion, has paved the way for cooption of indigenous initiatives within the state apparatus, creating the framework of legitimizing the initiatives of pro-development activists. In the process of cooption, a degree of compromise with cultural heritage and environmental sustainability has emerged rather to be obvious. Here, the indigenous society encounters tensions from within. These tensions have been compounded with localized emerging consideration of the indigenous culture, their heterogeneity and the diverse levels of social and economic development. These have contributed towards the construction of forming divergent identities and and shaping up of diverse collective mobilizations. Thus while the sustained mobilization and rejuvenated identities form solidarity in terms of historical experience to develop resistance and politically question the social issues of injustice and persistent marginalization, emerging state perspective on reconciliation, integration and development on one hand, the same context indigenous identity is reformulated to legitimize the said state perspective on development and reconciliation on the other. However, despite such differences, sustained mobilizations on land rights and cultural and political autonomy, and the common experience of historical oppression and neglect and concern for culture and heritage contribute to articulate and rejuvenate their identities that link their historical association in the country. These identities are in the process of creating space for their engagement with Australian society by maintaining autonomy and respect for of each other's culture. It is effectively reflected in the articulation of Roy Dootch Kennedy the Chairperson of SPATE:

> We need a major change in the mindset that is a mountainous thing and not going to happen so immediately ... While taking about assimilation you

are to take care of indigenous values as well and you are to connect the country through their cultural heritage, language ... The government should now have serious dialogue with us ... The journey begins now.

In this changing trajectory, the processes of formation of identity and solidarity among the indigenous people, as pointed out by various scholars, is affected by the emergence of an indigenous middle class and the overwhelming tendency of that class to become absorbed professionally into the government (Jones and Hill-Burnett 1982, 224; cf. Merlan 2007), and the increasing welfare dependency of a large section of the indigenous population. However, neither the pattern of middle-class emergence nor their welfare dependency has been uniform in Australia. They are posited with eclectic social and economic processes and differentiated levels of economic development and engagement with the state and the civil initiatives. There have also been varied quanta of mobility and migration. Thus, the process of social and cultural integration, economic development and political empowerment at the grass-roots level through the local land council have produced multiple identities of the indigenous people which are in the process of constant construction and reconstruction, formation and shifting. Within these processes, in terms of historical experience, while all the indigenous people remained fixed to resistant identities; in terms of contemporaneous reality, one section shifts from resistant to legitimizing identity. These identities get solidified in a new context (Melucci 1992, 1996; Pizzorno 1978), interact with historicity (Touraine 1981), develop an interface with choice (Sen 1999) and get shifted from resistant to legitimizing processes (Castells 1997). In the context of collective mobilization, while the conservationists are tended to be guided by a subjectively moral commitment to nature and culture and indigenous values and unity and symbol, a section of pro-development protagonists are inclined to be guided by the urge for achieving immediate interest — rational calculations of earning revenue for their immediate economic betterment. These eclecticities are not as much because of cultural and geographic specificities of the indigenous people of Australia, as they are for the colonial oppression and injustice that destroyed their symbiotic relations between culture, land and nature. Hence, they look for all available resources and at times diverse mediums to reconstruct their place and identity for their sustenance and empowerment in Australian society. Thus, despite the formulation and transformation conflicting identities, resistant to legitimizing or the vice versa, there have remained a continuity in the dynamic of indigenous identity which is their nostalgia and inner urge to re-establish their inherent linkage to nature, culture and autonomy. Their inherited primordial identity gets priority over all acquired identities within the overall processes of colonization and globalization. Hence out of the sustained pressure of colonization and globalization, there has been the resurgence of a strong feeling of community among them. To quote Castells:

> Within this arrangement sustained colonization and oppressive globalization have pushed vast sections of the population take recourse to primordiality and form 'the identity for resistance' leading to the formation of communes or communities. They construct collective resistance against unbearable oppression, usually on the basis of the identities that were apparently defined by history, geography or biology, making it easier to essentialise the boundaries of resistance. (Castells 1997, 10)

5
Globalization, ICTs, Networks, Work, Culture and Identity

Reflexivity in an Emerging Knowledge Society

In the wake of introduction of economic neoliberalism, advancement of economic globalization and proliferation of ICTs, India stands today at the epochal transition from the pre-given agrarian and part-industrial societal frameworks towards a knowledge society. By bringing in unprecedented economic and technological transformation, and social and cultural momentum, this society has set in motion new patterns of work participation and occupational mobility, new interconnectivity among individuals with enormous flow of information and knowledge, and new avenues of choice on the one hand and new forms of hierarchy, exclusion and marginalization on the other. Although these transformations and dichotomies are influenced and accompanied by the traditional entities of caste, ethnicity, gender, and rural and urban divides, the increased interconnectedness and access to knowledge has helped people to widen their choice of economic and social lives and articulate new identities and social reflexivity. Significantly, the exercise of these choices often helps them to surpass traditional role performance and meanings and to articulate new aspirations, questions and criticality to the pre-given structure of domination. Hence, these identities have acquired reflexivity in the emerging knowledge society, and in the wake of its transition from the pre-given society, these have emerged to be very transformative in nature, seeking multiple expressions. Against this backdrop, this chapter will examine the emerging dynamics of identity formation in the context of the emergence of the knowledge society in India by highlighting the key dimensions of the knowledge society and its interface with ICTs, fast expansion of the service sector and new patterns of work participation, penetration of knowledge jobs, and spatial and occupational mobility therein. By locating individuals within the unequal space of occupational hierarchy, expansion of a new socio-cultural milieu, marginality and construction of new social networks and interactivity, it elaborates the processes of construction of solidarity and fluidity in identity that respond to the structure of subordination as a conscious act of reflexivity. This chapter is based on data collected from both primary and secondary sources.

Knowledge Society and Its Key Dynamics

The progress of human society has remained intrinsically linked to the production, dissemination and application of knowledge, paving the way for its civilization journey. Although every human society has used knowledge for its progression, survival and sustenance, the knowledge society distinguishes itself from other societies by nurturing, exploiting and integrating knowledge as the key resource to all the domains of its activities. Some of the key dynamics of the knowledge society such as the mass production of knowledge, replacement of traditional work and workforce, expansion of globalization and ICTs, and discontinuity of old and construction of new identities are elaborated further.

Mass Production of Knowledge for Wealth and Employment by Cultivating Human Mind

This society is widely characterized by mass production, the dissemination and use of knowledge for the generation of wealth and employment, the formation of a new social order and aspirations, building new frontiers of social networks and solidarity, the shaping up of a new framework of social relations and culture, the inculcation of new interests and identities, and the creation of new space and pace of development for its members in society. The foundation of this society is erected on the creative potential embodied in the human mind that is harnessed by inculcating appropriate human capability through formal education and skill. This capability is exploited, disseminated and put into wider use through ICTs in a globalizing environment. In this society, knowledge acquires a value-added meaning that transforms the man of knowledge into a new man of power with redefined responsibilities (Drucker 1968, 249). By reinforcing the human mind as the site of power, the knowledge society makes power both identified and diffused (Castells 1997, 359–60).

Transformation of Knowledge, Identity and Replacement of Traditional Workforce

The economic structure of the knowledge society develops a global network of wealth, power and identity (Castells 1983, 1997); transforms knowledge as the main means of livelihood of the largest group of the population (Drucker 1968, 249–50); ushers economic and social transformation at a global scale; creates new economic appetites, aspirations and demands (Porat 1977); and replaces muscle by mind (Toffler 1990, 8) and agricultural and industrial workers by knowledge workers.

Distinguishing from Agricultural and Industrial Societies

The knowledge society brings striking changes in most of the key areas of society and distinguishes itself from the agricultural and industrial societies. Some of these distinctions are shown in Table 5.1.

Table 5.1

Comparative Features of Agricultural, Industrial and Knowledge Societies

Key Areas	Agricultural Society	Industrial Society	Knowledge Society
Key resources	Natural resources	Physical labour	Mental, intellectual capability
Source of power	Land, animal and physical	Steam engine	Internet
Key tools	Plough and hoe	Machine tools	Information and communication technologies
Major products	Foods, other basic services	Industrial goods and services	Data, information, knowledge, ideas

(Table 5.1 continued)

(Table 5.1 continued)

Key Areas	Agricultural Society	Industrial Society	Knowledge Society
Major working categories	Agricultural workers	Industrial workers	Knowledge workers
Market	Localized markets	National and world market, colonies	Global market
Major source of GDP and employment	Primary sector	Secondary sector	Tertiary sector
Major social movements for social change	Peasant, tribal, localized unity	Labour, factory or organization class based	Larger issues connecting people locally and globally on the issues of environment, women, ethnic, gay, lesbian, etc.
Bases of social identities	Communitarian, consolidated	Secular economy partly consolidated	Multiple-global, widely diffused
Forms of social mobility	Slow pace of mobility widely conditioned by primordial arrangements	Fast pace of mobility, widely vertical	Fast pace of mobility both vertical and horizontal
Forms of spatial mobility	Very limited, predominantly rural to rural and mostly for non-economic purpose; insignificant incidence of immigration	Fast mobility for a limited section of people from rural to rural and rural to urban areas for both economic and non-economic purposes; immigration for a limited section of population	Extensive mobility from rural to urban areas and from urban to urban areas, predominantly for the economic purpose; unprecedented incidences of immigration
Pace of change	Very slow	Fast for a limited section	Very fast and all encompassing

Source: Author's own.

This new era has been described interchangeably as Knowledge Society, Information Society, Information Age, Electronic Era, Global Village, Technetronic Age, Post-industrial Society, Third Wave, Networked Society and many other such terms, we prefer to call it a knowledge society. Knowledge is produced in the human mind as an interrelated processed product, and in this society, knowledge acquires an operational and commodity value and becomes a factor of economic growth (Machlup 1962). In the knowledge society, the relationships between ideas, data, information and knowledge are not discrete and hierarchical; rather more of a spiral cyclical one that develops a higher spiral cycle continuously. They are subject to multiple uses and are put in the common basket of knowledge for application and generation of wealth and employment.

Transforming Human Being as Bearers of Explicit Knowledge

A knowledge society is founded on the basic trust of human potential and on their innate capacity to be knowledgeable. In this society, human beings are the key resource as they are the bearers of key capital, that is, knowledge. This society transforms human beings, triggers their creative reflection and converts the 'tacit knowledge' that they possess into 'explicit knowledge' for the creation of new meaning and its mass production through increasing significance on formal education, skill and training (UN 2005, 36–37).

Using ICTs and Globalization as Key Constituents

Revolution in ICTs and globalization are crucial co-constituents. They are indispensable for the sustenance and expansion of the knowledge society that has posited humanity to 'face a quantum leap forward' (Toffler 1980, 348; Toffler and Toffler 1995, xi) and have enabled people to be part of large-scale knowledge networks through computer, World Wide Web networking, Skype, emails, blogs, Twitter, Facebook, SMS, MMS and the like in this society (Melucci 1996, 8), paving the way for replacing the pre-existing 'mass society' (Dijk 1999). Globalization and ICTs have brought into being an unprecedented flow of goods, services and mobility of ideas, information, and images of human beings across space with unprecedented speed. These have ushered in a 'networking form of organization across the globe with flexibility and instability of work, and individuation of labor through the constitution of a space of flows and timeless time' (Castells 1997, 1), and 'a unitary framework of experience across the globe, yet at the same time new forms of fragmentation and dispersal' (Giddens 1990, 4–5).

Envisioned to Be a Progressive, Planned and Rational Society

The knowledge society has been widely envisioned to be a progressive, planned and rational society that would replace high risk with low risk, promote a caring and participatory environment, reconstruct the state to be unnecessary in future, empower the powerless by challenging the traditional structures of control, reduce hierarchy and promote democracy (Cohen 2003, 51–67; Evans 2004, 11–14) to eradicate human toil, social class divisions and ideologies of antagonism (Gorz 1982).

Brought Discontinuity, Disorientation, Conflict and New Identities

The knowledge society brings varieties of restructuring and alteration in the pre-existing societal arrangements, discontinuity with the past (Dracker 1966), real-life shockwaves, dizzying disorientation in social institutions and an alternative consciousness (Toffler 1970, 161). It has produced new power structures and new forms of exclusion, polarization, inequality and social asymmetry, and has inculcated new areas of interest, new identities, social movements and a new landscape of conflicts and a political category of a new underclass (Castells 1997, 11; 2001, 60–61). It has created categories of upwardly mobile and powerful knowledge-rich, and downwardly mobile and disempowered knowledge-poor; it has divided society digitally, produced new social boundaries and fragmentations, and constructed new varieties of social identities. These identities are formed, according to Castells (1997), based on an increasing realization among social actors about the loss of control over lives, environments, jobs, economies, governments, countries and ultimately over the fate of the earth and about the new forms of domination. Hence, the emerging knowledge society has not produced a uniform collective identity; rather, social actors with unequal and diversified control over resources, institutions and socio-political processes have tended to promote diverse identities. The knowledge society has also brought in new forms of domination. To Castells (1997), the knowledge society has produced the following interrelated forms of identities to respond to the logic of domination and loss of control over lives:

Legitimizing Identity: This identity is predominantly introduced by the dominant institutions of society to extend and rationalize their domination vis-à-vis a social actor. These are used to sustain social order and to maintain status-quo through patriotic, religious or consumerist orientations.

Resistant Identity: This identity is generated by those actors that are in positions/conditions that are devalued and/or stigmatized by the logic of domination, thus building trenches of resistance and survival on the basis of principles that are different from or opposed to those permeating the institutions of society.

Project Identity: Social actors on the basis of whatever cultural materials available to them build a new identity that redefines their position in society, and by doing so seek to transform the whole structure. This identity challenges the hegemony of the dominant class at several levels. It proposes an alternative to the existing forms of rationalization, commoditization and consumerism and poses fundamental challenges to late capitalist modernity (Castells 1997, 8).

Ludic Identity: Castells has also highlighted the arrival of ludic identity that locates subjectivity in the luminal anti-structures of late modern mass culture which privilege privatized hedonistic indulgence and mass-mediated forms of escapism and/or simulated contestations that allow subcultural withdrawal of self and identity from the larger society, what has been called 'retreatism' (Longman 2010).

To Castells (1997), these identities are neither nor produce unified outcomes, and these are neither progressive nor regressive identities except in its historical context. The legitimizing identity generates a civil society, that is, a set of organizations and institutions as well as a series of structured and organized social actors, 'which produce, albeit sometimes in a conflict manner, an identity that rationalizes the source of structural domination'. The identity for resistance leads to the formation of communes or communities. It constructs forms of collective resistance against 'other unbearable oppression, usually on the basis of identities defined by history, geography or biology, making it easier to essentialize the boundaries of resistance'. Here, the examples of are religious fundamentalism, nationalist self-affirmation, etc., 'the expressions being exclusion of the excluder by the excluded. The project identity, according to him, produces subjects' (Castells 1997, 10).

The knowledge society is taking shape in India on a pre-given foundation that is socially divided in terms of caste, ethnicity and gender, and geographically in terms of villages, towns and metro cities, economically in terms of rich and poor, and politically in terms of dominant and dominated groups. While the spread of modernizing, developmental and globalizing forces is eclectic, based on the aforementioned considerations, the penetration of the knowledge society has added to this unevenness in many ways. In this backdrop, to suffice the objective of this chapter, information collected from four metro cities, Delhi, Mumbai, Kolkata and Chennai, four district towns, Meerut in Uttar Pradesh, Balurghat in West Bengal, Nagercoil in Tamil Nadu, Thane in Maharashtra, and three cluster of villages from Kumarganj Block in West Bengal, Bhagawanpur in Uttar Pradesh and Killiyur in Tamil Nadu, focusing on a cross-section of 2,700 people from diverse caste, tribal, gender and economic backgrounds is used. In order to provide a macro picture, a good body of secondary sources of information is also used in this study.

India: The Shifting Direction towards a Knowledge Society

India inherited a predominantly agricultural society from the British after Independence. Society was widely characterized by dependence on agriculture for employment and wealth generation, low productivity of land, lack of industrialization, persisting unemployment, heightened poverty, illiteracy, social inequality, stagnation and the feudal domination of large segments of population. It emphasized the immediate need for agricultural modernization and industrialization as the panacea for all social and economic ills. Accordingly, it initiated a plethora of new initiatives including those of the land reforms, agricultural modernization, and rapid industrialization until the 1980s under the regime of centralized planning, rigid economic discipline and a state-controlled business environment for export promotion and import restriction. These programmes, however, brought only partial success in agricultural modernization and rural development and very limited progress in industrialization. Over the decades, the transitional dynamics of India were widely characterized by a chronic low rate of economic growth, regular budget deficit, inflation, high rate of unemployment, labour unrest, large-scale industrial sickness, increasing trade deficit, a huge burden of indebtedness on international funding agencies, frequent unrests by peasants, workers, farmers, etc., and the increasing pressure of population on traditional resources. At this point, while the world had been experiencing the new technological and economic choices and the proliferation of the knowledge revolution, India in the early 1990s opted for the path of economic liberalization and adopted the ICTs-driven globalized knowledge revolution as a new opportunity to ignite its human resources for a new future and 'to steer the society to a new direction'. The state emphatically asserted that 'we missed the industrial revolution but we should not miss the information and knowledge revolution ... Leapfrogging into knowledge era looks imminently possible today for the societal transformation of India in the twenty-first century, which is going to be the century of hope for India' (Planning Commission of India 2001). The structural adjustment programme (SAP) that paved the way for domestic market liberalization and private investment in key sectors of the economy helped the state to bring in huge private and foreign direct investment in the information and communication technology and private investment in education. Now, huge infrastructure for road and transport, IT hubs and business processing, tour and travel, banking and insurance, health and education, entertainment and recreation are being created with unprecedented speed. ICTs links are established in every corner of the country, both through state and private initiatives. 'Digital India 2015' has been a new slogan to pave the way for a vibrant knowledge economy in India.

Contemporary India experiences phenomenal expansion of educational institutions from 103 universities and 3,604 colleges in 1970–71 to 712 universities and 33,023 colleges in 2011–12. Over the years, the number of students enrolled in higher education has increased from 20 lakh to 259 lakh. Now more than 20% of the student population goes to the doorstep of higher and technical education. The GER at secondary level has gone up to 65%. The educational background of the workforce has also phenomenally increased.

In the 1990s, less than 0.5% of the population had access to the Internet. Now more than 35% of the Indian population has access to the Internet, 91% to mobile telephones. Mass and new social media has brought new opportunities for networking, new patterns of work participation, new capacity for mass production, dissemination and use of knowledge by the largest segment of population, 65% of whom belong to the age group of below 35 years. All these have brought not only new momentum in the economy by creating new varieties of jobs but also a new phase of economic growth and social arrangement in the country.

The economy that was stagnating below 4% rate of economic growth in the pre-1990s has experienced above 9% economy growth in the 1990s. Over the years, work participation in agriculture has declined to 49% and its contribution to GDP to below 13%. Despite several state-sponsored initiatives, India has not been able to emerge as an industrialized nation. This sector accommodates 24% of the workforce and contributes to 26% of the GDP. Today, however, India experiences phenomenal expansion of the service sector. It contributes 65% of the GDP and accommodates 27% of the workforce of the country. Its growth rate surpasses that of the agriculture and industry, and it has registered above 10% growth in the last fiscal year (Government of India 2014). The fast shift of the economy towards the service sector is linked to the expansion of knowledge economy in the country.

Education, ICTs and Emerging Nature of Work Participation: Empirical Reflections

Although India has a knowledge-based past, the social foundation of this knowledge was neither mass-based nor inclusive in its caste-ridden society. In contemporary India though, the scope and condition for mass production and exploitation of knowledge and proliferation of non-agricultural jobs have significantly widened. However, one is yet to see whether such scope has been uniform or eclectic across the metro cities, district towns and the villages and among the cross-section of the population irrespective of their caste, tribal and gender backgrounds.

Access to education, formal training, ICTs and service-based jobs have played a crucial role in the expansion of the knowledge society. The present study shows that the quantum of spread of literacy and education, ICTs and non-agricultural occupations like business and service have been diverse among the metro cities, towns and villages and among different social groups. Table 5.1 shows that villages have more illiterates than the district towns and metro cities. As far as the literates up to XII standard are concerned, their representation in the working population has substantially increased across the space, even though the urban areas have an advantage over the rural ones. However, as far as the graduate, postgraduate professionals and technical degree holders are concerned, they have highest concentration in metro cities, followed by district towns and then villages. The general category, OBCs and women from all social groups have a higher degree of representation in high educational qualifications than those of the STs and SCs (see Table 5.2 for details).

Because of pre-existing spatial divides, metro cities have higher degree of penetration of landline telephone, mobile, computer and Internet than the district towns and villages respectively. However, mobile telephone has a higher extent of penetration across the grid. Similarly, the significance of spatial difference among cities, towns and villages has been minimal

Table 5.2

Level of Education by Caste and Gender in the Metro Cities, District Towns and Villages

Levels	Category	Metro	District Town	Village
Illiterate	General	Nil	Nil	Nil
	OBC	3.5	3	13.3
	SC	13	4.8	19.7
	ST	Nil	40	50
	Women	Nil	14.3	18.0
I–XII	General	38.8	50.2	69.7
	OBC	66	49.2	56.3
	SC	64.7	65	67.6
	ST	20.6	12.5	10.6
	Women	23.3	42.2	71
UG + PG	General	36.5	37.8	27
	OBC	19.7	36.3	27.7
	SC	12.8	21.2	12
	ST	29.2	2.5	6.6
	Women	49.2	32	11
Technical	General	24.7	12	3.3
	OBC	10.8	11.5	2.7
	SC	9.5	9	0.7
	ST	Nil	Nil	Nil
	Women	27.5	11.5	Nil

Source: Study Team 2010.

where access to radio and television are concerned (see Table 5.3 for details). Corresponding to the educational and ICTs divides, the proportion of workers engaged in business and service and the proportion of knowledge workers to total workers have been highest in the metro cities with 64% and 49.8% followed by district towns with 60.8% and 39.5% and the villages 42% and 25% respectively. At the nationwide level, the proportion of workers engaged in business and service has been 56.6% and the proportion of knowledge workers to total workers has been 39.5% (for details, see Table 5.4). These show a positive co-relationship of a higher degree of urbanization with higher educational qualification; higher extent of educational qualification with higher degree of penetration of business and service activities; and higher quantum of business and service activities with higher degree of penetration of knowledge jobs and vice versa. Such correlations also have positive relationships with the inherited social inequality in society depicted in the traditional caste, ethnic and gender backgrounds of the workers. The emerging knowledge society in India sees the phenomenal proliferation of knowledge workers across the space with difference intensity. It also finds the continuity of the old knowledge workers such as those of the teachers, lawyers, judges, doctors and health agricultural extension workers with the emerging body of new knowledge workers, who are dealing with ICTs, media, business processing, and host of related activities which have emerged in the wake of globalization and information revolution in recent decades. The details of such jobs are described in the fourth section of this chapter. The form and extent of penetration of knowledge jobs, however, are largely conditioned by the pre-existing patterns of caste, ethnic and gender divides in society and their related educational attainments and access to ICTs.

Table 5.3

ICTs Penetration in the Selected Metro Cities, District Towns and Villages

Place	Telephone	Mobile	Computer	Internet	Radio and/or Television
Metro cities	58.8	92.7	20.6	10.7	82.3
District towns	39	76.15	9.8	5.8	75.4
Villages	14.5	77.4	2.5	1.2	81.2

Source: Study Team, 2010.

Table 5.4

Proportion of Knowledge Workers in Relation to the Service/Business and Total Workers

Place	Gen % of Workers in Bus + Ser	OBC % of Workers in Bus + Ser	SC % of Workers in Bus + Ser	ST % of Workers in Bus + Ser	Women % of Workers in Bus + Ser	Total % of Workers in Bus + Ser	% of Knowledge Workers in Bus + Ser	% of Knowledge Workers to Total Workers
All metro cities	88	61	46.5	25	53.8	64	73	49.8
All district towns	95.3	68.8	41	02.7	52.3	60.8	61.5	39.5
All villages	53.3	63.3	24.3	6.0	26.7	42	43	25
Average of total	78.86	64.36	37.26	11.23	44.26	55.6	59.16	38.1

Source: Study Team, 2010.

Because of their higher degree of access to higher and technical education and ICTs, the general categories have higher degree of access to knowledge jobs than the OBCs, SCs and STs across the space. Table 5.2 shows that in the metro cities, 70% of the workers from the general category are engaged as knowledge workers. Their representation as knowledge workers in the district towns is to the extent of 58% and in the villages 50%. Such representations as knowledge workers in the metro cities, district towns and villages for the OBCs are to the extent of 52%, 48% and 30% and for the SCs 28%, 25% and 20% respectively. Significantly, 50% of the workers from the ST group are in the knowledge job in the metro cities, 20% in the towns and 8% in villages. High concentration of the STs in knowledge jobs in metro cities is mostly because of the fact that mostly, the educated ST population migrates to the metro cities and they are able to avail the benefits of reservation policy in getting jobs in this sector. Women have high concentration in knowledge jobs in the metro cities with 48%, followed by district towns with 40% and villages with 18% (see Table 5.2 for details.) In general, across the space, it is seen that as social status declines, the work participation of knowledge workers also declines.

Tables 5.4 and 5.5 clearly show that knowledge work is spreading at a faster rate in the metro cities than in the district towns, more in the district towns than in the villages; that business and service activities have been good hosts for the knowledge jobs; that access to education and ICTs is positively linked to the access to knowledge jobs; and that historically inherited inequality grounded in traditional caste, gender, ethnic and spatial divides has a positive correlation with the unequal spread of knowledge jobs. These tables have also shown that at the national level, 38.1% workers are engaged in knowledge jobs, indicating that 61.9% of the workers are in non-knowledge jobs, 50% of the non-knowledge

Table 5.5

Proportion of Knowledge Workers in Relation to Total Workers in Metro Cities, District Towns and Villages by Caste and Gender

Place	General	OBC	SC	ST	Women	Overall
Metro cities	70	52	28	50	48	49.8
District towns	58	48	25	20	45	39.5
Villages	50	30	20	8	18	25

Source: Study Team, 2010.

workers are from cities, 60.5% from towns and 75% from villages. It also shows that though knowledge jobs are expanding fast along with an increasing access to education and ICTs among people, these have not replaced the non-knowledge jobs and their social and economic significance. Both types of jobs coexist and contribute to construct new patterns of job hierarchy, mobility, marginality and identities in the emerging knowledge society.

Knowledge Work, New Hierarchy and Mobility

Knowledge work can't be sustained in isolation. It needs huge support at the initial stage for its arrival and sustenance. Thus, it generates employment opportunities for service providers and supports service providers and manual workers of various sorts. In India, foundation for knowledge work is in the making. Occupationally, it is at a fast transitional phase, and has created a new occupational hierarchy across cities, towns and villages, putting knowledge jobs at the top in this arrangement as shown below:

> *Core Knowledge Workers:* A host of jobs have been identified as knowledge jobs such as those of teachers, researchers, doctors, entrepreneurs, health workers, real estate executives, insurance agents, typists, computer operators, and agricultural extension workers and professionals engaged in ICTs, in banking, retail and the like services, media, business processing, tours and travels, software and hardware engineering. Having emerged as the core categories of knowledge workers, they get higher income and social and economic security. They are predominantly represented by the upper and the middle strata of the caste groups across the space and experience very high quantum of upward mobility.
> *Linked to the Core as Support Services Providers:* Labour contractors, transport providers, electronic and electrical technicians, office peons, etc., many of whom are the intermediaries and arrange support services for the knowledge industries. They include both skilled and semi-skilled workers, are highly flexible and transitional categories and experience vertical occupational mobility, earning

a high amount of income. They are also predominantly represented by the upper and middle strata of the caste groups, even though a very small section of the lower social strata is integrated there. Many of them are transitional categorized, earn higher income and experience high volume of upward mobility.

Linked to Periphery—Manual Worker: They include both unskilled and semi-skilled workers such as fitters, carpenters, drivers, rickshaw pullers, security guards and mechanics, and unskilled manual workers of all sorts like construction labour, etc., whose quantum of activities have increased with the expansion of knowledge economy. They are also predominantly represented by the lower caste groups, even though a very small section of the upper caste groups are found there, especially in the urban areas. They predominantly experience occupationally horizontal mobility, high level of social and economic insecurity and earn very low levels of income.

The new occupational hierarchy has evolved as a human pyramid, whereby small sections of core workers (knowledge workers) and their support service providers exploit emerging economic opportunities and maximize their economic interests, reinforcing their social significance by occupying the top and the middle segments of this pyramid. At the bottom of the pyramid is the vast mass of manual/unskilled workers who provide varieties of physical labour for the growth and sustenance of this society and its organizational structure. This occupational and social hierarchy has been sharpened with the increasing gap between the core knowledge workers who are knowledge rich, upwardly mobile and informed, on the one hand, and the knowledge poor, who are stagnant, uninformed and spatially and horizontally mobile on the other. It comes closer to the observation that knowledge society has widened class divides between the knowledge haves and the knowledge have-nots, (Touraine; cf. Lyan 1986) and between the empowered 'information-rich' and the 'information-poor' (Castells 1996, 67) in the globalized world.

In general, the quantum of upward mobility has been higher in the metro cities and district towns than in the villages, more for the upper castes/strata than for the lower castes/strata, more for the educated, trained and knowledgeable than for the non-knowledgeable. Significantly, most knowledgeable are from the pre-existing dominant sections of the society. The emerging knowledge society, by enhancing the scope of vertical occupational mobility of the knowledgeable, who are predominantly from the pre-existing upper sections of society, and by widening the space for horizontal mobility of non-knowledgeable, who are from the lower sections, has widely reinforced pre-existing social hierarchies. It has also brought into being new form of imbalances in occupational mobility by injecting varieties of uncertainties in new jobs and new forms of marginality through horizontal mobility. The expansion of this society has been accompanied by an environment of job insecurity and loss of liberty for certain knowledge workers, service providers and manual workers through the culture of contract labour and outsourcing of several of key activities of the organization. Notwithstanding new economic movements, the work situation for both types of workers is conditioned by an economic boom and recession in the developed world, beck and call work relation, lack of employment security, stress, long working hours lack of freedom and near absence of alternative choice. Therefore, within these emerging contradictions, a new pattern of marginalization is in the making.

Emerging Knowledge Society and New Forms of Marginality

We have discussed the dynamics and dimensions of marginality in the previous chapter dealing with peasant identities in India. Although the knowledge society has produced its own pattern of marginality, it has simultaneously reinforced many of the old facets of marginality in some form. Within this emerging world, marginality is shaped and extended for those segments of population who are not only deprived of the opportunities for education and skill development and access to ICTs but have also posited themselves in unequal, insecure and peripheral working conditions and social networks. In general, the knowledge society has produced:

> *Structurally Marginalized:* They are located within the structural arrangement of the knowledge society, and contribute to the expansion of this society without getting substantive scope of upward social mobility. They are represented by the migrant workers working in the informal sector, workers not getting

adequate access to education and ICTs, workers who are continuing to provide cheap labour remaining socially neglected, economically under paid, politically disempowered and historically cumulatively deprived, and such other categories. Historically inherited social inequality and deprivations have remained positively linked with a vast section of structurally marginalized.

Functionally Marginalized: They have acquired the marginalized status within the emerging functional arrangements of the knowledge society, even though they are posited with the possibility of upward mobility. They include knowledge workers working in insecure and stressful working conditions as contractual, ad hoc, non-permanent workers, educated and trained workers, but compelled to be employed in a low position and the like, informal workers working within the formal organization and many such categories. They are also deprived of many of the social security, child care, maternity and the like benefits. For many of the functionally marginalized, historically inherited deprivation and inequality provide an added disadvantage.

Neo Marginalized: They are not marginalized historically but have acquired this status because of reshuffling of the economic and opportunity structure. They include the sizeable section of general and the middle class who have not been able to acquire the required education and skill and do not have adequate access to ICTs for several reasons and people of all categories who are unable to get integrated with the emerging consumer culture, lifestyle and the ICTs-driven competitive socio-cultural milieu.

On many occasions, these marginalized categories appear to be mutually inclusive as many dimensions of their marginality are historically cumulative and socially relational. While the traditional facets of marginalization have remained ingrained with the pre-given socio-cultural values, the emerging facets of it are legitimized by strict adherence to the rule of law that discourages trade unionism in workplace, encourage culture of hire and fire, and effectively demonstrate the global threat of recession. The new facets of marginalization in this emerging knowledge society are being legitimized by the rising culture of silence, passivity, anonymity and collective withdrawal of dissent from real public space and through the emerging consumer culture and new socio-cultural milieu of this society that encourages more fluidity than solidarity in social lives.

New Socio-cultural Milieu in a Pre-existing Segregated Society

Along with the expansion of economic neoliberalism, education, ICTs and emergence of new occupational hierarchy on the one hand, and marginalization of vast section of people on the other, a metro/urban-centric, youth-focused, fast-changing fashion and consumption-oriented global socio-cultural milieu is in the making across the space in India. Widely driven by ICTs, it has revolutionized all areas of social activities, including those of business and shopping education and socialization, networking and collaboration, career counselling and mobility, health care and beautification, matrimonial and friendship financial transaction and banking, tour and travel, music and arts, spiritualism and religion, collective mobilization and advocacy, and all other areas as one needs in his/her day-to-day existence. This socio-cultural milieu has helped to convert the world into a site of production and consumption of information, and to make public addicted to it all through their active time either to be active agents or passive consumers of it. By injecting a culture of competitive consumerism, it relentlessly endeavours to reproduce consumerism by socializing people in a global culture embedded in consumerism, minimizing the space between personal and public through cyber-centric interaction.

Within the thick of such socio-cultural momentum, societies in India experience the arrival of a new-generation youth who are product of economic liberalization, globalization and ICTs. They are socialized in the ICTs boom and intensify social interaction and networking with increased speed and frequency through text messaging, voice mailing, commercial advertising, e-mailing, e-charting, Facebook posting, blogging, twitting, Skyping, wave casting and host of such social and new media activities. These have created a social milieu of closeness through intensive interaction in a virtual world—the ideal expression being 'out of (web) site out of mind'. Being active in a virtual world is widely described to be active in the social world. It is posited to be described as a symbol of high modernity, forward-looking world view, cosmopolitanism, universality, globality and knowledgeability.

These e-credos are highly pro-adaptive to the ICT-driven culture. They are like the 'digital natives' of America as described by Prensky (2001) and electronic credo, rather 'e-credo', of India with deep-down orientation to ICTs-driven consumerist lifestyle, desire to have the latest brand of ICTs gazettes, branded clothes, body wire and motor vehicles under their possession at an early part of their lives. They are the emerging ambassadors of 'consume and throw' culture who have little guilt feeling of conspicuous consumption. They live in the present through consumerism, at times against the lifestyle of their parents and grandparents who prefer to live in future even at the cost of the present.

They are available not only in the virtual world but also in real life, forming varieties of community within a community who extensively use ICTs to communicate, socialize and engage meaningfully across the space to produce a youth-centric social milieu sustainably. They practise new cultural idioms preferring 'Yo' handshake over hello or 'namaste', western fast food—pizza, burger, pasta—over local dishes, cappuccino coffee over local drinks like lassi, use innovative and different vocabularies and abbreviations such as 'pop' for papa, 'mom' for mammy, 'sis' for sister, 'bro' for brother, 'princy' for school principal, 'LOL' for nonsense, 'IDK' for 'I don't know' and varieties of new-age words/vocabularies as language of interaction. They decorate body with tattoos, adorn distinctive branded attire and keep themselves ready with state-of-the-art electronic gadgets and smart and confident body language to make their presence felt in public domain distinctively, different from the rest. They try to represent them constantly through selfies 24×7 in their defined social world. They redefine traditionality in a new context and place laptops, notepads, iPods, pen drives and mobile phones in front of Goddess Saraswati for blessings instead of notebooks, books and pens as was the practice traditionally. They expand new horizon of friendship regularly in the virtual world, but seldom know the people in the neighbourhood. They are ready to be socially sensitive and make a huge hue and cry in the virtual world that has emerged to be a powerful force to reckon with. Although they are predominantly visible in the mega cities and in the urban areas and among the upper social and economic strata of society, their emergence has been quite explicit even among the lower socio-economic strata and in the rural areas with a low intensity. They from the core of the new smart community being highly adaptive to the emerging socio-culture milieu set in motion by the knowledge society whose orientation to life is widely guided by the understanding that you only live once (YoLo).

They have become the reference point and the face of the emerging knowledge society, being the *techno-addicts* of knowledge era. They inject more fluidity than solidarity to the pre-existing social order; their lifestyle itself represents an apparent criticality to the traditional social order; they develop contestation to many of the pre-existing realities and largely contribute to the fragmentation of everyday reality. Significantly, the middle-aged professionals, academicians, entrepreneurs and others who have both the desire and the capacity are profoundly tended to be integrated with this socio-cultural milieu and are in the process of getting acclimatized with this techno-centric culture as both addicts and moderates. These e-credos and these segments of population have emerged to be the driving engine and flagbearers of the information age.

Although the e-credos are spreading across the space, they are not a homogenous category. Their pre-given locations in a specific spatial, caste, ethnic, gendered and the like groups widely condition the construction of their world views. Hence, there has been their diverse integration with the society.

The emerging cultural milieu similarly has been unable to integrate a large segment of society, especially the structurally marginalized within its own ambit. In effective terms, they have emerged to be a loose nod of this cultural milieu by compulsion and not by choice. In the process of interaction and mobility, many of them lose not only the required space to preserve, practise and promote own cultural choice but also become dependent on the market-driven available alternatives on which they seldom have a control. Within the emerging economic and social milieu, this section of people has emerged to be the outsiders from within, and survive as global 'marginal man' who resides in urban areas as immigrants, and in rural areas as native but are integrated effectively to none culturally and politically. They are posited to be consumers of global goods and services, viewers and listeners of entertainment industry and culture, and followers of elite-centric politics mostly at the cost of loss of their own cultural identity. The traditional cultural mosaic of Indian society that is layered and fragmented has been layered and fragmented further with the emergence of new socio-cultural milieu, even though whole society is circumscribed by global consumerism. Notwithstanding the increased layering and limited inclusion in the global consumerist milieu, an imposition of Western/global cultural practices over the localized ones has emerged to be a reality.

Integration with Knowledge Society and Its Varied Patterns

The knowledge society has developed new logics of integration in society. Among the various parameters of integration, the extent of access to higher and technical education, ICTs, knowledge jobs and managerial/supervisory positions in the organizational hierarchy have emerged to be the crucial ones since these are immediately linked to mobility and have achieved status in society. As people are unequally posited in relation to access to these indices there have been varied patterns of their integration with the knowledge society.

Knowledge jobs show a positive correlation with high level of education and skill, higher degree of urbanization, high caste and ethnic backgrounds and vice versa. The general category population in all has got 'high' degree of integration with knowledge society in metro cities, district towns and villages by getting a very high degree of access over high and technical education, ICTs and high degree of access over managerial and non-managerial positions in knowledge jobs. The OBCs are in the process of fast integration with knowledge society. By the overall indicators, they have high level of integration in the metro cities and district towns and moderate level of integration at the village level. The SCs have a moderate level of integration with the knowledge society in metro cities and district towns and a low level of integration in the villages. The STs have in all a high level of integration with the knowledge society in the metro cities and low level of integration in the district towns and villages. Awareness about the policy of protective discrimination among a section of the SCs and STs and their migration to the urban areas have contributed to such integration in the urban space. Women, on the other hand, have a high level of integration in the metro cities and district towns and a low level of integration in the villages. However, knowledge jobs in general have become gender-friendly. In all, a higher degree of integration with the knowledge society is positively linked to higher degree of mobility in society. Significantly, the emerging form of mobility and extent of integration to the knowledge society has remained conditioned by caste, ethnicity and gender consideration and circumscribed by spatial locations (see Table 5.6 for details).

Sustained Social Divisions, Diverse Opportunities of Social Networking and Formation of Multiple Identities

The increasing flow of information and access to ICTs and increasing quantum of migration and mobility have brought new opportunities and

Table 5.6

Dominant Patterns of Integration with Knowledge Society by Various Social Groups across the Metro Cities, District Towns and Villages

Place	Indicator	General	OBC	SC	ST	Women
Metro cities	Post-secondary education	Very high	Moderate	Low	High	Very high
	Access to ICTs	Very high	Very high	Very high	High	Very high
	Knowledge job (non-managerial)	Very high	Very high	Moderate	High	High
	Managerial/supervisory position in knowledge job	Moderate	Moderate	Very low	—	Low
	Overall	High	High	Moderate	High	High
District towns	Post-secondary education	Moderate	Moderate	Moderate	Very low	Moderate
	Access to ICTs	Very high	Very high	Very high	Moderate	Very high
	Knowledge job (non-managerial)	Very high	Very high	Moderate	Very low	High
	Managerial/supervisory position in knowledge job	High	Low	Very high	Low	Moderate
	Overall	High	High	Moderate	Low	High
Villages	Post-secondary education	Moderate	Moderate	Very high	Low	Very high
	Access to ICTs	Moderate	Moderate	Moderate	Low	Moderate
	Knowledge job (non-managerial)	Very high	Very high	Low	Low	Low
	Managerial/supervisory position in knowledge job	High	Very high	Very high	Low	Very high
	Overall	High	Moderate	Low	Low	Low

Source: Author's own.

Note: Indicators in terms of access achieved position: Very High 60% and above, High 50–59%, Moderate 30–49%, Low 20–29%, Very Low 19% and below.

contributed to form new networks in the society to exploit those opportunities. However, persistent social inequality, construction of new hierarchy, new forms of marginalization and uneven integration with the emerging knowledge society have contributed to the formation of new varieties of social networks.

New Opportunities and Networks

Social networks have always remained a powerful informal collective arrangement for developing interconnectivity among its members to enhance, exploit and maximize their individual and collective interests. Usually, all social networks work parallelly which are formed based on caste, class, ethnicity and professional and the like affiliations. The dominant sections of the society having higher degree of access over connectivity and information use their networks more than those of the others who have lesser degree of access to connectivity, resources and information. In the knowledge society, use of ICTs has brought a paradigmatic shift in the dynamics of social networking as it has provided the scope and condition of social mobility for all segments of the society across the geographical space. However, the emerging knowledge society is posited in a contradictory situation. The emerging networks are ICTs-enabled and formed immediately based on economic and social interests to harness the opportunities which are proliferated across space. Although emerging social networks tend to have a cross-cutting alliance, domination of the dominant social groups prevails over the rest. Previously, the upper strata of the society formed the dominant social networks based on extensive face-to-face and postal and limited telephonic communications to exploit the available resources. They also used their social and cultural capital for these purposes. On the other hand, devoid of cultural and effective social capital, the lower strata had very limited networking potential and seldom had any parallel networks with wider access and very often they were dependent on the upper strata to get connected with the wider world and to get access to any new livelihood options and opportunity. In fact, traditionally, those networks were predominantly elite-centric, top-driven and controlled and used only by the dominant sections of the society. Now, ICTs have helped forming multiple waves of networks which function parallelly for all segments of the society, and at times, these networks criss-cross the boundary of each other's networks. These networks are no more local; rather, these are interconnected with a wider society for a wide variety of flows and interactions and opportunities. Hence, there are multiple networks that intersect with the logic of each other's functioning as shown below. These networks function based on their caste/class, gender and spatial considerations and on the form and extent of access to ICTs by the members.

1. The upper and middle strata/castes of the rural society developing networks within their own space and with the upper strata of the district towns and the metro cities and vice versa for business, investment and new economic interests, education and matrimonial, and other issues of political and social interests (mediated by all varieties of ICTs and social media).
2. The lower strata/castes of the rural society developing networks with their counterparts in the district towns and the metro cities and vice versa and within their own space, for seeking information about employment opportunities, possibility of migration, small business, loan, marriage, medical help, etc. (mediated predominantly by mobile phones and limited use of social media).
3. Upper and middle strata/castes across the space frequently using the network of the lower strata/caste to get information about labour, services, land and other resources, and avenues of new investment. Being the dominant section, they easily get access to such networks (mediated mostly by mobile phones and limited use of social media).
4. Lower strata/castes of the villages, district towns and metro cities using the network of the upper strata (very infrequently though) within their own space to get information about employment, wage rate, loan and other opportunities on daily basis. Being the dominated section, they have very limited access to such networks (predominantly mediated by mobile phones).
5. Women of upper/middle strata/castes developing networks within their own metro cities, towns and village spaces for employment, matrimonial, social ceremonies, social get together etc. (predominantly mediated by mobile phones and limited use of social media).
6. Cross-caste/strata and cross-space networks developed by e-credo across the villages, towns and metro cities and vice versa for education, employment, friendship, art, music, culture, profession and enrichment (mediated by all varieties of ICTs and social media).

Although these networks are not exclusive or fixed, in the present juncture of the society, these are getting extended further, cutting across the local, regional and national boundaries and also getting reformulated to suffice social economic and political interests of the people in society. Significantly, the bases of formation of these networks are founded on the pre-existing caste, class and gender segregation on the one hand and emergence of new economic opportunities and expansion of ICTs on the other. These networks are reflective of the dynamics of domination and marginality, and construction of identity and their fluidity.

Connectivity and Fluidity in Identity

Within the emerging patterns of social divides, marginality, diverse forms of social integration and criss-crossing networks of interconnectivity with the wider world, the rising knowledge society experiences the formation of diverse identities in the form of resistant, legitimizing, project, ludic, submission, passive, anonymity to flexibility.

Legitimizing Identity

The emerging knowledge has produced a thin but powerful community of status quoists who have been able to harvest maximum benefit out of emerging social connectivity, networks and new avenues of economic opportunities because of their pre-existing social and economic status in the society. They are predominantly from the upper strata/castes, have reproduced a large section of core knowledge workers and service promoters from among them and have emerged to be the key beneficiaries of this society. They take advantage of their pre-existing social networks and ICTs to maximize their economic interests and to consolidate their social and political position in society. Many of them reinforce traditionality in everyday life by encouraging traditional ways of life, practising caste prejudice at least in personal life, horoscope, encouraging caste-based marriage, practice of dowry, adherence to religious dogmas and by intersecting religion with politics etc. They encourage participation in the rituals of new religious sects and *baba*s (personalized religious cults) by making use of their social networks and reinforce each other's legitimacy. They use the support of the dominant institution of the society to rationalize their domination, and in turn become active agents of legitimizing institutions of the society. In all effective terms, they make a mix of tradition and modernity by using ICTs, new media and other institutional apparatus in society and project them as the change agents and dominant progressive force of the society. They constitute a significant section of the society and their proportion is on increase across the space.

Redefining the Context for Resistant Identity

The increasing connectivity and the networks have opened up the possibilities for new economic opportunities, migration and occupational mobility, new frontiers of freedom, choice and friendship for the marginalized sections of society. Unlike those of the traditional 'one-to-one' employer–employee relations, there have emerged the possibilities of multiple employers–employee relations. Workers now move for employment across the geographical space and also enjoy a good deal of choices and freedom. These have helped to break the geographic and many of the social barriers for being and becoming parts of larger social and economic processes on the one hand and to bring in good deal of disorientations in the pre-existing social relations on the other. For many, migration and occupational mobility have brought the opportunity to break the bondage of primordial domination and pre-existing barriers marginality.

The emerging networking, mobility and interconnectivity, however, has helped the resurgence of subjugated networks, knowledge and identity at the grass roots which were either dormant or remained un/underused or unrecognized. The traditionally marginalized now relocate their resources, strength and knowledge to get interlinked with wider world. By developing networks for alternative choices, they also develop a critique of the present world and articulate a resistance against the traditional forces of domination. As their marginalization was legitimized within the primordial arrangement of ethnicity, caste and gender, they have been aware of the political and economic significances of their primordial identity. They now privilege primordiality as it keeps them grounded to their roots and nostalgia through social, ritual and festive intercourse; helps them recollect and recast common memories of neglect, subjugation and exploitation; constructs meaning for them of their political participation; and gives them concrete identity in the world of decontextualization and fluidity. It is, however, not to say that the knowledge society reproduced primordial identities for a political or economic goal but to say that historically inherited deprivations and domination, which have a primordial root, have significantly retained their association with the collective identity formation in this age. The marginalized people of the knowledge era have inherited varieties of deprivations and dominations which were historically inflicted on them and were legitimized through the primordial hierarchies. These deprivations and dominations are now questioned by the subordinated groups and they develop resistance against the primordial dominant group through varieties of resistance.

Besides following their primordial cultural root through increased interactivity, they also assert their identities as slum dwellers, workers, peasants, farmers, forest dwellers, displaced persons, etc., and try to get integrated with variety of economic and political forces for assertion of their newly discovered identity and to develop resistance against domination of various sorts. They simultaneously form new bondage of solidarity with diverse groups. Significantly, the language of such resistance against the dominant group is multifaceted and is manifested in one or many of these forms in everyday life: avoidance, non-recognition in public place, mimicking, non-showing of traditional respects, critiquing and developing contestation individually or collectively and participation in organized movements.

Project Identity

ICTs function as a double-edged weapon; while they liberate a section of people, they also help consolidate areas of conservatism and absolute. Religious fundamentalist leaders and their followers propagating extremist views are the cases to this point. They construct and sustain their identities as a project to retain the traditional structure of authority unquestioned in a new social context. They use ICTs-enabled network for creating a community of excluders by excluding the others. They endeavour to retain their conservative and fundamentalist ethos and even try to change the whole structure of the society and even want to redefine society as in accordance to their thought and beliefs as a political project as per their dictum. The project identity is now getting formed through interactive social media across the space on everyday basis. Their community of followers is also on the increase because of aggressive mobilization on the one hand and grouping primordialization and parochialization in society on the other. These identities often use the primordial collectivities of castes, ethnicity, religions and regions to inculcate the sense of pride, hate and insecurity, especially for political goals.

What is significant is that social progression in India has been accompanied by host of contradictions and tensions between the forces of secularization and primordialization. A part of such primordialization is in the process of being co-opted by communalism and religious fundamentalism. This is widely reflected in the increasing manifestations of religious fundamentalist forces and identities who use all high-end ICTs to propagate their medieval dictum, causing tensions, conflicts and disharmony in the very existence of the emerging knowledge society—a knowledge society which is supposed to be progressive, secular, inclusive and rational.

Ludic Identity: The knowledge society has produced a thin layer of people with ludic identity, who want to enjoy the world here and now with conspicuous consumption undeterred by environmental, neighbourhood, societal, cultural and the like concerns. Although they are relatively young by age, educated and predominantly from the upper and upper middle strata of urban India, their size is gradually increasing across the space. They want to be globally linked, locally uprooted, get flowed in the latest world of material and non-material fashion for me, myself and mine.

Identity of Silence, Passivity and Anonymity: The knowledge society experiences the proliferation of identities of silence, passively and anonymity, whereby a large chunk of population prefers to remain silent spectators or passive in attitude for taking a position, asserting their identity and entitlement. Their public assertion only repeats the phrase that 'nothing can be changed'! For a section, this is strategic and deliberate to be legitimizing through silence; for another, it is simply lack of awareness or apathy to dominant public discourse; while for a vast section, it is a fear of loss of livelihood or the level of comfort they achieved. They altogether form the corpse of silent majority in society. Many prefer to be free riders, while some prefer to remain anonymous. Lack of integration with the emerging forms of connectivity and networks, burden of traditional bondage, lack of appropriate information and understanding, etc., widely contribute to such identity of silence, passivity and anonymity. However, these are not fixed, but rather transitional in nature and look for appropriate moment to be a part of a visible assertive process.

Multiple Identities: The emergence of the knowledge society has kept a section of society to be socially, economically and politically undetermined and in a state of constant flux. The burden of information overflow, increasing fragmentation in social order caused by migration, occupational mobility, the emergence of multiple social and cultural interactivity, and high rate of penetration of new and social media now help to form new image and reconstruct the social reality and social identity on a daily basis for this section of people. Hence, for many, there is neither a uniform image nor a common identity as there are multiple choices in employment, network, social and cultural practices, and political affiliation. They switch from primordial to secular and vice versa as a matter of convenience. They predominantly represent themselves through multiple identities, which are contradictory in one context and complementary in another. These are predominantly conditioned by individual choice of interest. Access to information, ICTs and increased interconnectivity have made these people smarter, clever, goal-oriented, rational and choice based. Although a section of these flexible identities apparently depicts them as inclusive and dynamic, in essence, they use, rejuvenate and reconfigure their identities as a means to an immediate interest. They are never fixed, unavailable to take fixed ideological, political or collective position, and appear more to be a fuzzy than consolidated in all collective engagements.

The Emerging Fluidity in Identity: In the knowledge society, collective identity as reflection of collective solidarity has emerged to be problematic as social collectivities which are usually understood as well-knit 'community' get loosely organized, are loosely formed without being founded in specific locale, and many a time are independent of geographical boundary, based on temporarily perceived ideals and interests, cross-cutting many a time contradictory interests and goals. This fluid and fuzzy membership makes the social order and the pre-established communities very weak in this society.

Socially, the knowledge society is widely characterized by unpredictable mobility of people as fluids that have no clear point of departure or arrival (Castells 2007) on designated physical location (Melucci 1996, 8), 'new forms of fragmentation dispersal' (Giddens 1991, 4–5) and mobility of population, objects, images, information, and wastes and their virtual travel and movements as social reality (Urry 2000) and emergence of virtual organization (Deane 1980). Within these emerging complexities, social systems increasingly manifest fluid-like characteristics and become increasingly subject to shockwaves of fluidarity rather than solidarity, public experience of self rather than collective identity (Urry 2000; cf. McDonald 2002). The knowledge society in India has emerged to be a part of a world that experiences process of integration with a wider world that is getting fragmented socio-culturally through the construction of multiple identities. The expressions of multiple identities take the forms of primordiality for legitimizing resistance and project on the one hand and ludic passivity, anonymity, silence and fuzziness on the other.

As the society in India has emerged to be part-agrarian, part-industrial, part-knowledge-based, part-local and part-global, it stands today within the momentum of multiple interactivities among multiple and diverse forces, structures and processes, causing the proliferation of multiple identities. The knowledge society is yet to be fully formed in India. It is in a fast transitional phase and finds itself in a whirlpool of multiple socio-cultural realities which have unsettled many of the pre-existing social forces. Herein, the contemporary social realities appear to be more fluid than consolidated as ever.

In India, along with the first expansion with the forces of globalization, ICTs, education and socio-cultural disembeddedness, multiple identities are in the making at the grass roots. Social collectivities are formed based on economic class or professional, ethnic, regional, caste, gender, environment, human rights and related interests and identities with same sets of people getting collectively engaged on diverse issues, interests and identities. By increasing interconnectivity with the wider world, they have emerged to be highly flexible as social collectivities that are regularly mobilized on the principle of fragmentation at one end and unification at the other, and are in the processes of continuous renewal and rejuvenation and are of crystallization of a composite culture of reflexivity, resonance and resilience. These flexible identities are shaped as reaction to sustained marginality at one end and receptivity to new world views at the other that have emerged out of the expansion of education, literacy and enhanced virtual and physical connectivity.

The society in India is posited to unfurl a great transformation from its predominantly agrarian to a knowledge-based society. This transformation has been accompanied by a shift in the organization of production, political ideology of the state, and the relationships between the state, market and people on the one hand and shift in the patterns of work participation, networking and in the process of construction of collective identities on the other. The state by accepting the neoliberal path of economic transition has promoted national and transnational corporations to bring in new patterns of work and work culture, migration and mobility, media and consumerism. By generation of new economic momentum, the state and the corporate world have promoted the knowledgeable to be at the core or near to the core of the economic pursuits of this society; the migrant, unskilled and manual labourers who are predominantly drawn from the rural areas from across the country are relegated at the social and the economic margin. The knowledge society has brought new structure of exclusion and domination in society, and many facets of these exclusion and domination have retained their association with the primordial entities of caste, tribe and gender. Apparently, reinforcing of primordiality and pre-existing forms of inclusion, exclusion and domination has brought despair and crushed the hope associated with new aspirations. However, the emerging knowledge society by bringing in new networks and interconnectedness and occupational choices and by increasing the flow of knowledge and information has made even the most vulnerable mind to be reflexive from within. It has ushered a brave and smart world that enables even the marginalized to rejuvenate old identity, construct a new identity and become part of multiple identities to question the structure of domination. It is in the process of developing knowledge, capability and choice by igniting each human mind to be the source of its key capital. Such ignited mind is now in the process of forming and rejuvenating identities for critical reflection. In contemporary India, critical reflections are in the making at the grass roots to produce a collective identity of resilience and resonance. The process of liberalization is in the making, and critiquing the existence has just begun. Even a marginal manual worker now not only asks: What is to be done? What would be the returns? He or she also suggests how it is to be done. They no more accept their marginal status as a part of destiny, but a product of neglect, denial and capacity deprivation. They look for alternatives being reflexively identified with multiple identities.

Knowledge has always been power. However, the centre of power has been diffused in knowledge of society as it has been placed in human mind in terms of their acquired capacity. This power is produced through diverse discourses and connectivity founded on the emerging culture of free exchange of information. Culture, being conditioned by the structural arrangements of economic inequality, unequal sharing of power and authority, primordial arrangement of hierarchy and emerging patterns of marginality still produces layers of discourses. These discourses produce individualized individuals on one hand, on the other hand self-reflexive communities both in the cyber space and and in the real life that have brought into being a space for choice in terms of capacity. Hence, the emerging knowledge of society is credited to create a space for inculcation of discursive identities across the social layers to explore all choice, liberation and self-expressions through diverse means.

6
Ethnicity, Nationality, Citizenship and Identity
Accelerated Binaries and Complementarity of Differences

Introduction

The interrelationships among the identities of ethnicity, nationality and citizenship have emerged to be eclectic across the societies as the essence of these identities gets negotiated and constructed through specific and wider social, cultural and political and historical considerations. Besides having varied trajectories of evolution, they are made subject to diverse usage, making their interface to be contradictory and overlapping at one end and complementary at another. Furthermore, despite having distinctive orientations and essence, these identities are neither compartmentalized from each other nor do they stand alone by themselves. This makes their relationships to be more complicated and at times unpredictable. Ontologically and existentially, ethnicity is the oldest among all these identities and it is inclined to retain its primordial and cultural inclination. Although as an entity it stands by itself for its specific primordial expression, it undergoes frequent processes of transformation and reconstruction on cultural, political and geographic considerations. Nationality, on the other hand, is founded on construction as an identity, even though at times ethnicity is understood in a national term. Many claim that nationality as construction is as ancient an innovation as human civilization. However, in its modern incarnation, it has started taking shape only in the 17th century after the failure of the universality of the Enlightenment project of Western Europe. It is founded on the imaginary subjective and emotional construction of geo-political, cultural and emotional solidarity of people, even with the desire to die for its sanctity. Citizenship has also evolved through several stages since the 17th century. It is founded on rational and legal orientations. Notwithstanding the diverse historicity and essence, and orientations and inclination, the domains of operation of these identities are interlinked, and they are in a continuous process of getting evolved, transformed and contextualized with the transformation in the economic, technological, socio-cultural and geo-political circumstances of the society. Hence, there have been diverse usages and practices of ethnicity, nationality and citizenship, and diverse interfaces among them, cross-culturally.

In a multicultural and multiethnic state like India, relationships among these identities have acquired a complex shape when one is asserted prevailing over the others, or privileged at the cost of the others for political, economic or cultural considerations. These complexities are again compounded when these identities are made subject to multiple interpretations by the politicians, academia and social activists alike. Hence, an attempt is made to see the interface, overlapping and conflicting positions of these three identities in the contemporary society.

Understanding Ethnic Groups

Ethnicity is as old as human civilization. It is an organizing principle of describing a collectivity based on common religious beliefs, history, language, territory, descent, race, shared culture and other such inherited principles. Although many of them overlap, they depict distinctive identities based on belief in inherited common origin. As Max Weber (1978) elaborates, ethnic groups are formed on the foundation of cherished

> ... belief in their common origins of such a kind that it provides the basis for the creation of a community. This belief may be based on similarities of external custom or practices or both or on memories of colonization or migration ... It is constituted simply by the belief in a common identity. (Runciman 1978, 364)

All human groups are believed to have distinctive origins in one way or the other. While some of these beliefs on origins are historically verified, same are parts of oral history and some belong to the domain of mythology. The foundations of common origin have gotten complicated with the incidences of migration, displacement and conquests in human history.

Thus, there is no universal way of describing ethnic groups. These are eclectic in terms of both the situation and the description of the situation. For example, in Africa, it is not a tribe in their homeland that is referred to as ethnic group but the uprooted migrant tribes in the urban areas. In the case of Europe, the term of nation or nationality is widely used to describe an ethnic group because of the attachment of people to their homeland. In Australia, ethnicity is widely applied to describe the immigrants, foreigners and non-citizens of specific racial origins (Castles and Miller 2009). In India, the term ethnic is often used to denote traditional tribal groups. However, of late, it has been a subject of diverse usage to describe social group in terms of their affiliation to specific linguistic, religious minority, regional geographical, etc., groups. Thus, across the world, many principles are added for identifying and constructing ethnicity that provide this social category an amount of their continuity and exclusivity in the society, and provide the context to juxtapose it with the category of nation.

Multiple Principle of Identifying Ethnicity

Ethnicity not only exists, it is also constructed. While to the primordialists these principles are fixed, and their attachment is immutable and irresistible, to the constructionist they are matters of construction, are contextually negotiable, flexible and variable, are matter of strategy and are constructed to suffice specific interest(s). Hence, there are contradictions between a subjective attachment on the one hand and the rational interest to be pursued through essentialization and construction of an ethnic identity on the other. As ethnicity is founded on multiple organizing principles of a common origin, it often involves the intersection of same sets of people criss-crossing each other's boundaries of common origin. For example, Bengalis and Tamilians possess distinctive identities constructed through linguistic principles. These identities get reconstructed when the linguistic boundaries get reconstructed between these groups in terms of their affiliations to various religious beliefs and practices of Hinduism, Islam, Christianity, etc. On many occasions, they have to make choice. While in one such situation, the choice may be conditioned by subjective value of one's association with one specific ethnic identity, in another situation it may be guided by rational calculation of interests with another ethnic identity. Hence, Barks (1996) has talked about the 'ethnicity in the heart' and 'ethnicity in the mind' to show that interests and ethnic identities are interlinked, and that at times silence of ethnic identity is required to be understood in relation to articulated or hidden interest. Although ethnic attachments do not necessarily determine the people's choices, the significance of ethnicity in matters of choice can't be ignored in toto (Barks 1996; cf. Jenkins 2007, 1478). Again, it appears that neither of them are absolutely exclusive; rather, they tend to be mutually inclusive as the socio-cultural, political and economic realities of construction of ethnicity frequently overlap. Hence, uniform conceptualizing of ethnicity has become a difficult proposition. Oommen (1997) has identified five different ways of conceptualizing ethnicity by the scholars.

First: a relatively small group sharing common cultural traits and tracing its descent to a common ancestor (e.g., Francis 1976).

Second: a self-defined group based on subjective factors surrounding past history or present existing conditions, cultural traits for the creation and maintenance of boundary vis-à-vis the others (e.g., Barth 1969).

Third: an interest group including the racial, religious and linguistic ones competing for benefits from the welfare state or using ethnicity as a resource (e.g., Glazer and Moynihan 1963).

Fourth: an identity-seeking instrument by the people of multi-racial and multicultural societies (e.g., Horousitz 1985).

Fifth: a device to seek psychological unity based on common origin linked to blood (Devos and Ross 1975; cf. Oommen 1997, 36).

However, despite such over lapping trends and an amount of flexibility in its construction and expression, there is always the element of continuity and exclusivity in the existence of ethnic group.

Continuity and Exclusivity

The continuity of an ethnic group is achieved through intergenerational transmission of culture, tradition and institutions (Stone and Piya 2007, 1457). These are usually ensured through distinctive processes of enculturation, socialization, education, adherence to values, norms and customs of its institutions, and practising of specific ways of life that provide the basis for their exclusivity in society. The shared sense of ethnic exclusivity is built on cultural similarities and differences, and they are sustained through the practising of discrete cultural markers such as distinctive language, specific notions of shared decent, co-residence, religion, historical narratives of discrimination, conquest or other shared experiences to express claim over the legitimate right to govern a specific geographical area (Hechter 2000; cf. Olzak 2007, 1465). No ethnic group remains in isolation despite having a degree of exclusivity of its own. Hence, ethnicity involves ethnic relations between people who are seen to be different, as well as among those who are seen to be the same. It is through these 'we' and 'them' that membership criteria and boundaries of community and region are fashioned (Jackeins 2007, 1476). In fact, this identity of 'we' grounds an individual in a circumscribed collective identity. Thus, ethnicity is simultaneously a collective and individual phenomenon. Even the personal ethnic identity is collectively reified and publicly expressed' (Geertz 1973; cf. Jenkins 2007, 1975).

Ethnicity and Nation

The boundaries of ethnicity often overlap with race and nation. Very often, ethnicity interfaces the notion of nation when the term nation is explained following the Greek word 'ethnos' which refers to people living and acting together in a manner that might be applied to people or a nation. However, a nation is more than ethnicity. When a nation is to be understood through an ethnic group, it is to be understood as a politically mobilized, self-conscious ethnic group linked to a specific territory. It is mobilized with the goal of forming a political unit to exercise autonomy or preserving a political unit in which this ethnic group is the predominant or extensive political force (Jenkins 2007, 1475; Stone and Piya 2007, 1457). It, in fact, indicates the potential of an ethnic group to be a nation.

While for Smith (1986), a collective name, a common myth of descent, a shared history, a distinctive shared culture, an association with a specific territory and a sense of solidarity are essential features of ethnicity, to Oommen (1997), ethnicity shares all these features except territory. 'When an ethnic group identifies itself with a territory because of ancestral/ imagined or immigrated association and adopts the same as their homeland and transforms their "outness" into the "ins" they became a nation' (Oommen 1997, 36; 1990, 163–82).

The relationship between ethnicity and nation could be not only overlapping but also sequential. To Oommen (1997), when an ethnic group acquires legitimate moral claim over a territory, it becomes a nation, and when a nation secures political jurisdiction in its homeland, it becomes a state. Thus, nation comes before the state formulation. The processes of transformation of ethnicity into a nation state go through several steps that begin with formal policing of the boundaries of community and region by formal powers of individuals and groups, followed by the acceptance of national identity claims in a formal package that includes citizenship, a passport, political rights and duties, etc., by formal power and authority (Jackeins 2007, 1476). There is also the opposite process of transformation of a nation into ethnicity caused by conquest, colonization, immigration and dislocation of ethnic group from one original country, region or nation, that is, a homeland. To him, ethnification of a nation takes place when it does not have the resources for state formation, that is, a homeland having political authority over it (Oommen 1997, 36).

Situationally, however, in many countries, ethnic homogeneity in terms of a common language, culture, tradition and history is emphasized to form the basis of a nation state. In this context, immigration and ethnic diversity are often seen as a threat to such an idea of the nation because they create a community without common ethnic origins. The position of immigrants, who are designated as ethnic groups, is often marked by a specific legal status of that of the foreigner on a non-citizen. The differences are frequently summed up in the concept of ethnicity or race (Castles and Miller 2009, 14–15). Hence, in specific cultural contexts, the relationships between ethnicity and nation become rather dichotomous.

The relation between ethnicity and nationality has emerged to be very complex and sensitive in the contemporary world. At this stage, it is rather imperative that we develop a comprehensive understanding of the ideal nation and nationality.

Understanding Nation and Nationality

The word 'nation' has been used diversely across time and space and has acquired diverse connotations. It owes its origin in the Latin verb *nasci*, understood as 'to be born', and is which means 'a group of people born in the same place'. While in the European universities of the late middle ages, 'nations' were the students who came from the same region or country, to the French writers of the 18th century, nations are the people of a given country. In prevailing usage in 'English and other languages, however, a "nation" is either synonymous with a state or its inhabitants, or else it denotes a human group bound together by common solidarity' (Rastow 1972). Nation is, however, more than a common solidarity; it is solidarity for emotion, action, love and sacrifice for the country and its inhabitants, and solidarity for being and becoming a collective identity; it is also simultaneously used as an urge for solidarity against the others. Over the centuries, however, philosophers and social scientists are yet to resolve the puzzle: What binds human groups together for such a solidarity? What makes people to make the supreme sacrifice and to kill each other for such an identity? Has there been a national solidarity without having the identified others? Hence, different principles are invoked to delineate the identity of nation.

Nation Founded on Sympathies for Cooperation

J. S. Mill (1861/1958) has invoked the elements of sympathy and cooperation among people to encapsulate the ideals of nation. To him (1861/1958), nation is a portion of mankind who are united among themselves by common sympathies to cooperate with each other more willingly than with other people, and to cherish the desire to be under the same government by themselves (Mill 1861/1958, 16; cf. Rastow 1972). The ideal of a nation is also linked to the formation of a principle and a conscience of high order as elaborated by Renan (1992).

Nation Founded on a Moral Conscience, Soul and Spiritual Principle

To Ernest Renan (1992):

> A nation is a soul, a spiritual principle. One is the past, the other is the present. One is the possession in common of a rich legacy of memories; the other is present consent, the desire to live together, the desire to continue to invest in the heritage that we have jointly received. The nation, like the individual, is the outcome of a long past of efforts, sacrifices, and devotions. A nation is therefore a great solidarity constituted by the feeling of sacrifices made and those that one is still disposed to make ...

These moral conscience and spiritual principles are not constructed mechanically. He puts human being in the centre of all conscience and principle. To him,

> The race, language, interests, religious affinity, geography, military necessities do not suffice to create such a spiritual principle because man

is a slave neither of his race, his language, his religion, the course of his rivers, nor the direction of his mountain ranges. It is a great aggregation of men, in sane mind and warm heart, created a moral conscience that calls itself a nation. (Renan (1992)

Nation as an Imagined Community

One of the most powerful articulations of the ideal of a nation has come from Anderson (1983) when he describes a nation to be 'an imagined community'. To him, a nation is an imagined political community and imagined as both inherently limited and sovereign. It is imagined because the members of even the smallest nation will never know most of their fellow members, yet in the minds of each lives the image of their communion. It is imagined as limited because even the largest nation has limits, boundaries, beyond which lie other nations. No nation imagines itself coterminous with humankind. Ultimately, it is this fraternity that makes it possible, over the past two centuries, for so many millions of people, not so much to kill, as to be willing to die for such limited imagining (Bandedict 1983, 57).

No imagining can be formed and sustained without some identified elements of commonness of and for the group to be designated as a nation. Hence, the ideas of commonness as debated by E. H. Carr (1939) are worth mentioning. To him, a nation founded on the possession of commonness, close contacts and feeling, and as a human group, which is specifically the nation, is in the possession of

1. The idea of a common government, whether as a reality in the present or the past or as an aspiration of the future.
2. Certain characteristics (like language) clearly distinguishing the nation from other nations and non-national groups.
3. A certain degree of common feeling or will associated with the picture of the nation in the minds of the individual members.
4. A certain size and closeness of contact among members.
5. A defined common territory (Carr 1939, 7).

Nationalism, in its present form though, has originated in the Western world in the 17th century and has also moved to other parts of the globe subsequently. While such a movement has been observed by a section of Western experts as being an import and imposition of higher Western culture on the rest of world, leading to the formation of a nation state and attainment of liberation, it has also been seen as an evil on the earth and also as a universal struggle for justice by many Indian thinkers and scholars.

Nationalism as Imposition of Higher Culture

To Gellner (1983), the process of achieving the ideal of nationalism entails

> [G]eneral imposition of a high culture on society where previously low cultures (and) ... the establishment of an anonymous, impersonal society, with manually substitutable atomized individual, held together above all by a shared culture of this kind, in place of a previous complex structure of local groups, sustained by folk cultures reproduced locally and idiosyncratically by the micro-groups themselves. (1983, 57)

Nationalism Passes through Folkloric to National to Mass-based National Movement

While Gellner's formulation implies a nation state and nationalism to be congruent, Eric Hobsbawm (1990) asserts otherwise. He elaborates that nationalism is related to territorial state and ... nationalism comes before the nation-state is formed; nations are 'constructed essentially from above', and 'national consciousness' develops unevenly among social groups and regions of a country, wherein the popular masses—workers, servants and peasants—are the last to be influenced by it. To him, national movements have passed through three phases from cultural folkloric to national idea and then to mass-based national movement. He elaborates:

> In nineteenth-century Europe ... Phase A was purely cultural, literary and folkloric, and had no particular political or even national implications ... In phase B, a body of pioneers and militants of "the national idea" and political campaigning for this idea emerged ... Phase C began when nationalist programmes acquire mass support ... The transition from phase B to phase C is evidently a crucial moment in the chronology of national movements. Sometimes ... it occurs before the creation of a national state; probably very much more often it occurs afterwards, as a consequence of that creation. (Hobsbwam 1990)

However, Hobsbwam was very critical on the issue of formation of nationalism in the Third-World countries. To him, in the Third World, nationalism does not take shape even after the formation of a nation state (Hobsbwam 1990).

Over the years, nationalism has taken a diverse course in terms of both content and its operations. The Western scholars have made distinctions between progressive and reactionary, benign and malign, Western and Eastern, civic and cultural, liberal and illiberal, etc., type of nationalism to emphasize on the supremacy of Western civic form of nationalism over ethnic/cultural form (Spencer and Wollman 1998, 255–57). In general, emphasis has been on the civic elements of nationalism, that is, on 'historic territory, legal-political community, legal-political equality of members, and common civic culture and ideology based on standard Western model of the nation'. However, 'all nationalisms are found to be double-faced, looked both forward and backward, both healthy and morbid. Both progress and regress are inscribed in its genetic code from the start' (Ignatieff 1993; Nairn 1977, 347–48; cf. Smith 1995, 99). Spencer and Wollman (1998) argue that there would always be 'the existence of the outsider, the "Other" in nationalism for creating and recreating the conditions in which supposedly "good" forms of nationalism may turn "bad"'. The use of binary oppositions seems ubiquitous in many areas of social and cultural analysis. If we are to grasp the realities of nationalism, we may need to transcend the sort of dualistic approaches (Spencer and Wollman 1998, 256). However, at many places in the contemporary world, these binaries have appeared to be real and there has emerged the tendency of privileging the cultural nationalism as a political ideology, over the civic form of nationalism.

Foundation of Nationalism in Indian Sub-continent

Hobsbwan's criticality about state of nationalism in the Third World is very explicit. In fact, in the Third-World countries, the concept of nation has become a contested category. It has been widely pointed out by a large section of the Third-World scholars that nationalism has evolved within the framework of the modernization project of the West, expanded with the expansion of capitalism and the decline of the colonial state, and that it is having a Western bias which posits the Western form of nationalism as a universal part of progression and relegates the East to be incapable of imagining the formulation of nationalism on their own terms. However, nationalism has gained ground in the Third World not because of acceptance of Western liberal tradition but because of their fiercely anti-imperial stand (Aikant 2006, 170). In this context, the perspective of Indian thinkers on nationalism is extremely relevant.

Nationalism as Universal Struggle for Justice: As against Anderson's formulation, Gandhi defined nationalism as a part of universal struggles of humanity for justice and equality. He was against armed nationalism and hatred against anybody in the name of nationalism. In his own words: My love, therefore, of nationalism or my idea of nationalism is that my country may become free, that if need be the whole of the country may die, so that the human race may live. There is no room for race hatred there. Let that be our nationalism (Gandhi 1947, 171). He also wrote in *Young India* in 1925:

> It is not nationalism that is evil, is the narrowness, selfishness, exclusiveness which is the bane of modern nations which is evil. Indian nationalism has struck a different path. It wants to organize itself or to find full self-expression for the benefit and service of humanity at large (Gandhi 1925, 18).

In fact, he was a patriot and a humanist. He writes:

> For me patriotism is the same as humanity. I am patriotic because I am human and humane ... And a patriot is so much the less a patriot if he is a lukewarm humanitarian ... (Gandhi 1921, 16)

Nationalism a Menace: Tagore (1950) was disturbed by the increasing fragmentation of the world and the growing lust for economic interest and political power in the name of nationalism. To him:

> A nation, in the sense of the political and economic union of a people, is organized for a mechanical purpose. It is an end in itself. It is for self-preservation. It is merely the other side of power, not of human ideals ... The Nation, with all its paraphernalia of power and prosperity, its flags and pious hymns, its blasphemous prayers in the churches, and the literary mock thunders of its patriotic bragging, cannot hide the fact that the Nation is the greatest evil for the Nation ... (Tagore 1950, 5–18)

He again says:

> The Nation has thriven long upon mutilated humanity. Men, the fairest creations of God, came out of the National manufactory in huge numbers as war-making and money-making puppets; ludicrously vain of their pitiful

perfection of mechanism ... It is the aspect of a whole people as an organized power. Nationalism is a great menace. (Tagore 1950, 26, 66)

Like Gandhi, Tagore was also a patriot, and a humanist. He was worried about the tyranny of power and encaging of liberty by the shallow motive of power. He was for the liberation of humanity as reflected in Gandhi's perspective on nation.

Nationalism as a Project for Normalization of Difference, Domination and Producing Consent: Partha Chatterjee (1994) questioned Anderson's arguments. To him: 'If nationalisms in the rest of the world have to choose their imagined community from certain "modular" forms already made available to them by Europe and the Americas, what do they have left to imagine?' Highlighting the changing trajectory of nationalism, he analyses that though in 'the 1950s and 1960s, it was a feature of anti-colonial struggles in the Third World, by the 1970s it had become a matter of ethnic politics of killing each other making 'nationalism as a dark, elemental, unpredictable force of primordial nature threatening the orderly clam of civilized life'.

To him, while contesting the 'colonial power nationalism was essentially a cultural 'normalization' project based on universalist justificatory resources produced by post-enlightenment social thought' that could not make the distinctions of language, religion, caste, or class a matter of indifference to itself. The national post-colonial modern liberal-democratic state has tried to ignore these differences and also showed indifference to these concrete differences for acquiring its legitimacy to rule. 'Hence the presence of populist or communitarian element in the post-colonial state is necessitated by the elite domain to have 'the real presence of an arena of subaltern politics over which it must dominate ... for the purpose of producing consent'. This domination produced innumerable fragmented resistances of the subaltern group to the normalizing project to show the 'limit of the universality of the modern regime of power, limit to the post Enlightenment discipline of knowledge, and to claim our freedom of imagination' (Chatterjee 1994, 4–13).

Besides such limitations, Chatterjee (1993) also finds crucial contradictions in the character of Indian nationalism that rejects 'the alien dominator nevertheless tries to imitate and surpass them by his own standards', again, while India rejects ancestral ways which are seen as obstacles to progress and yet also cherishes them as marks of identity

(Chatterjee 1986, 2). Indian nationalism however endeavours to overcome these contradictions

... by resorting to a process of imitating the West, accepting the latter's superiority with regard to material progress, while affirming itself as being spiritually superior, even in a position to export its spirituality to the west, and thus drawing a claim for autonomy on this basis. (cf. Raghuramaraju 1993, 1435)

Nationalism as Product of Inherited Indigenous Commonness of Indians

In India, of late, there has been strong claim, especially by the Right wing political thinkers, to redefine the background of Indian nationalism in terms of inherited common features. Savarkar (1923) locates the roots of Indian nationalism on the claim of inherited common race, land, history, language, culture and common 'others'. Savarkar elaborates that Sindusthan/Hindusthan is founded on 'one nation and one race—of a common fatherland and therefore of a common blood'. Hindus are the descendants of the 'Aryans who made their home on the banks of the Sindhu ... developed a sense of nationality ... and actually brought the whole land from the Himalayas to the Seas under one sovereign sway' and that Hindusthan is a land of Hindus who had to face the attack of Arabs, Persians, Pathans, Baluchis, Tartars, Turks and Mogul invaders for centuries. It was through this prolonged furious conflict that the people of India became intensely conscious of themselves as Hindus and were welded into a nation. To him, the Hindus are one because they own a common *sanskriti* (civilization) of Hindu culture, and Sanskrit has been the chosen means of expression and preservation of that culture and the history of this race. To him, Mohammedan or Christian are the common others for they are not and cannot be recognized as Hindus (Savarkar 1923, 4–12, 43, 92, 115). Savarkar, however, asserted that Muslims were the real enemies of the nation, and not the British. To him, the development of Western science, technology, industry and knowledge systems in India is to be used for achieving material prosperity and for making bombs and weapons, in order to 'militarize Hindudom', and there is a need to 'Hinduize all politics' and 'militarize Hinduism' (Savarkar 1964, 46; Keer 1966, 142; cf. Raghuramaraju 1993, 1936–37).

Critiquing the Ideal of Commonness

The Right wing formulation of Indian nationalism have emphasized on the homogeneity over heterogeneity and pluralism. They have again emphasized on cultural nationalism over secularnationalism. India, however, is built on a plural cultural, religious and linguistic foundation, and Indian nationalism has always stood for a plural cultural framework for inter-connectedness among people as nationalized subjects, and for justice, fraternity and equality for each other. 'Nation is understood in India in terms of civilizational unity, belief and cultural heritage of the people that is grown out of the freedom of acceptance and rejection. Thus, even within the ritualistic and religious orthodoxy, the heterodox systems have coexisted in India. It is a mistaken belief that unity of a nation is incumbent upon homogeneity' (Aikant 2006, 175). In fact, there has been an uneasy tension between cultural nationalism (or communalism as it is known in India) and Nehru's vision of secular nationalism as interpreted by the Congress party. Chatterjee (1992) points out that many of the themes that run through the contemporary rhetoric of Hindu extremist politics were integral parts of the historical imagining in the 19th century of India as a nation. The fragile consensus of 'nationness' in India which emphasizes on the singularity of nation formation to legitimize the centrality of a nation state 'will always have available for its sectarian use the common resources of a single national history of the Hindus' (Chatterjee 1992, 112). Many critics of the Hindutva-driven nationalism point out that the self-avowedly 'Hindu nationalist force' is now not only defining the Hindu foundation and character of the Indian nation and trying to emerge as 'foremost defender of the Hindu community, but also redefining the minority religious rights not as a mark of democracy but as unwarranted privilege for the minority group. The idea that India has a comparative culture, made up of numerous religious strands, as well as non-religious cultural currents and is all greater for it, is simply anathema to the forces of Hindutva' (Brass and Vanaik 2002, 2). To many, such view simply reinforces the majoritarian politics through homogenization of cultural, economic and political practices by ignoring the distinctiveness of history, religious beliefs and practices, food habits, languages, and norms and values of small groups, including those of the tribes in India. In this context, it is relevant to see position of tribes within the homogenizing nationalism in India as an example.

Tribe and Nationality in India

The plural foundation of Indian nationalism is not founded on a majoritarian totality, but on the mutual interaction among various communities that horizontally links them by respecting each other's distinctive identity and cultural autonomy. However, at times, this interaction is interpreted as a process of integration of small cultural groups and identities, not with the society but with the dominant majoritarian community.

The tribes in India have remained an integral part of the plural foundation of Indian society through their distinctive cultural and religious practices, use of language, dress, foods, rituals and customs. However, there has been a view that in the process of interaction with the majoritarian groups, the tribes in India are undergoing a process of acculturation; that they are getting integrated to Hinduism and that this integration can be measured by degrees of their integration with the majoritarian Hindu society. Accordingly, they have been described by G. S. Ghurye (1963) as 'property integrated', 'loosely integrated' and 'not more than touched by Hinduism' to remain as imperfectly integrated as the 'backward Hindus'. Here, Hinduism has been the reference point, and non-integration has been accepted as a sign of backwardness. Such views, according to Xaxa (2005), by depriving the tribes of their autonomous space of mobility and transformation, privilege homogenizing Hindu nationalism. Hence, through the identification of the tribe as Hindu, the tribes are not only denied of their autonomy but are also in the hierarchical structure of the caste system, paving the way for loosing of their distinctive identity. Hence, Xaxa (2005) argues that the advocates of Hindutva, by conceiving the tribe in terms of religion only, often overlook the distinctiveness of the tribal language, social organization and way of life. Although the tribal and the Hindu own natural religion, the tribes cannot be denied of their distinct identity and autonomy. Hinduism is based on caste, and a tribe can be Hindu at the risk of losing the tribal status (Xaxa 2005, 1364). India has experienced phenomenal proliferation of ethnic discontents in the country in the form of separate statehood based on language, religion, tribal or indigeneity, regional autonomy, etc., movements. Notwithstanding these criticisms and the persistent discontents, there is no denying the fact that there has been a process of adaptation to Hindu ways of life or to Hindu cults by sections of the tribes in India, for example, the Bodo-Rajbanshi tribes of Assam, Rajbanshi of North Bengal, Manipuri of Manipur, Bhils of Rajasthan, etc. These have impacted the interface between ethnicity and nation.

Secular Nationalism, Persistent Inequality, Primordiality and Contradictions

The process of formation of national identity in India encounters forces of Westernization, colonization and secularization on the one hand and the prevailing religious and cultural practices on the other. In the predominantly traditional/primordial social and cultural foundation, secularism expanded in India as result of the Western impact and not of colonial impact. The ideal of secular India was promoted by the Western-educated elite who derived inspiration from Western thought and got stimulus from religious reform movements and the anti-colonial struggle. The ideal of a unified national identity out of multireligious and cultural diversities demanded a clarified relation between religion and nation state. The fundamental question was whether or not there would be demarcations between state and religion, and whether Indian nationalism will be founded on majoritarian Hindu state or whether it would be founded on religious pluralism. It is very clear to Mahatma Gandhi, the Father of the Nation, that despite being a Hindu majoritarian state, India can't and should not be a majoritarian theoretic Hindu state. It, However, is not to be devoid of the universal accommodative philosophy of Hinduism. Despite the pressure that emerged out of the creation of a theocratic Pakistan and the resurgence of religious fundamentalism in the Indian subcontinent, he was in favour of the separation of state from religion. He wrote:

> Free India will be no Hindu raj, it will be Indian raj based not on the majority of any religious sect or community, but on the representatives of the whole people without distinction of religion ... They would be elected for their record of service and merits. Religion is a personal matter, which should have no place in politics. (Gandhi 1947, 277–78)

He further writes:

> I do not expect India of my dreams to develop one religion that is to be wholly Hindu, or wholly Christian or wholly Mussalman, but I want it to be wholly tolerant, with its religions working side by side with one another (p. 257) ... The state has nothing to do it (religion). The state should look after the secular welfare, but not your or my religion. That is every body's personal affairs. (p. 278)

Gandhi advocated not for religious division but for co-existence of multireligious and cultural entities in free India. His emphasis was for an India that would be free from divisions between 'masses and classes'.

Religious indoctrination in a newly formed independent state which is conditioned by sustained poverty, social divisions, illiteracy and practice of regressive tradition will not only bring social segregation, intolerance and hatred in society but will also bring destruction to the inherited plural and accommodative foundation of this society. Hence, the alternative was secularism.

For Jawaharlal Nehru, in a country like

> India, which has many faiths and religions, no real nationalism can be built except on the basis of secularity ... We have not only to live up to the ideals proclaimed in our Constitution, but make them a part of our thinking and living and thus build up a really integrated nation. That does not mean absence of religion, but putting religion on a different plane from that of normal political and social life.

He has also forcefully asserted that any other approach rather than secularism in India would mean the breaking up of India (Nehru 1983, 330–31). He was for religious co-existence in terms of several cultural ingredients of secularism lying deep-rooted in certain aspects of the Indian historical tradition.

Although historically India has been a country of many religious faiths, none of them existed in isolation from each other. Rather, there have been efforts to bring in synthesis through various reform movements spearheaded by various saints and spiritual leaders. Hence, Nehru has always emphasized on the strong spiritual and moral legacy of the saints and sages of India that has always provided 'a moral foundation and certain moral concepts which hold together our ideals and our life in general' (Nehru 1965, 530–36). A secular state, says Nehru, 'does not obviously mean a state where religion is discouraged. It means freedom of religion and conscience including freedom for those who have no religion, subject only to their not interfering with each other or with the basic conceptions of our state'. Although Nehru was concerned with the practice of secularism, he was also deeply concerned with the problem of inequality in society. He was looking for its eradication through the idea and practices of secularism. He writes: 'The word secular, however, conveys something much more to me, although that might not be its dictionary meaning. It conveys the idea of social and political equality' (Nehru 1965, 327). Here Ramila Thapper points out that the Indian definition of secularism talks of coexistence of all religions. In contemporary India the coexistence of religion exists, but their equality is yet to be established. Hence secularism is less evident. To her, state and state patronage do not invariably distance themselves from religious organization, in fact some time they are closely tied together (2016, 30).

Although the spirit of secularism expanded in India under the influence for the West, the contexts of its emergence between the West and India were clearly different. In the West under the impetus of Religious Reformation, Industrialization and the Democratic Revolution, the state was separated from religion as there was a direct clash between the state and religion. However, Indian secularism has grown not with direct clash with religion as in the West but rather 'as an integrative concept, transcending religions on the one hand and tapping the unifying forces promoted by the secularization process within the religions of India themselves on the other. Indeed, Indian secularism acts as a bridge between religions in a multireligious country via the secular concept of equality (Joshi 2007).

As secularism is flourishing in India in a different context from that of the West, there is a need to understand the facets of Indian secularism without segregating religiosity, tradition and primordiality from secular practices. Rather, these are to be understood in terms of their complementarity as practised in Indian society since ages as the tradition of religious pluralism and tolerance provides the space of such complementarity. Hence, the strand of thought that does not recognize the relevance of multiple traditions and their historical existence in India stands at odds against the practice of such complementarity. In the context of prevalence of the historical tradition of religious pluralism and tolerance, Madan (1997) points out that secularization that propagates separation of sacred from its stands at odds with its religious tradition in India. The Western ideology and practice of secularism stand apposite to the beliefs and practices of communities and social groups in India. To him, different religious movements of saint tradition have always propagated for tolerance and peaceful coexistence against the tendency of fundamentalism. He (2006) further propagates for the participatory pluralism that recognizes incompleteness of social group in the absence of others.

In India, while for many, everyday existence is essentialized in terms of economic and social inequalities, and political deprivations, the realities of ethnic diversities, the philosophical foundation of coexistence and religious tolerance has remained available for misinterpretation and misrepresentation by the sectarian forces. Neither the dream of the Father of the Nation for the eradication of difference between the 'masses and classes' nor Nehru's idea of 'social and political equality' is realized in its full sense. Rather, eradication of poverty, unemployment and livelihood insecurity is yet to be realized for millions; proper education and training, and spirit of science and rationality are yet to reach the doorsteps of each household, feudal domination and practice of caste linguistic, regional, racial and gender oppressions and discrimination have remained the realities of life for large segments of population. These are also accompanied by huge divides in society wherein a limited few get enormous command over resources, power, income, information and social status, and the vast majority have emerged to be marginalized and devaluated notwithstanding the ideals of equal citizenship rights in society. The process of nation building in many ways depicts a fractured image of India. Hence, while the historical tradition presents pluralism and existence of primordial identities, in the contemporary society, social and economic deprivations and inequalities acquire interface with primordial collective identities. Importantly, primordial identities have acquired a political meaning in political mobilization both for people and the politicians. Hence, there is a need to understand the content of citizenship in India, its evolution and interface with primordiality.

Significantly, India is also experiencing a contradiction between civil and cultural nationalisms in the genealogy of modern post-colonial state formation. At times, they are so entangled that it is impossible to neatly demarcate each other. Many of these contradictions are assumed to be resolved within the ideal of common citizenship in the country that recognizes secular individual rights at one end and their primordial group rights on the other. Citizenship as practice, ideals and identity is still evolving in India, having its interface with nationality and ethnicity questions, even though it has been institutionalized within the constitutional framework of the state.

Citizenship

Citizenship as the embodiment of special legal rights and entitlements, duties and obligations of the people in relation to the state and people themselves is shaped through the engagement of people with state for centuries. It is indeed a Western innovation and still under the process of refinements based on situational experimentation. In the present juncture of its shaping-up, it has integrated several key elements to it which have evolved over the centuries.

Elements of Citizenship

Based on West European experience, T. H. Marshall (2009) highlights that citizenship that currently embodies civil, political and social rights has evolved over the last three centuries sequentially.

1. The civil rights which deal with the individual freedom, that is, liberty of person; freedom of speech, thought and faith; the right to property, right to conclude valid contracts, and the right to justice, etc., took birth in the 18th century.
2. The political rights which delineate the right to participate in the exercise of political power, adult franchise, etc., came into full expression in the 19th century.
3. The social rights that assert for the right to economic welfare and social security, right to share the full social heritage and right to live the life of a civilized being according to the standard prevailing in the society got momentum in the 20th century (Marshall 2009, 149).

Citizenship Rights and Obligations

Citizenship rights are founded on three important paradigms: *individualistic* founded on individual liberties and welfare entitlements; *political* founded on civic duties and obligations which are practised in the public spheres; and *collective* identity paradigm founded on the assumption of a predominantly cultural set of common values and traditions converging in a common sense of belonging (Giesen and Eder 2001; cf. Gosewinkel 2010, 140). Citizenship in a modern state not only confers sets of legal entitlement to the members of the state but also demands good civil behaviour, political and collective obligation for active engagement in the polity and more passive commitment for commonly shared values and convictions of citizens and of civil society (Gosewinkel 2010, 141). To Marshall, citizenship rights are earned through innumerous struggles in history. Now, 'it is a loyalty of free men endowed with rights and protected by a common law. Its growth is stimulated both by the struggle to win those rights and by their enjoyment when won' (Marshall 1997, 15).

Ideally, citizenship has a territorial aspect as full membership of a citizen can be realized within a defined territory of a nation state that regulates the right to residence as a pre-condition for naturalization and citizenship. Citizenship rights of a citizen are usually derived from birth or stay in the territory of a nation state (Gosewinkel 2010, 143). They evolve with the evolution of the nation state. In most of the developing countries, citizenship rights are evolving out of their traditional past. Hence, they encounter the contradiction between the individual citizenship rights and primordial collective rights.

Citizenship vs Primordial Collective Identities in India

Although citizenship in India owes its origin to the British rule in India, Indian's social conditions along with its ideas, beliefs, values and customs have shaped the identity of citizenship in this country. Marshall (2009) has shown that Europe was a capitalist and class-based society when citizenship was introduced. However, India was a caste-based and predominantly feudal society when the idea of citizenship was introduced in this country. Citizenship as an ideal of democracy is based on equality, while caste is based on hierarchy. Hence, Beteille (1999) points out that though the British were the first to introduce the idea of citizenship in India, the idea of equal citizenship between themselves and their native subject was missing. During the colonial period, Indians were subjects and not citizens, and it was only after the Independence that the rights of equal membership with equality of status and opportunity were unequivocally introduced in India through the Constitution (Beteille 1999, 2588). The relationship between caste-based social arrangement and citizenship has remained antithetical in India. Being predominantly a traditional society, the identity of an individual is largely articulated here through his or her location in the traditional collectivities of caste, region, religion, tribe and other ethnic groups in India. Despite the introduction of modern institutional arrangements such as parliamentary democracy, modern bureaucracy, citizenship, etc., India has not been able to break itself from its traditional past in identifying the social collectivities and isolating individual rights from collective rights on secular credentials. It is not to say that modern and secular professional collectivities such as those of citizen, class, professional groups, etc., are missing from Indian society. Rather, their presences are overshadowed and underprivileged by primordial collectivities on many an occasion. However, Beteille points out that within the parliamentary democratic framework, rights of citizenship in India are rights of individuals and not of collective identities without consideration of race, caste, creed or gender. As mentioned in the Constitution, he also makes it explicit that the individual rights are the same for all Indian citizens (Beteille 2008, 40).

The Constitution of India has provided the space of individual rights through Articles 19 to 22 of the Constitution. Article 19 ensures the individual right to freedom (freedom of speech and expression; to assemble peaceably and without arms; to form associations or unions; to move freely throughout the territory of India; to practise any profession, or to carry on any occupation, trade or business). Article 20 provides protection to an individual in respect of conviction for offences. Article 21 provides protection to an individual of life and personal liberty. Article 22 provides protection to an individual against arrest and detention in certain cases.

The Constitution of India also provides the space for collective rights through Articles 15 and 26. Article 15(4) permits the State to make special provisions for the advancement of any socially and educationally backward classes of citizen or for the Scheduled Castes and the Scheduled Tribes. Article 26 gives 'every religious group a right to establish and maintain institutions for religious and charitable purposes, manage its affairs, properties as per the law.'[1]

However, operationally, there have been encroachments of collective identities in the domain of individual identities. There has been a contradiction between the secular individual identity and the primordial collective identities. In this context, it is important to mention that the Constitution of India has made special provisions for historically neglected caste and tribal groups for their social mobility and for their betterment in the society. Over the decades, India has seen the proliferation of assertions and rearticulating of collective identities to claim collective rights in the form of caste and communities. These assertions have brought new dynamics in Indian society. Many of these claims and assertions are accommodated within the domain of collective rights through the policy of protective discrimination. To Beteille,

> [O]ur constitution assigns pre-eminence to the individual as citizen, but our politicians, legislators and even judges seek to advance the claims of castes and communities in the name of social justice ... While assigning primacy to the claims of the individual as citizen, the constitution did make some special and transitory provisions for certain severely disadvantaged sections of society. Those provisions have been greatly extended, especially

---

[1] See http://www.gktoday.in/articles.

in the last 20 years, and they now threaten to 'eat up' what is due to each individual as citizen ... Collective identities based on caste and community have been given a new lease of life ... (Beteille 1999, 2589)

It is widely noticed by scholars that the group rights that are recognized by the Constitution of India have been exploited by the political parties with sectarian purpose and electoral calculation. Such usage of group rights has further conservative sense of religious affiliation and polarization (Khilnari 1997). Although the Constitution of India propagates for impartiality while the State engages with citizens in promoting and protecting their group rights, such engagements are widely seen as majoritarian intervention or minority appeasement. In contemporary India, political parties publicly express their religious affiliation and promise benefits of the State in favour of their respective communities (Singh 2016, 5–6). The contradiction between individual and collective rights (read as individual and collective identities) has brought significant contradiction in the secular facets of Indian nationalism.

These have caused frequent encroachment on the secular and primordial identities which are reflected in the intersectionality between the identities of ethnicity, nationality and citizenship in India.

Experiences of Intersectionality, Difference and Complementarity in India

In India, citizenship rights, nationalist imaginations and ethnic solidarities are still evolving and getting continuously reconfigured and transformed within the transitional processes of tradition and modernity, globalization and localization, and primordialization and secularization in the society. Despite its transition to the new economic, technological and political era, traditional social divisions that have their roots in the religious, sectarian, caste, linguistic, cultural and regional, etc., primordial foundations have remained a reality. These primordial ethnic identities are reconfigured, reproduced and rejuvenated in everyday life to suffice varieties of social, economic and political purpose. They act as instrument and force situationally. Furthermore, in the democratic state, while citizenship is used as an instrument of equality for individuals, ethnicity and nationality are often invoked by states to confer or deny collective equality (Oommen 1997, 38). Within these processes, these identities experience continuous process of consolidation at one end and fragmentation on the other. Let us examine some of their dynamics below.

Overlapping Boundaries and Social Inequalities and Privileging of Ethnicity and Primordiality: The plural social foundation of India that is traditionally erected on primordiality and ethnicity is also arranged unequally, which promotes social segregation. In a multifaceted system of inequality that is conditioned by traditional social hierarchy, inequality and deprivation, cultural segregation, and primordial subordination, where development initiatives have failed to secure life and livelihood of millions and where primordial affiliation operates at the highest level both implicitly and explicitly, the identities of nationality and citizenship tend to get prevailed over by ethnicity in the routine of lives. As these inequalities have remained cumulatively associated with the ethnic foundation of society, many tend to find ethnic justification for their persisting plights in society.

Development Deprivation and Ethnicization of National Identity: Although ethnicity is predominantly a primordial cultural identity, many of the ethnic claims for autonomy and special provision for protective discrimination are rooted in the development deprivation, cultural neglect and political apathy against their effective integration in the political mainstream of the society. Altogether, these produce discontents and sustained political mobilization to transform their primordial cultural entities into a political identity. Many of them have emerged as sub-national identities within the democratic and federal mosaic of the State. These have impacted the interface between ethnicity and nation. Here Oommen (2002) has witnessed two contradictory trends. To him, independent India has witnessed the 'state-centred nationalism' that conflates state and the nation and recognizes the sovereign state as the crucial nation maker and the 'state-renouncing nationalism' characterized by demands for cultural and fiscal autonomy within the federal polity, movements for separate province and identity-seeking ethnic movements. He also observed that while the 'nationals' are asserting their cultural identity and demanding better economic entitlements within their homeland vis-à-vis the ethnicities, the tension between all India single citizenship and multiple national identities is getting exacerbated (Oommen 2002, 272).

Exercise of Citizenship Rights in Ethnic Term: In India, identification of social collectivities on primordial credence gets patronage among the politicians of most ideological pursuits. The political parties seldom avoid an opportunity to cultivate their support base in

Ethnicity, Nationality, Citizenship and Identity 183

primordial ethnic terms. Most of the established political parties, who even vow in the name of secularism, very often than not give due credence to ethnic background while nominating candidates for election in terms of ethnic/caste/regional, etc., primordial composition of the concerned seat. They also appeal for vote from the citizens tacitly on these considerations. Although a generalization is difficult, it is widely observed across the country that citizenship rights for adult franchise, etc., are also exercised both implicitly and explicitly in primordial terms. The pre- and post-election media analysis of voting patterns of election invariably reveals such truth. From the citizen's side as well, the act of exercising adult franchise in terms of non-primordial credentials has become an ideal only of a thin minority.

Increasing Significance of Primordially within Formal Organizations: As the process of secular and formal institution building has been very weak, and achieved merit and established rules and procedures always do not get due respect, covert lobbing based on ascribed credentials for benefits and positions of all sorts mostly gets privilege over the former. Hence, a political affiliation on proximity through primordial consideration comes into play in a big way at most levels. When often 'whom you know politically' and 'what you are primordially' and not 'what you are' in achieved or formal substance is important for getting accepted or rejected, the secular credential of citizenship and the philosophy of equality as attached to it frequently become a casualty for a common man who are otherwisely not connected to the given power structure.

Even sections of the enlighten middle class, who are supposed to be the bearers of secular citizenship, resort to caste, regional or religious identities for lobbies for this upward mobility. They, even in the state-run government organizations, first start lobbying based on primordial credentials, and organize and mobilize their support base within these secular organizations tacitly on primordial consideration. They then try to control the organization to secure their own benefits and distribute benefits and favours out of turn among their followers, again on primordial considerations. In the process, they weaken the organization, its institutional sanctity and the ideals of equal citizenship rights.

Ethnicity as Response against Domination: At the grass-roots level, many primordial identities also work as a counter hegemonic force to redress social imbalances. While the hegemonic forces try to retain their control over the institutional arrangements of the society and their functioning takes recourse to primordial identities either tacitly or explicitly, the dominated group also use their primordial resources to develop resistance against such domination by rejuvenating their primordial identities. Formation of associations based on primordial credentials of caste, language, religion, region, etc., across the country is a testimony to such resistance against domination. Gradually, they demand for share of power through the assertions of their primordial identities.

Increasing Fluidity and Connectivity through Ethnicity: In real life, a large segment of the society have emerged to be socially fragmented, culturally uprooted and politically fragile, and their social identities has become more fluid than consolidated in the wake of neoliberal globalization, high rate of mobility and migration, extensive usage of ICTs and virtual communication, and growing individualism. Many feel a lack of depth and solitude with the socially constructed or formally provided identities. Hence, an overwhelming section of people fall back on primordial ethnic identity to remain grounded in the society culturally, while a section tends to use it as a tool for the fulfilment of immediate political aspirations and economic interest. They also tend to perceive the ideal of citizenship and of nationalism through a primordial route. The political entrepreneurs in the country also find an opportunity in the consolidation of primordial identities, and in many ways promote the same for an immediate electoral gain.

Practice of Ethnic and Cultural Pluralism in Articulation of Nationality: Nationality is in fact multifaceted, as it embodies a variety of civic and cultural dimensions in it. Nationality has a civic dimension in India. In everyday cultural discourse of nationality, the well-articulated framework of 'unity in diversity' of people is invoked on a daily basis to place emphasis on the culture of accommodation and tolerance, give and take, fraternity and justice, and pluralism and integration. Here, solidarity is formed by respecting ethnic and cultural diversity as a facet of richness of Indian traditional ethos, and diversity is celebrated by grounding the nation on the empirical realities of coexistence of multiple faiths, cultural practices and ethnicities and by linking bit by bit each citizen of the diverse groups into the plural socio-cultural fabric of this nation.

However, the neo-cultural dimension of nationality tries to underprivilege diversity by imposing the ideals of commonness in culture, religion, language, territory and civilizational unity. It tends to derecognize and demolish the diverse specificity with a hegemonic monolith construction. It tends to use the culture, economy, geography and history to construct solidarity against the 'others'. It constructs the 'we' by overshadowing the diversities and differences that exist in society, and it also directs this 'we' against the defined 'others' by becoming an ideology. It creates binaries as we versus the others as well as differences in terms of cultural and civic, etc., orientation. While a cultural nationalism as a community sustains itself against the 'other' by constructing 'we' as ethnically, linguistically and/or religiously distinct from others, 'good' or civil nationalism creates loyalties based on an allegiance to citizenship rights, fundamental freedoms and equality (Greenfield 1993, 4; Ignatieff 1993; cf. Banerjee 2002, 54). India transits between the two as one tries to make it a political choice, the other a way of everyday life.

Limited Spread of Civic Nationalism: In India, in one form or the other, everybody is made aware of their cultural primordial positioning not only in the neighbourhood interaction but also in the formal official documentation. It makes ethnicity to be an identity that stands and exists for all. Furthermore, though a large chunk of Indian population uses a part of political right by exercising adult franchise as citizen, a vast majority of them are seldom able to exercise their social and civic rights that form the core of civic nationalism. Here, citizenship rights and their full potentials are fully exercised and enjoyed predominantly by the enlightened middle class, and civic nationalism has remained an ideal for limited segments. Several cultural, economic and political hurdles still stand firm against the spreading and sustaining of the spirit of civic nationalism among all sections, especially among the poor, slum dwellers, peasant, tribes and such other groups explicitly, even though they are active agents of the civic dynamics of nationalism. In routine discourse, while cultural nationalism is the property of all, civic nationalism is for limited section of people. However, India is fundamentally a multicultural nation. Here, one group feels its incompleteness in the absence of the others (Madan 1997), and in everyday life, only a limited section is touched by the spirit of commonness against the 'others'—the real or the imagined. Although the normalization project of Indian nationalism has not been able to eradicate the economic, social, demographic, cultural, etc., differences among the social groups, it has rejuvenated the old and produced new varieties reflexive collectivity in society who interpret culture in inclusive and accommodative terms.

Imitation of Western Cultural Nationalism in Indian Context: The Western concept of cultural nationalism appears to be inadequate to explain nationalism in India in terms of binaries. Here, an amount of mix between cultural and civil nationalism has remained to be a reality. It is very often difficult to distinguish between the two as primordiality and ethnicity have remained deeply intertwined with varieties of civic practices. It has been observed that the micro- or local-level, cultural/ethnic differences often get overshadowed by the sweeping resurgence of national identity during exigencies and mega events of the country. These were well depicted during the Independence struggle against the British; the Indo-Pak wars of 1947–48, 1965, 1971 and 1999; the Indo-China War in 1962; and so on. Even in the event of disaster and natural calamities, and action against external aggressions, India expresses collective sentiments. During sports events such as cricket, football and hockey matches and Commonwealth, Olympic, Asiad, SAARC, etc., games, such unity is constructed. Such sweeping resurgence of national identity is in fact episodic and short-lived, founded on binaries against others and having upward and downward swinging of consolidation and collective expression depending upon the exigencies and the nature of collective events. Everyday discourse of nationalism, however, is founded on love for *desh* (native land) that dissolves the binaries and accommodates all varieties of diversities together without having an identified 'other' from within. The broad framework of traditional love for *desh* idealizes the imagination of inclusiveness, cutting across the boundaries of caste, class, religion, language, ethnicity, etc., of a place in which people have nurtured themselves. Beyond the *desh,* there is *pardesh;* but these are not founded on binaries. The *pardeshis* are welcome as *atithi* (guests) as *atithi devo bhava* (guests are gods). This is not political choice, but an everyday cultural practice. The spirits of nationalism, civic or cultural, that have penetrated in India as parts of Western ideology, have remained multifaceted and are yet to be fixed in either of these forms as it is made to frequently move like a pendulum from cultural character at one end to civic at the other. This movement continues as the secular credential of the citizenship has remained fluid and ethnicity gets privilege over the rest, though tacitly but firmly. Within this swinging, what has remained fixed is the love for *desh* as unaltered, that can neither be demolished nor constructed through the construction of exigencies or binaries, but can only be reinforced through the practice of constitutional citizenship.

Conclusion: Coexistence with Diverse Complementarities

Contemporary India posits herself within unprecedented and ever expanding flow of interconnectivity produced by ICTs and social media, mobility and migration and exchange of ideas and thoughts among the people across the society. These have expanded the scope and conditions of individuation and reflexivity and social and political choices despite an increasing quantum socio-cultural decontextualisation among the people. Hence the identities of ethnicity, nationality and citizenship are to negotiate with new and diverse forces, and gradually move from the arena of a 'given' to negotiated identities with host of contradictions and complementarities.

Resurgence of Cultural Nationalism and Nativity: Politics and Culture of Global Society

Globalizing India now experiences the proliferation of cultural nationalism. Right wing Hinduism has been the expression of such nationalism. This, however, has got a political overtone in certain thoughts and action that aims to alter the pre-existing facets of nationalism in India.

Many political commentators like Bajpai (2017) cite the incidences of religion charged election campaign (in UP most recently); 'love jihad' allegation against Muslim men; 'ghar wapsi' conversions; beef bans; killings of Muslims accused of eating, storing or transporting beef, murdering of rationalists and intellectuals; attack on art, literature and films; clashes on college and university campuses; arrests of students on sedition charges; assaults on students from the North East; etc.; highlight the gradual Right wing takeover of Indian polity. To Bajpai, such takeover would be through election and constitutional changes, sustained campaign of micro level, and vigilant-led cultural assaults against minorities and the liberals. The resurgence of Hindu nationalism, however, is seen not as a sudden and localized phenomenon but rather many having its root in the vote bank politics and its practice by various political parties. Verma (2017) points out that some political parties 'that reflexively genuflect before the altar of secularism have blatantly used Muslims as a vote bank in order to win elections, but done very little to address the real needs of the community'. They have also indulged into majority appeasement politics through various means. The Bharatiya Janata Party on the other hand has tirelessly worked to consolidate a Hindu vote in opposition ... In the ensuing turbulence, sane voices—both among Hindus and Muslims—were sidelined, while extremists grabbed the headlines.

The resurgence of Hindu nationalism in India is not an isolated phenomenon. Srinivas (1992) points out that Hinduism has encountered several forces throughout its history. In the middle age it has encountered the Muslim. Since the 19th century, it has encountered the British and the Christian missionary attacks which were usually severe on the entire gamut of its institutions, practices, values ideas and beliefs. To him Hinduism has changed over the centuries. 'In the last few decades Hinduism has had to cope with certain momentous changes such as the division of Indian sub-continent into India and Pakistan ... The establishment of Pakistan was preceded and followed by the brutal killing of millions of innocent Sikh, Hindu and Muslim men, women and children, and the rape and abduction of innumerable women. That period also saw the establishment of a Jewish state in Israel, and Buddhist states in Sri Lanka and Burma. It also witnessed the rise of Islamic fundamentalism in a vast region extending from the Atlantic coast to the Pacific. How can Hinduism remain immune to all these forces and events?' As Hinduism is responding to several forces it has acquired a political connotation too along with its cultural meanings and practices. Now cultural organizations like the RSS and VHP and the political parties like the BJP (evolved from the earlier Jan Singh and Hindu Mahasabha) have as their aim to protect the interest of Hindus, Hinduism, and India (1992,10–11). There has also been responses of Hinduism from the grass roots towards such forces being the manifestations of a way of life on one hand and ethnic identity on the other. Such identity is also one the one hand linked to varieties of social, economic and political interests.

In the post-neoliberal globalized world, there have been upsurges of nationalist tensions, coupled with flare-ups in xenophobia and nativism. Although the process started long back and all around, the Brexit in UK and the election of Trump in the USA speak the real rise in the neonationalism. Prakash (2017) narrates that in many parts of the contemporary

Ethnicity, Nationality, Citizenship and Identity **189**

world, for example, in South America, North Africa, the Middle East, the Balkans, South and South East Asia, democratic elections have given rise to authoritarian, ultra-nationalist regimes, which are quick to 'eviscerate the civil liberties, and the rights of the opponents to their nationalist programme'. In the 1980s, Ronald Reagan demanded that Mikhail Gorbachev destroy the Berlin Wall. Thirty years later, Trump proclaims that the world needs more walls between nations. To him, the neo-nationalist propagate their own world view with the help of globalization's ultimate tools: the Internet and social media. They focus their energies on the manifold possibilities for communication, rallying and sharing provided by the Internet. Their campaign is supported by international bodies, their overtone for economic and political liberalization go hand in hand. Here the traditional politicians are simply not as well connected as the new nationalists. In fact a new era is in the making both in the political and technological terms.

Attempt to Reorient Traditional Ethnic Cultural Framework to Consolidate the Fuzzy Identities and to Supplement Techno-economic and Political Transformation

In contemporary India, the identities of ethnicity, nationality and citizenship are posited within the multiplicity of economic, technological, social, cultural and political transformations. In the wake of neoliberal economic globalization, fast penetrations of ICTs and social and mass media, the ever-growing consumerism and resurgence of ethnic and Right wing political assertions, the social and cultural life of average individuals are getting re- and deconstructed on an everyday basis. As the conventional social bondages are becoming increasingly weak, profound desires of self-expressions getting repressed, ignored and devalued, and persistent inequalities, feudal dominations and social segregation getting redefined in the emerging new contexts, the individualized individuals are increasingly experiencing a good deal of fuzziness in their identity than a consolidated solidarity. Within this fuzziness, they find a meaning of their collective expressions, loosely through their ethnic identity. As development deprivations, social injustice and political dominations have remained linked to primordiality and ethnicity, many use this as a political opportunity to construct majoritarian and minoritarian identities in politics in the name of indigeneity. Hence, India experiences an unprecedented surge of neo-nationalism at time in the form of hyper-nationalism. It uses new and social media for the arousal, construction and sustenance of cultural nationalism. It speaks about the indigenous religion, culture and belief, and simultaneously the significance of economic neoliberalism. It brings the priests of temple to preach economic growth. It talks of traditional cultural ways of lives and propagates for smart cities, roads, highways, digital India, cleaning India, skilling India, big business and high-end investment, *sabka saath aur sabka vikas* (together with all, development for all) as road maps for development. Notwithstanding the new developmental discourse, the tendencies to construct binaries between social groups in terms of their location to specific ethnic groups are being shaped at the grass roots. There have also been the unfortunate manifestations of these binaries in many parts of the country. Now the arrival of neo-nationalism have set in motion a new churning that posited to standardize the plural foundation of the society with a common cultural nationalism. Neo nationalist narratives now tend to redefine and reassess the interrelationships between ethnicity, citizenship and nationality.

Development Deprivations and Persistent Inequality Making Multiethnic Underpinning Available for Political Manipulation

India is essentially a multi-lingual, multiethnic and multicultural country. These groups are also unequally posited in terms of their level of economic and social development. Although during the Independence struggle the significance of such diversity was ignored while responding to the exigencies, and nationalism became a normalization project both during the Independence struggle and thereafter, it has not emphasized on a common cultural framework. The normalization project of post-Independence India has propagated for equality, fraternity and justice, and has asserted for secularism, socialism and democratic republic, through constitutional and progressive legislative measures. As this normalization project is yet to accommodate the aspirations of all sections of people and to ensure the social and economic freedom by overshadowing the significance of primordial and multiethnic underpinning at the grass-roots level, these are widely made available for mobilization and manipulation, mostly because of their capacity-choice-development and mobility deprivation. In India, along with the protests and revolts of peasants, farmers, forest dwellers, displaced persons, etc., for a vast section of population collective assertions are also articulated and staged based on ethnic/primordial identities. Ethnic and other localized upraises, however, are not only seen with suspicion, but many a time, these are also designated as 'others' by the state and the opponents. The process of ethnicization of protest can be eradicated by eradicating poverty, deprivation and non-integration and by attacking the cause of poverty, illiteracy and non-integration in effective terms, and not by their syndrome alone. It is not to suggest the annihilation of ethnicity, but to preserve the ethrived diversity as a part of rich Indian tradition by providing each ethnic group equal opportunities for social and human development so that patriotic and nationalistic spirits are inculcated among all these groups through the normalization process. Such a process should provide equal space and pace for nurturing and accommodating nationalism and preserving specific cultural ways of lives of each social group.

Traditional Cultural Framework Still Stands for Cultural and Religious Pluralism and Incompleteness in the Absence of Others

The historical tradition of India suggests that the interface among ethnicity, nationality and citizenship in India needs to be understood not in a homogenizing rigid unitary framework of one religion, one language and one culture, but in terms of a flexible foundation of multiculturalism and religious pluralism. Such flexibility has provided the space for the coexistence of these categories with diverse complementarities, despite the realities of secretarial interventions at times and places.

The firm reality of Indian society time and again shows that though India is largely a traditional and spiritual country, its traditional spiritual ethos is seldom internalized to give it the expressions of cultural nationalism. As a homeland of four great religions of the world—Hinduism, Jainism, Buddhism, and Sikhism—and innumerous native tribal religions, as an accommodative host of other major religions such as Islam, Christianity, Zoroastrianism and a fertile ground for proliferation of religious syncretism and rich saint tradition, India is historically founded on universal spiritualism and cultural accommodation than on absolute homogenized identity, being a land of *sarva dharma sambhava* (all religions are equal) and *vishwa kutumbakam* (world as one family). Hinduism, which is followed by the vast majority in the country, is predominantly used as a liberal way of life for the accommodation of multiculturalism than as an expression of dogmatized insulated communitarianism. Hence, the Hindu way of life is not a reflection of sectarianism, but a reflexive universality.

Although ethnicity is constantly making its imprint on citizenship and nationality, and it has remained a blockade for the emergence of secular citizenship and civic nationalism in Western sense of the terms, in every reality, it has remained difficult to isolate them culturally. In fact, the Western prescription of secularism is yet to get cultural rootedness in Indian society. As Joshi (2007) points out,

> [S]ome of the basic failures of contemporary Indian secularism arise from the lack of rootedness in the Indian cultural traditions which, to a large extent, still mean the Indian religious traditions. To ignore that Indian religions and the Indian cultural traditions are closely intertwined is to ignore basic historical and sociological facts and processes.

Madan (1997) also points out that the Western ideology and practice of secularism stand apposite to the beliefs and practices of communities and social groups in India. Hence, there is a need to understand the diverse traditional beliefs and cultural practices, not in terms of practice of narrow communalism and fundamentalism but in terms of tolerance and peaceful coexistence against the tendency of fundamentalism as propagated in the saint tradition in India. Hence, emphasis on Western cultural nationalism not only upholds the existence of a majoritarian nationalism, but also use the Western sense of binary between majoritarian and minoritarian tradition, or civic and cultural nationalism out of a context and for a limited political goal. Such emphasis is largely a misplaced priority.

Preexistence of Patriotism as an Emotional and Cultural Unity

Popularly, India is more of a country of patriots than a state of nationalists. As Nandi (2006) elaborates, while nationalism is still evolving, for a large section, it has remained to be a folkloric, cultural and patriotic phenomena by remaining non-specific, non-ideological 'presuming the existence of communities based on religions, castes, sects, linguistic affiliations and ethnicity other than the country. Such phenomena expect the state to serve the needs of a society and a culture, not the culture and the society for the state' (Nandi 2006). In fact, in everyday existence, India experiences the innumerable interaction of the patriotic citizens. Their affiliation to the country is non-ideological; their outlook is constructed/developed not keeping in mind hostility against 'others', but their love for their local community and culture pre-existed the modern society as peasants, farmers, workers, artisans and members of various ethnic groups. Their patriotism provides the foundation of a plural society and culture in India and the foundation of a multi-national/multiethnic society therein. Hence, the idea of nationalism that existed since ages in India was predominantly used in a patriotic form with a tendency to move towards universality as a part of multicultural/plural ways of lives.

To Eric Hobsbawm (1990), nationalism evolved from a cultural folkloric to a national idea and then to a mass-based national movement. To him, in the Third World, nationalism does not take shape even after the formation of a nation state (Hobsbwam 1990). Although political nationalism as a Western import gradually took shape during the Independence struggle against the British, civic nationalism as a reflection of patriotism was a part of the great tradition of Indian society that connected the people through multiple cultural threads since ages. Although most citizens of the country are the bearers of elements of civic nationalism, in contemporary India, political nationalism as an ideology has a thin presence in most citizens. Hence, to Nandi (2006), nationalism at this level is a viable ideological entity mainly among the small minority of the urban, educated and modern citizen in India to whom the principles of the older way of life have become shaky (Nandi 2006).

Imposition of Binary and Homogenization Putting Limits to Patriotic Imagination and Inherited Plural Foundation of Society

In India the tendency to interpret the traditional plural religious and cultural framework in terms of unitary homogenizing framework put several limits to the inherited collective morality and human obligation. It threatens the plural foundation of the society by identifying 'others' from within. It makes a man from within to an enemy of a man from within. These incidences only make the apprehension of Tagore (1955) true that 'nationalism is a great menace and nation is the greatest evil for the humanity'.

Nationalism is a cherished ideal that is to be achieved by making careful selection from traditional cultural heritage linking it to the aspiration for justice, equality, fraternity and dignity of citizen in society. It also involves act of upholding these traditions and practicing them through idealism, emotion and sentiments for creating a conscientious human community. If a nation is to be a soul and a spiritual principle founded on rich legacies of memories as thought of by Renan (1992), or if it is to be an imagined community with the image of their communion as propagated by Anderson (1983), or if is to be an effort for establishing an impersonal society with shared culture as propagated by Gellner (1983), or to be a good nationalism as elaborated by Greenfield (1993) and Ignatieff (1993), the multicultural, multiethnic, multireligious foundation of Indian society is to be protected. The good legacies and memories of coexistence, forming of communion across the social groups, long tradition of sharing and of give and take provide the foundation of Indian nationalism and not the declaring of the imagined 'other' even from within. As Gandhi writes: There is no room for race hatred here. Let that be our nationalism (Gandhi 1947).

The foundation of India's common man's identity that is widely located in spiritualism, animalism and innumerous folkloric traditions of primordiality, also finds a space for nurturing within the constitutional foundation of brotherhood, fraternity and secular citizenship in India. The Constitution of India has empowered the people to assert for secular citizenship for equality, justice and development, and simultaneously made commitment to preserve and promote diverse linguistic, religious and cultural practices. Efforts so far have been not to impose hegemonic cultural assimilation on all group, but to promote civic culture in public space by ensuring equality, rule of law and justice for everybody and also to show equal respect to all cultural and religious groups. Efforts are also in the making with people's initiative from below for inculcating a culture of secular citizenship and civic nationalism through a process of compartmentalization between secular and primordial in public discourse and simultaneously accommodating and showing respect and providing equal treatment to all cultural and ethnic groups as part of historical diversities as realities of India. The challenge, however, remains as to how such compartmentalization, complementarities and culture of accommodation to be retained in contemporary India. The answer in all possibility lies with the inculcation and assertion of citizenship rights to ensure the nation building process.

In India, neither secularism nor nationalism, and neither its religious ethos nor its culture, are matters of alternative political choices imposed from above. These are parts of the historical heritage that belong to the people of the country, whose use are conditioned by the Constitution and its liberal democratic practices. The contemporary world experiences the surge of nativity and reverse protectionism and in many parts of the world, those are mobilizing the social and political forces from within to construct a sense of threat, real or imaginary, and organize a host of strategies to thwart such threats. The foundation of liberal multicultural India now experiences a paradigm shift in its political culture with the surge of ethnic revivalism. These ethnic revivalisms in many ways are linked to the development deprivation, social exclusion and political subordination of vast segments of the population. Now India as a nation is to address three immediate challenges: First, to define and accommodate the debate on cultural nationalism in terms of the prevalent multicultural fabric of the society. Second, to minimize ethnicization of poverty, inequality, injustice and development deprivation at all levels and fronts by addressing the real cause of ills of Indian society so that India becomes free from the division between the masses and classes, as propagated by Gandhi. Third, to uphold the spirit of secular citizenship by providing a sense of belonging to the nation to all citizens with ensured justice, equality and fraternity.

In India ethnicity and patriotism (*deshbhakti*) are indigenous categories, while nationalism and citizenship in the modern sense of these terms, are the western imports. In essence ethnicity expresses itself as the foundation stone of cultural pluralism. In the normal course these are not expressed as binaries, even though many of these identities have emerged as expressions of protests against their isolation, injustice and marginalization in society. Patriotism also has not traditionally been the expressions of binary while developing imaginary and real love for the country. However modern nationhood as achieved by India in 1947 through the division of the country has got founded in bitter experience of communal divides for the common-man. Though in last 70 years India has made significant progress in science, technology, education and diplomacy, the deep rooted problems of poverty, un-employment, ill health, poor housing, feudal domination, social segregation, etc., have not been effectively eradicated for vast segment of population. Hence, while partition of the country on religious line has been understood as a major cause of such problems by a section of population, ethnicization of poverty, inequality and domination remained a reality for many. These objective conditions have created a social space for invocation of ethnic identity as a justificatory tool for underdevelopments and neglects. Very often subjective perceptions are also politically constructed both implicitly an explicitly in terms of binaries. Under these conditions the secular citizenship as enshrined in the constitution seldom get its full expressions as the realities of ethnicity have remained ingrained in everyday discourse in one form or the others. As long as the differences between the masses and the classes are not eradicated as propagated by Gandhi the ideals of equal citizenship will be casualty to ethnicization of identity. Here lies the significance of the 'constructive programme' of Gandhi that call for ensuring communal unity, undertaking constructive work, removing untouchability, prohibition, adoption of Khadi, ensuring village sanitation, new and basic education, promoting provincial languages, ensuring economic equality for kisan, labour and Adivasis, lepers, students and initiating civil disobedience as nonviolent means of protest. To him "the constructive programme may otherwise and more fittingly be called construction of Poorna Swaraj or complete Independence" by truthful and non-violent means' (Gandhi, 1943: 33). In fact eradication of the differences between the masses and classes is the corner-store for the realization of equal citizenship, full expression of patriotism and in making ethnic identity a reflection of reflective cultural pluralism in India.

7
Partition, Alienhood, Migration and Shaping Up of an Indian Identity

The Cost and Joy of Being Patriotic

Introduction

A collective identity is formed, gets transformed, consolidated and deposited in a person based on his or her long-drawn composite lived-in experiences that are acquired through varieties of social processes and situations that he or she encounters in the society. Experiences that are gained, sustained and internalized through the processes of upbringing and socialization, enculturation and interaction, compromise and negotiation, subordination and marginalization, assertion and resistance, incidences of threat and isolation, persecution and stigmatization, and association and fulfilment play crucial roles in shaping up such an identity in a person. Although social forces condition the expression of role performance and construction of meaning of an identity, many conscious individuals exercise their choices for the expression of such identities prevailing over all such conditionings, even going against the resurged social and political undercurrents of the society. Many uphold such identities as these get deposited in them as purpose, meaning and principle of life, even paying several situational costs, and enjoy their reflexive action as a part of their commitment to society and their own self. Many average Indians have got their entity transformed into such reflexive identity by experiencing the trauma of partition of the country, followed by victimhood of religious fundamentalism and communal violence, alienhood, isolation in a majoritarian theocratic country, and subsequent migration and marginalization in new set-ups, but have survived against all such odds by developing resistance through everyday experiences. Many of them have also experienced intense individualized cooperation from Hindu and Muslim neighbours during their alienhood in the hour of crisis. In the growing-up process, many such Indians have been transformed to be multiculturalists, religious pluralists and liberals upholding good memories of inter-community Hindu–Muslim cooperation in hours of crisis with the tolerant, multicultural and plural ethos of India. Through the lived-in experiences and the reflexivity they have acquired in their upheld identity, they assert that communal annihilation of man is committed not by another man or a community but by communal force.

India has achieved its nationhood after prolonged struggles against the British in 1947 that resulted in division of the country, creating a Muslim nation of Pakistan (with its two constituents—West and East Pakistan) and a secular nation of India. The division of the country and creation of two nations brought unimaginable miseries for vast sections of population who immediately experienced a high degree of uncertainty, hopelessness, physical threat, mass exodus, murder, riots, burning and destruction of houses and property, gang rapes and harassing of women and children. These created enemies out of old friends, 'we' and 'they' community of refugees and natives, and felt communities of majority and minority in the name of religion on each side of the border. It was, however, not a one-time phenomenon. Those who stayed back in the newly created theocratic states were to encounter everyday threats, undergo the experience of humiliation and alienhood and get resocialized in a new political culture as a religious minority in the name of nationalism. For many, it has remained a life-long experience of alienhood on the one hand and relocation in a new nationhood on the other. What is the nature and form of alienhood that a child has undergone with his family as a religious minority in the newly created nations? How do the experiences of alienhood contribute to construct an imaginary notion of nationalism that remains on the other side of the border? How are the threats of physical attacks, plights of migration and prolonged separation from the family are handled by a lone religious minority in a majoritarian state and as refugees in new nation—the nation of their dreams? How do the native communities react in a situation of communal aggression, threat and violence, and the receiving communities react to the forced migrants in a new nation? How do the old good or bad collective memories contribute towards the construction of a nationalist or a patriot identity in a person of such communities? How do such identities react to the resurgence of communalism and sectarianism in contemporary India?

This chapter aims to answer these questions by presenting such an identity based on a biographical account of an individual who has undergone the processes of alienhood during early days of his childhood and adolescence, and sufferings along with other members of his family in East Pakistan against the backdrop of partition of India (1947), post-partition turmoil, disintegration and imposed migration of his family from East Pakistan to India. It further narrates the process of his resocialization and growing up in remote villages, attaining adulthood, acquiring education in a multicultural environment in India and the gradual process of getting associated with larger social groups and formal organizations in towns. The chapter also describes the processes of transformation of identity of this individual from that of an alien religious minority in East Pakistan into a secular patriotic one in India. Positing him in a wider socio-political context and citing contradictory processes and his experiences of trauma and pleasure, threat of communal violence and friendly support, separation and reunion, isolation and integration, immigration and settlement, and marginalization and mobility, the chapter narrates how this individual intersected the identity of alienhood, nationality, ethnicity and citizenship in the process of his growing up, acquiring adulthood and association with a wider society in the Indian sub-continent. Anonymity of this individual is maintained for professional reasons.

Here begins the journey of a common man.

The Trauma of Partition in Early Childhood and Dreaming India as *Nijer Desh* (Own Country)

He was the seventh of eight children of his parents, born 10 years after the partition of India in a lone Hindu family located in a remote village in the extreme southern part of East Pakistan (now called Bangladesh). This family was surrounded by a numerically dominant friendly group of native Muslim families on the one side and a sizeable number of hostile and aggressive anti-Hindu Muslim refugee families on the other. The Muslim refugees were migrants from India, especially from Bihar, who had migrated to that village in the aftermath of the India–Pakistan partition in 1947. These families had their culturally distinctive rituals and religious practices, clothes and languages, and their attitudes towards each other. He grew up there as a child under the shadow of communal tension in the early 1960s in a neighbourhood of these mixed communities.

As he started getting sense of himself as a child, he found himself to be conditioned by several dos and don'ts to be observed along with other siblings at home. He was growing up there in the company of 8 people: his eldest brother of around 18 years of age, third and fourth brothers having a little age difference with him, his youngest brother, mother, widowed *Pishima* (father's sister) and his father. While his eldest sister was already married in another part of East Pakistan, his second brother and second sister were sent to India for study and were staying with their relatives. At home, all children were habituated to the practice of a conservative Hindu culture regularly reflected in the performance of various rituals, choice of food and clothes and also in the usage of language.

His house was located within a lashing green orchard and a little away from the river of Ganges. A tall bamboo fence covered with varieties of creepers formed the long wall for that house to mark its separation from the rest of the villagers. Within this boundary there was another inner boundary that covered the whole household and its living arrangements. Only relatives and close friends and neighbours were allowed to enter into this boundary. All children of the house were to spent their time inside this boundary except for the school hours and the play times. His mother would get up invariably before the sunrise and regularly mop the house with cow dung and after taking bath being covered in wet clothes pour holy water of the river Ganges on the *tulsivite* (a small earthen podium inside the house with a *tulsi* sapling on it) and would offer *pranam* (traditional salute) to the rising sun to mark the beginning of the day. His father was also an early raiser. After completing his morning walk and taking bath in the river Ganges would recite *Gaytri mantra* (vedic sacred message) in front of the tulsivite to mark the beginning of his day. Children were to get up very early in the morning and and to start studying before the sun rise. There were two hearth in the house. One was for them and the other was for their widowed Pishima. His mother would cook only fish and vegetarian food (absolute no to chicken and *halal meat* locally termed as *jobo* (meat through Islamic method of slaughtering animals). Invariably, every evening she would wear fresh/washed clothes to blow a conch and light a *diya* (small lamp) in front of a *tulsi* plant as mark of her devotion to Hindu gods and goddesses. All children were to follow the instructions of the elders for taking bath twice a day, changing clothes after coming from the outside and speaking only *bhadra bhasha* (pure Bengali language) as against the *chalti bhasha* (common language) spoken by the children in the neighbourhood. His mother was a true homemaker and an effective teacher at home. Besides remaining busy with the household chores, she would make the children study. She would also leisurely narrate stories from Hindu epics such as Ramayana and Mahabharata and of Lord Krishna and other Hindu gods and goddesses. His *Pishima*, who got married at the age of 7 and became a widow at the age of 9 was living in one corner of the house following the strict principle of Hindu widowhood by wearing markin (rough white clothes), maintaining shaved head, eating only boiled food, etc. However, she was the best friend to all the children at home and the best storyteller in the night for them.

His father was popularly known as 'Doctor babu' to all the villagers as he was a medical practitioner by profession. Being the only doctor in that area, he always got extra attention from the villagers. He was a disciplined patriarch who, being a big landlord and a good medical practitioner, had in-depth rapport with the members of all communities. However, his public life was highly compartmentalized from his personal one that was guided by a strict Hindu code of conduct, such as keeping a sacred thread on his body, wearing only *dhoti kurta*, maintaining a Hindu calendar for all rituals and ceremonies and daily worshipping Hindu gods and goddesses including nature worship. Though he remained busy throughout the day with his patients, tenants and regular friends (who were mostly from the Muslim community), he interacted with the children without fail in the morning and evening as part of his daily routine. He regularly taught them English and mathematics, shared news of his choice from Bengali newspapers and most importantly inspired them with the stories of freedom fighters. Under his strict instructions, children were not allowed to take food in neighbours' houses nor were they allowed to play with the neighbourhood children, except for children from selected native Muslim families. There were a few *lethels* (traditional security guards) in the house, who looked after the children once they went out of the house to play.

In early 1960s, the social backdrop of that village was full of communal tensions arising out of news and fictions on border tensions between India and Pakistan and China. Importantly, much of this was diverted against the Hindus of this area. As there were communal tensions in the neighbourhood and incidences of frequent stoning of their house, forceful plucking of fruits from their gardens, forceful grazing of cattle in their courtyards and making of verbal threats of various sorts to their family by the refugee Muslim neighbours, they were made to feel as if they were in an alien country through their everyday experiences. A psychological wall was created between the Muslim refugee neighbours and their family.

His mother, *Pishima* and other senior members in the family always prevented them, at time even physically, from mixing with the neighbourhood boys because of their foul language and nasty and rustic gestures. However, despite all these restrictions, this little boy had covertly developed friendships with all boys in the neighbourhood and played with them all rural childhood games. In the event of getting noticed by the elders in the family, he was not only withdrawn and given bath in cold water as an act of purification but also given physical punishments in the form of twisting hands, fingers, ears and even caning on the hips. However, the result was not up to the expectation of his elders.

Regular Ridiculing: Although he was inducted in games by the neighbourhood children, he had noticed even in those childhood days that he was often addressed by the refugee Muslim children as *Kafir* and *Malaun* for any of his silly mistakes in the game. Although such utterances generated amusement for everybody in the game, neither he nor his then playmates knew the actual meaning of such terms. However, at home, once he used these terms to address his immediate elder sibling unaware of their meaning and implication. The result was of unexpected magnitude: after all rebuke and interrogation, he was strictly prohibited from interacting with the children in the neighbourhood.

Until Class II, he studied at home along with his brothers. For his admission in Class III, he was sent to an old *madrasa* school (being converted into a junior school), the only primary school in the neighbourhood. Two of his siblings were already studying there in Class 5. There, along with Bengali, he was taught Urdu, parts of Koran and also the national anthem of Pakistan: *'Pāk Sar Zamīn Shādbād...'*. There, he again had regular encounters with another group of Muslim refugee classmates who regularly addressed him as *Malaun* and *Kafir*, blocked his path and movement within the school and made him sit only in the back row of the class, which, according to them, was meant for *Malaun* and *Kafir* students like him. Over and above, he was instructed by those boys not to complain to anybody about them. He gradually started feeling lost, humiliated and lonely in the school. Although his class teacher, known as *'Moulavi Master'*, was very friendly with him, he was unable to express his psychological plight due to some unforeseen fear. For this lonely isolated boy, school was not an attractive place for learning and playing; however, he had no option but to go to this school due to parental pressure.

Despite an increased quantum of his interaction with other students in the school, the tag of *Malaun* and *Kafir* remained attached to him.

As more boys started using these terms for him, he started feeling more humiliated, but did not get any remedy. He started sharing his humiliation with his elder brothers, who also experienced similar taunts and humiliation in the school. They gradually started sharing these incidences with their parents. Their mother was deeply disturbed by listening to all these narratives. This little boy noticed his mother listening to their narratives very carefully, hiding her tears with one edge of her sari and also repeatedly and firmly pronouncing: 'Everything will be alright when we will go to our *nijer desh*—India'. He became so happy to know that there is an end to it and he has a country of his own–India. He was unable to fix himself on the question of *nijer desh*. He was silently but very carefully listening to the discussion at home regarding the future plan of their migration to India in the wake of heightening communal tension in neighbourhood. The publicly humiliated and internally confused boy started getting a ray of hope in the utterances of his mother and discussion at home. He started constructing an image of India that according to his mother was a *Ramarajya*—a country with no hatred, no poverty, no quarrel, and where all were treated equally. He gradually started identifying himself more to be an Indian than to be a Pakistani or as a *Malaun* or *Kafir*. His home environment made him construct an illusionary image of an Indian child of his own understanding in him than to be anything else. However, his slip of tongue about his newly discovered identity invited more hostility from the refugee playmates in the village and classmates in the school.

The more this boy was getting isolated from the neighbourhood and school playmates, the more he was coming closer to his mother who would invariably project an ideal and moral image of India in front of the children at home. Although his mother's love for India was very expressive to them, she was never a hater of the other community. She was the *naya bhabijan* (newly married wife of elder brother) to most of the native Muslim neighbours. Her best friend was a Muslim woman—the village counsellor's wife. In her daily talk with the children, she always advised them to remain grateful and respectful to these Muslim neighbours who had helped them in the extreme moment of attack on their family. Based on experience, his mother always said: 'Everybody is not communal or anti-Hindu. It is only a few who create it for their interest while others get carried away'. Although this little boy had not seen the partition of the country, he had learnt and seen in that early age the fear, anxiety, humiliation and physical threat that a religious minority community faces in a majoritarian state, where a country was partitioned on religious lines.

He had simultaneously learnt from his mother and his widowed *Pishima* the incidence of communal mob attack on their family. However, he had also learnt from them the courageous help of the Muslim neighbours to protect their family when they were attacked by the refugee Muslims. This incidence was often narrated to them not only as an example of inter-community relationship but also as a spirit to uphold such relationships in future.

The Violent Attack on the Family: A Repeated Story and the Aftermath

It was immediately after Independence and the partition of India in 1947 that most of the Hindu families left the village for India. They found that with the partition of the country, the inherited mutual trust and traditional sense of bonding and belonging in that multireligious neighbourhood had started waning. They emerged to be fragmented and devastated. His father and *Pishima* were neither ready nor convinced of this partition. His mother was at an advanced stage of pregnancy. Their inseparable attachment to *pitribhite/vastuvite* (parental land) and fear of loss of life and property prevented them from migrating to India despite heightening communal tension and increasing flow of forced cross-border migration across these newly created nations. Above all, his father's childhood friend and many of the neighbourhood Muslim families came forward to assure them of help in the event of any threat to their lives. Ultimately, this small family of that time (consisting of his father, mother, 19-year-old widowed *Pishima*, 6-year-old eldest sister and 2-year-old eldest brother) decided to stay back in East Pakistan and to try their destiny to live as a Hindu minority in a newly formed Muslim majoritarian state. However, within a few months, destiny took a new turn to test the strength of the Hindu–Muslim friendship bond.

One morning in late 1947, a huge crowd of Bihari Muslims/refugees led by a few locals gathered in front of their house. They were abusive, aggressive and hostile in their attitude and started anti-Hindu slogans. They set fire to the waiting room of his father's dispensary and told him to vacate the house and leave for India immediately or else all would be burnt to death. His father got shaken by looking at the pale, insecure, grim, shocked and hapless faces of his wife, widowed sister and innocent toddlers at home. He requested the crowd to give them at least six–seven days'

Partition, Alienhood, Migration and Shaping Up of an Indian Identity 205

time to vacate the house as his wife was at an advanced stage of pregnancy. The crowd was non-compromising, allowed them only a few hours to vacate and sat in front of the house for getting its possession within the prescribed time. They also set fire to one part of the outhouse and started pelting stones inside the house. Unable to bear such tension, his mother got labour pain and collapsed. His *Pishima* started taking care of his mother and of the screaming helpless children as much as she could do. Shouting and chaos engulfed the house. Ignoring all the risk and tension, however, few Muslim women from the neighbourhood came to the house from the backyard to take care of his mother.

Undeterred by the tension, threat and chaos going inside the house, his father kept on repeatedly pleading and requesting for more time from the crowd, but in vain. His repeated pleading that continued for around an hour or so only produced amusement and encouragement for the attackers, and frustration, pain and helplessness in him. As the refugees were getting more and more aggressive and started advancing towards the inner part of the house, his father decided to give up and got mentally ready to vacate the house to save at least the lives of the family members at all cost. He again got frightened upon seeing a large convoy of bullock carts carrying more than 100 club-wielding people rushing towards the house. He became highly despaired and went inside the house and closed the main door of the house to protect the family from a huge attack. However, he was surprised and amused to see that these people on bullock carts were neighbours, friends and well-wishers, who were led by his childhood Muslim friend and his reliable Muslim *lethels*. As they came closer to the house, they started shouting loudly:

> Doctor babu! We have come; please open the gate and come out. Don't be afraid of these scoundrels. We are here to help you. We will not allow an innocent Hindu family to be touched even. *Naya Bhabijan*, you are sister. We will give our life for you.

This move for the protection of a Hindu family was indeed organized by a Muslim *lethel* of his father who rushed to his father's childhood friend, an influential Muslim landlord in the neighbouring area, for help without informing anything to his father at that moment. Muslim neighbours also came out who jointly surrounded the house to overpower the aggressively attacking refugees and finally drove them away to restore the safety and security of this lone Hindu family in that trouble-torn village. His father came out of the house to be greeted and assured by his childhood friend and the lethels and neighbours there. Within the house, the chaotic moment also came to a halt as the neighbourhood Muslim women quickly formed a barricade against the entry of any outsiders there.

His father's friend made the refugees and their leaders commit that they would not even try to enter the premises of this Hindu house. It was an emotional reunion of Hindu and Muslim neighbours and reposing of trust and mutual feelings for each other. For the sake of their childhood friendship, his father's friend and the local Muslims also appealed to his father not to leave for India as long as they (his father and his father's friend) would remain alive. His father publicly accepted that appeal and lived up to it until his friend and that lethel were alive in East Pakistan and thereafter in Bangladesh.

The Everyday Threat and Frequent Visits to India

This episode of 1947 brought a deep sense of threat and persecution, especially in the minds of his mother and for other siblings of this boy. This episode was also repeatedly told to the children who were born after 1947. It created a sense of threat for all. He had seen his father strictly instructing all the children not to play outside the courtyard of the house, not to speak to outsiders, to come back from the playground before sunset and to keep the main gate of the house tightly closed at all times. There was always a sense of tension and fear in the house as some neighbours were threatening them regularly with abusive language: 'Go to India fast, else you will be butchered here soon. You *Kafirs, Malauns* have no business here; leave Pakistan soon ...' The tension was getting increasingly high, especially during the nights. The tension had reached such an extent that even the sound of wind blowing or movement of wild animals or birds would make all the children rush to their mother or *Pishima* to hide out of fear. In the event of somebody knocking on the door late in the evening or at midnight (which were repeated phenomena because of calls from patients for his father), everybody would wake up and sit around a lantern (which was the only available source of light in those days). He had also seen few of their neighbours forcefully breaking the boundary/fencing of their house, plucking fruits from their garden and even pushing huge number of their cattle inside their boundary to develop quarrel with them, especially in the absence of his father.

His father was always firm and undeterred by these tensions. He would always console the family members, saying, 'This is nothing. My friend and neighbours are there to help. Nothing will happen; they are only a limited few and they speak only out of frustration. Moreover, our lethels are also there ...' His father would also frequently utter: 'I am committed to my friend, my patients and to my widow sister'. His father was also convinced that 'this artificial division of the country would not last long. Netaji Subhash Chandra Bose would come back soon and would unite the whole of India again'. In discussions about migration to India, his *Pishima* would toe the line of his father, while his mother was convinced that the whole family would have to migrate to India if lives were to be saved, children were to be educated and a dignified life to be lived. She would frequently utter: 'Neither can I listen to the vulgar language of our neighbours regularly nor can I see the grim faces of my children anymore!'

This little boy had seen his mother weeping frequently after listening to the tales of everyday humiliation from her little children. He had seen her mother having heated arguments with his *Pishima* and his father who, according to her, were unable to realize the threat to life and everyday humiliation and insecurity of the family. His mother's brothers were there in the northern part of West Bengal in India. His father was liberal enough to allow his mother to visit her brother's place in India as she desired. Two of his siblings (his second sister and second brother) were already sent there for study on her insistence. In the later part of 1964, his father again prepared passports and obtained visas for his mother and younger brother for travelling to India. Till this time, this little boy was never taken to India by his mother. He was told that it would be a long journey, and lots of enemies would be around on the road. He was always left behind in the custody of his *Pishima* to be taken care of in the absence of his mother. This time, however, he was more grown up, had developed more understanding about his surroundings and wanted to go to India to come out of his everyday humiliation and alienhood. However, his mother prevailed upon him with the promise that she would select a school for his study and bring a bright red shirt and black pants for him from India. The boy had no option but to accept the imposition with tearful eyes.

Loneliness and Intensification of Interactions with Muslim Neighbours

Many a time, absence creates a space that makes one realize the significance of the absentee in one's real life. It also provides a space for alternative understanding with in-depth sensitivity. In the absence of his mother, even though for only a short duration of three months, his seven-year-old self developed a new understanding of the world around him. He was now a big boy with his own understanding and got promoted to Class IV in the school. He found his father to be less authoritative, Pishima to be more caring and elder brothers to be more affectionate, considerate and less quarrelsome in the absence of his mother. His eldest brother who was studying in another school located around 10 km away from the village also left home to appear for his matric examination (Class 10), staying temporarily with a Hindu family there. Now he got more scope to interact and develop friendship with the neighbourhood native Muslim children, though his mixing with the refugee children remained restricted. Although he developed a tacit sense of apathy for the school and for some classmates in the school, he had little choice to discontinue. He experienced their increased aggression, as they called him *Kafir*, pushed him in the classroom, isolated him from games, etc. In the absence of his mother, he started feeling lonelier with each passing day, without getting much scope of expressing his frustration.

Meanwhile, as the days passed, he received a letter from his mother, stating that he would be taken to India next time for admission in a good school there and that she would be back soon with the promised gifts for him. His mother's letter gave a new boost to his personality. He saw an end to his plight in the school and among the refugee children in the neighbourhood. Out of enthusiasm, he went the next day to the school with newly acquired confidence and declared in the class that he would soon leave for his 'own country, India'. He also resisted the terms *Malaun* and *'Kafir* used for him by his classmates. It led to a scuffle in the class with the refugee boys, and he got a big blow on his face and a big cut on his eyebrow. He fell on the ground and started bleeding. The boys ran away as *Maulavi Master* came to his rescue. After first aid, he was sent home. His condition made his father very upset and very angry. His Pishima started weeping while two of his immediate elder brothers, being saddened and shocked by his condition, started removing his clothes, which had become full of blood stains. His father rushed to the school to lodge a complaint, but in vain. His father decided not to send him to school until his mother was back from India. His father's friend and many Muslim neighbours and friends came to console and empathize with this injured and traumatized boy and his father. After that incident, several of his Muslim schoolmates also started coming to meet and play with him in his house after the school hours. This episode made him firmly believe that even though they were a lone Hindu family there, they had good

Muslim friends to look after them and friendship was not based only on religion.

As he was not attending school, he started getting more liberty to play with the local children and to visit their houses. He started getting motherly and sisterly affection from the elderly women of these families. He and his playmates, besides playing local games, also shared mythological stories of each other's religions, which they had learnt from their parents and recited together the poetry of Tagore and Nazrul and varieties of folklore.

His mother returned from India after a long gap of three and a half months. He started getting a new sense of identity, faith and confidence in himself as he was repeatedly assured that he would be sent to India, his nijer desh, soon for his study. He found a new meaning to his existence upon wearing the 'made-in-India' red shirt and black pants with all pride to affirm his elevated status. He never visited India. He started running all around the village, wearing the newly acquired made-in-India clothes and showing them to his neighbours and friends with a sense of pride. Although his over-enthusiasm was met with strong rebuke from his elder brothers and cynicism from some playmates, he was overtly undeterred as India was his heaven of hope to break all barriers of alienhood, humiliation and stigma.

Indo-Pak Border Tension in 1965 and a Sudden Journey in the Midnight

As he was slowly getting ready to immigrate to India, history took an ugly turn that prompted a hurried migration of this boy to India. In the middle of March 1965, in the wake of increasing Indo-Pak border tension, rumours and information of violence against the Hindu families in the neighbourhood started spreading regularly around the area. The local miscreants also became active. Stone pelting on their house, especially in the night, became a regular phenomenon. The tensions got so intensified that movements of all members of this family got restricted to within the house only. Sensing some unwarranted situation, friendly Muslim neighbours also started patrolling their house along with the lethels. However, the tensions got intensified further with information that members of two Hindus families were burnt alive last night in a nearby village and that there might be an attack on this family any time. Many miscreants also started shouting anti-Hindu slogans in the early morning. His mother feared an attack on their family. His father's friend and several neighbours arrived quickly to assure his father of full protection and help. However, in view of heightening tension, it was decided that his mother would leave for India that night itself with three youngest children, while his father, his *Pishima*, and eldest and third-eldest brothers would stay back in East Pakistan for the time being. It was also decided that the journey would start very secretly and his father's friend would arrange all logistics for this journey. A *lethel* was instantly sent to bring back the eldest brother of this little boy from the boarding house for his protection.

This little boy saw his father and *Pishima* getting considerably tensed while preparing others for a sudden and forced journey. He also saw that his mother, though in a tensed and pensive mood, was firm like a warrior getting ready for an unwanted war. His father told all the parting members of the house that they were to leave the house in the middle of the night and in the guise of a Muslim family. All the children were instructed not to make any sound during the journey, to address their mother as *Amma* instead of *Ma*, to ask for *pani* (water) instead of *jal* and to address their elder brothers as *bhai* instead of *dada* (as part of the local Muslim vocabulary) to project them in public as Muslims. In the afternoon, his father's friend came again along with his wife and few other Muslim women. Those women gave his mother a black *burkha* (used by Muslim women to cover their whole body in public) to wear. They put a lot of *kajal* (black eye cosmetic) in his mother's eyes and eyebrows to darken them and put a big nose ring on her nose to give her the look of a Muslim woman. They also requested his mother to remove *sindur* (vermilion) from her forehead and red and white bangles from her hands as those were symbolic marks of Hindu women. As these were being removed, he saw that his heroine mother started sobbing and collapsed on the ground, saying, 'I am neither a Muslim nor a widow. I am a Hindu; please leave me alone. I will not go to India. I will die with my children and husband here'. Although everybody started weeping, his father again made an effective intervention to bring the emotionally charged situation under control to ensure that such preparation should not go astray.

Ultimately, the journey started in rows of bullock carts in the dark of the night. His *burkha*-clad mother sat on a covered bullock cart with her young sons. This bullock cart was escorted by two other bullock carts in the front and two at the back, surrounded by around 25 lethels carrying dim lanterns and clubs in their hands. The whole convoy was led by the age-old reliable Muslim lethel and his elder brother who was brought back home that evening. This little boy looked behind from the moving bullock cart to only find that his strong, tall father had mellowed and was holding the hand of his third brother with one hand and consoling his *Pishima* with another. His father was trying to say a few last words for that journey but was unable to say anything, and the journey started.

It was a late-night journey full of tension. His *burkha*-clad mother was trying to cover all the three children with her unmanageable burkha as a hen does to its chicks. His elder brother was standing firm on the gate of the coach with a tensed grim face with all the readiness to face any eventuality; so was the lethel. Whenever a new passenger was entering the compartment, they were getting alarmed. The little boy was so tensed that he was suspecting everybody to be an attacker and was getting up from sleep frequently. Even a small movement of anybody's arm was making him tensed. Although his *Pishima* and mother had taught him to chant and recite *Ram Naam* (Lord Rama's name) to overcome all fear, he was unable to utter the same due to the fear that others would identify them as Hindus. The only mode of communication with his mother throughout this journey was through her firm touch on his head. The shocked family was voiceless. Deep breathing, watery eyes and silence were speaking the language of their uncertainty, separation and frustration. Nobody was even asking for water or food, or expressing the need to relieve themselves; so deep was the sense of threat and suspicion among them. By around noon, after hopping on a train, they reached the last point of their journey—the Indian border.

What a relief!! All of them became very jubilant after getting down from the train as it was a new lease to life and achievement for all of them. They started talking to each other on natural and emotional terms. His mother removed the burkha and again put on vermilion on her forehead and white and red bangles on her hands to get back her married and motherly Hindu look. However, it was again a time of separation. His eldest brother and the lethel were to go back, undertaking the same ordeal. His mother held the hand of her eldest son and put it on the hand of the lethel and said to him: 'I am keeping my son in your custody. Protect him, take him home back and protect my husband and others who are alone there'. The lethel replied: '*Naya Bhabijan*, as long as I am breathing, nobody will be able to touch Doctor babu and your children. It is the promise of a *Musalman*. You go to India without any doubt'. The lethel and his eldest brother started walking back towards the railway station with tearful eyes to go back to their house in that village in East Pakistan. He along with his mother and his two immediate elder brothers started walking towards India without knowing that they were moving for a long ordeal and separation.

Arriving in India: The Dreamland

As the lonely four souls started moving towards the border, this little boy became very excited with each step towards India. He forgot all tiredness and tension and pain. Why not? He was going to enter in his *nijer desh*, his dreamland—India. He rushed leaving behind everybody to reach the edge of the Pakistani boundary, even though his mother advised him to walk slowly and stay together. He was surprised that he was stopped at the check post. East Pakistan Rifle guards asked for his identity. He replied: 'I am a Hindu and I am an Indian'. The security guards smiled at him. His mother followed him to show the passports and visas. All were allowed to enter India. He was, however, again stopped. This time it was by the Indian Border Security Force. Before they asked any question, he himself said: 'I am a Hindu and I am an Indian. My brothers and my mother are also Indians. We are coming to our country'. He was so happy that the Indian Border Security Force personnel hugged him, took him on their shoulders and gave him a few pieces of biscuits. It was a proud moment for him. His love, respect and feeling for India increased manifold. His brothers and mother who were always giving him extra attention, though liked his enthusiasm, advised him to remain contented. All of them entered India after completing all formalities at the border check posts.

He was looking all around. He was feeling like a liberated bird. He was thinking that all Indian children must be happy like him. He kept on looking all around—the blue sky, flying birds, green fields, silver rivers, grazing animals, glittering ponds, smiling people ... everything. To him, it seemed as if everybody was welcoming him to India. He forgot the pain of separation from his father, brothers, *Pishima* and his playmates. After undertaking two bus journeys of around three hours each and another ride on a bullock cart for another one and half hours, they reached in the late evening a remote unknown village in the northern part of West Bengal, located around 3 km away from the East Pakistan border on the other side. They received a warm welcome in the house of his maternal uncle and *didi ma* (mother's mother) where his second elder brother and second elder sister were already staying for study.

Getting Settled with Unexpected

This little boy was extremely happy that he was getting extra attention from his relatives, and that the strict instructions for 'dos' and 'don'ts' and avoidance and withdrawal from mixing with children were markedly absent there. Children were also trying to be friendlier than he initially expected. In case of anybody asking his name, he was excited to introduce himself as: 'I am a Hindu and I am an Indian'. Although his utterance was fun for others, it was a matter of pride for him, because to himself he had arrived in his own country. Shortly thereafter, as the days were passing and he was getting acquainted with the playing style, songs, foods, etc., a turning point came to his life.

It was around two weeks after their arrival in India, that is, in the second week of April 1965, that they were informed by a local police station that their passports had been confiscated by the administration and they would not be allowed to go back to East Pakistan immediately as the Indo-Pak War had broken out. They were also informed that the life of all Hindus in Pakistan was in danger. Accordingly, they were advised to stay back in India until further communication. Although his mother was mentally ready to stay in India for a longer period of time, she was not mentally ready to accept such uncertainly. There was no clue from anywhere about the safety of others in East Pakistan as all lines of communication were sealed. His mother, however, became courageous to see that the education of her five children was not affected in India. After a few days, she decided to send this little boy to the government primary school in this village, and his admission was finalized.

Refugee in Others' Eyes but Indian from Within

Despite the additional uncertainty in the family, this little boy became very excited with this information that he would go to school. To him, it would be a school with new friends where nobody would push him to the corner and would address him as a *Kafir* or a *Malaun*. Next day, he frequently started asking everybody about the school timings. The morning hours became too lengthy to wait for the school. He dressed up well, arrived at the school before time and reached his class with a slate and pencil in his hands. Without fail, he sat in the first row in the class. He was trying to be friendly with other students. As the class teacher entered the room, he stood up with all other students and said '*Aadaab*' (a form of greeting in Urdu) while the other students remained silent. As the teacher asked his introduction, he said very loudly: 'I am a Hindu, and I am an Indian'. The teacher took a backseat. The fellow students started whispering and after a few moments, the teacher asked the name of his parents. Before this boy could reply, some fellow students answered the teacher: 'Sir, he is a refugee ... a Pakistani refugee'. The little boy could not believe his ears. He started screaming: 'Oh no! I am an Indian, I am a Hindu'. The teacher smiled and after taking the class, he went away. The fellow students started whispering while he started repeating his proud identity. He tried to convince the classmates, but in vain. Other students declined to accept his utterance anymore. They asked him to sing the national anthem of India. He started singing the Pakistani one: '*Pāk Sar Zamīn Shādbād ...*' They asked him to sing the national song of India. He again failed and recited '*La illaha ...*' as he learnt in the madrasa school in East Pakistan. The result was obvious. The fellow students started laughing at him. He neither knew '*Jana Gana Mana*' nor '*Vande Mataram*'. His towering ego got deflated in a few moments. He felt highly humiliated and disturbed to be termed as a Pakistani refugee and returned home with a big burden of humiliation on his head. He stared weeping in front of his mother.

However, this boy never gave up. He was ready to do anything for his hard-earned Indianness. Overnight, he memorized the Indian national anthem '*Jana Gana Mana*' and the national song '*Vande Mataram*' as the first step to be qualified among the students for consideration as an Indian. He started asking his classmates the credentials he needed to be identified as an Indian. The answers were as vague as anything else to him. In his mind, India was for Hindus as Pakistan was for Muslims, as told to him in his school in East Pakistan. However, in this village school, he found several Muslim students in the class marked by their surnames and were not isolated by others. He also found students reciting in the class: '*Hindu, Muslim, Sikh, Isai—Amra sokole bhai bhai*' (We Hindu, Muslim, Sikh, Christians are brothers). The plural atmosphere of the school in particular and of the village in general gradually made him think of the world around him in different terms. The unitary and undifferentiated image of India that he constructed in his mind now started getting replaced slowly by a plural one. He was highly moved by the recitation of patriotic poetry by teachers that took the students on an emotional journey of love, brotherhood and sacrifice for the country. As he started getting naturalized with the plural surroundings and engaged with studies at the school, tension and uncertainly on the home front had reached a higher level.

Indo-Pak Political Turmoil and the Lone Family

Within two to three months of their arrival in India, relatives gradually became non-affectionate and non-cooperative, perhaps realizing that this family would be a burden on them for long. His courageous mother made separate arrangements for their stay and made her own space of autonomy to ensure that the education of the children does not suffer in the absence of their father. She was to take care of five dependents, including two high-school-going sons and one primary-school-going son, one marriageable daughter and one toddler. However, after all the money which she brought with her got exhausted, the economic condition of the family deteriorated within a few months. There was no immediate source of earning. Although around 20 acres of land was there, which she purchased on her earlier visits to India by selling her ornaments, none of the relatives were ready to provide true account of these lands and of their produce. The family was left high and dry. At that point, a big help came from a Muslim sharecropper from the village, who had taken parts of their land for cultivation under the sharecropping system. This sharecropper genuinely came forward to hand over the share that he retained with him. This was the only source of income until new crops arrived in the month of December/January next year.

By the time they arrived in India an eventful shocking period of six months had passed. However, they received no communication from their father. In the months of September and October 1965, while the whole village took on a festive look for *Durga Puja* celebration, this lone family became desperate to get information about the other members who stayed back on the other side of the border. The news of military hostility between India and Pakistan was a matter of regular discussion in the neighbourhood. In the absence of a newspaper or radio in the village, people visiting the local markets were the only source of information about this war and atrocities against Hindus in East Pakistan. They, however, brought more fiction than fact, which was sufficient enough to increase the uncertainty and sadness for this family. For the first time, they decided to celebrate *Durga Puja* very modestly and without any new clothes—a situation which is unimaginable for a Bengali family.

Additional Shocks: Meanwhile, his family got a huge shock with an unconfirmed information that his eldest brother had been arrested at the Indo-Pak border by the East Pakistan Rifle guards as he was illegally trying to cross over to India from the East Pakistan side. It was also added that the arrested person confessed that he was a Hindu young man and was carrying new clothes and gifts for his siblings and mother for the *Durga Puja* celebration. The family got further engulfed in sorrow, even though it was very difficult to confirm this information as lots of rumours were constructed surrounding this event. His mother was running from pillar to post to get confirmation of this news. The relatives were not of much help. In those moments of tension and uncertainty, the Muslim sharecropper again took an adventurist lead. He somehow sneaked into East Pakistan illegally, risking his life, and came back after a few days only to confirm the information that it was the eldest son of that family who had been arrested. The sharecropper, however, was unable to confirm the whereabouts of their father and the other members of their family who had stayed back in East Pakistan. This family very quickly emerged to be a loner and a subject of sympathy in the village, gradually becoming financially weak and unwelcomed by their close relatives.

His mother, however, became the sole saviour for all five dependant members in the family who would look to her virtually for everything. She became very bold in the face of all these challenges. She decided in early 1966, as the new crop arrived from the sharecroppers, to shift to a newly built house that was located around 3 km away from the village of their relatives and was situated near a bus stand and government schools. She repeatedly told her children: 'Don't get carried away by rumours, your father is alive. I have firm faith in him and in God. He will come soon to enquire about your study. Don't belittle me in front of him, you should study, study and study'. And they shifted to the new place with new challenges to encounter. In the absence of his father, his mother was trying to take focused initiatives for their study and academic progress.

Growing Up in a Multicultural Village

Life got a fresh start in the new house in a new village, even though this newness remained embedded with the accumulated sense of frustration, separation and insecurity. It was a multicaste and multiethnic village, where for the first time, this little boy also got an opportunity to interact with non-Bengali neighbours. In this village, he started going to a new primary school along with his younger brother. His immediate elder brother was given admission to the high school. His second eldest brother also joined the college in the local district town. Moreover, his mother married off his sister in a humble function. She also purchased a radio, which was the first radio in the village, to listen to Bengali service of BBC news, especially on Indo-Pak border tensions and relations. As the produce from the land was not sufficient, she sold her ornaments and a piece of land to ensure education for the children. Like his father, his mother would not only sit with them to supervise their study but also bring children from the neighbourhood to study with them without consideration of any caste, creed or religion. She regularly visited the school to know the progress of the children, though that was not a practice in this village. Every day, invariably over the dinner, they talked about their father and brothers whose whereabouts were not known to them for years now. He had always seen his mother weeping alone but not in front of them.

In this new village, he was given the opportunity to interact with and visit houses of all of his schoolmates and playmates freely and without any perception of threat and exclusion. He was as liberated as the other village children from all social and ethnic groups. He had taken the liberty by himself to play all sorts of games, run through the green paddy fields, jump in the pond to pluck lotus, ride on buffaloes with others and blow flute sitting under the shade of trees with his village playmates. Without hesitation, he ate food, especially on festive occasions, in the houses of all his friends. The restriction of *Bhadralok* (upper strata literati group of Bengal) and Hindu culture as imposed on him in East Pakistan was of no meaning to him in this new village.

Although his free bird character was appreciated by all his playmates, this was not appreciated by a section of the village elders. They complained to his mother about his overtures. They also said that in the absence of his father, this boy was getting spoiled as there was nobody to control him. One of the influential villagers also offered to regularly monitor this adolescent boy. They were also against the free movement of his mother in the village, especially her going to the school and the market. However, his mother became very assertive and said very clearly: 'My son has a God and he has a father, and he does not need a godfather. Don't worry, I will take care of him as his mother. I know myself and my responsibilities'. These village elders never liked the assertion of his mother and her strong sense of autonomy. They tried to create problems for this family, but she stood firmly against all these odds with all her calm and cool and firm conviction. However, as an immediate impact of these episodes, the movement of this boy got conditioned and he was allowed to play only with a limited section of the children and that too for selected games. He was wondering as to why such restrictions were imposed on him.

All were Indian there and all were friendly, so why such restrictions? He was made to realize over the next few months that there were hierarchies, social divisions and deeply embedded practice of exclusion in the village.

Breaking the Barriers of Caste Order

His mother was religious but liberal in her approach, having no faith in untouchability but with firm conviction on cleanliness and respect for each other's sentiments. These were not philosophical ideals to her but everyday practice. In his new house, he had seen his mother keeping three sets of glasses to serve water to Bhadralok, Muslims and others. The labourers were supposed to use the last category of glasses. On the question of this division, his mother always replied that *Boro Jat* (upper castes) would never take water in the glass meant for *Choto Jat* (lower castes), that is, if this was not respected, then people would not take water in their house. As a consequence, they would be isolated in this village. In East Pakistan, he was aware only of religion and not of *Jati* (caste). He knew that he was a Hindu, but not his caste. It was a new term or phenomenon for him. He knew neither the meaning of its significance or influence nor social impacts. He was not too sure whether the fact of his belonging to a particular caste was a matter of superior or inferior status or whether such association was a resource or a liability. It was puzzling and amazing for him to discover that he also possessed a caste besides possessing a religion through inheritance.

Out of curiosity, he started asking/enquiring about the caste background of his classmates/playmates. Although there was no practice of untouchability in the school, he found that all the students were aware of their caste background. At that stage of life, it was a discovery for him to see that his classmates were from many caste, tribal and religious backgrounds. He also realized that the children were not bothered about their caste and religious backgrounds. It was only the elderly persons from the clean castes who were protective of their castes.

He simultaneously realized at that stage of life that the labourers and domestic helps who were employed in their house were not only from poor but also from lower caste backgrounds. He also realized that irrespective of one's social and economic position, everyone had a sense of self-respect, and it was a two-way process. As his mother was carving out a space for her dignity and assertion against the will and domination of a few village elders, the labourers in the house were also asserting for their dignity. The little adolescent boy started encountering and experiencing the phenomena of poverty and domination and the practices of inequality, hierarchy, social restriction, stigma and domination in the village. He also saw resistance against these practices.

As per local tradition, the labourers were to clean their utensils after taking food in the house of an employer. But one day, after taking food, the labourers of their house objected to this practice, saying that it was a humiliation for them to clean their plate in the house of others. His mother, however, tried to convince them saying that since there were no other workers in the house and all of them cleaned their own plates after food, they should not mind doing so as members of the family. Their replies were again new to this boy: 'We have no problem to do it as your sons; however, our *samaj* (society) will boycott us if somehow they come to know about it'. Ultimately, his elder brother instructed this little boy to clean the utensils of the labourers as 'children have no caste' according to the elders. Although he did it happily for several months/years on a rotational basis with his brothers at home, assertion for dignity and fear for and domination of samaj appeared to be hard realities to him. He could personally realize that his heroine mother was working against all these odds to preserve and promote the well-being of their family in the absence of his father. And being a female, she encountered additional odds in this male-dominated village. These made him see that there were not only many castes and tribes in the village, but they were also present in layers of inequality and segregation despite being parts of same religious groups. He was puzzled that even though all of them were Indian, each of the groups' relation with other groups was conditioned by their own samaj. He found several contradictions and raised several questions both at home and at school.

Village Teachers, Spirit of Independence Movement and Paradise of Pluralism

As directed by his mother, the village school was the sole place of getting answers to his questions and a direction for his life. He found that his schoolmates were equally puzzled on the relationship between caste, samaj, religion and desh (country) and on their significance in their lives. Answers came from the school teachers, but these answers were of a different nature. The sensitive school teachers of this village were the real bearers of the spirit of the independence movement. There was an old bearded Muslim school teacher known to them as Nizam *Mastermasai* (teacher) and a clean-shaved Hindu teacher known as Saha *Mastermasai* who regularly inspired the whole class of students to dedicate themselves for the cause of the nation. Before they took their classes, they were making it a point to narrate the sacrifice of the freedom fighters—Shahid Khudiram Bose, Benoy Basu–Badal Gupta–Dinesh Gupta, Masterda Surya Sen, Matangini Hazra, Netaji Subhash Chandra Bose, Bhagat Singh, Mahatma Gandhi, Jawaharlal Nehru, Bal Gangadhar Tilak, Lala Lajpat Rai and many others—for the freedom of the country. In good spirit, these teachers spoke for hours about the plural essence of Indian cultural heritage. They highlighted the historical bond of Hindu–Muslim unity, need of social equality, dignity of labour and the need for dedication to society, nationality and humanity. Many a time while lecturing, they forgot about the school hours. They talked about social reforms and revolution for the eradication of ills in the Indian society such as poverty, ignorance, ill health and the practice of castes system with the help of education. They told the students:

> None of you are ordinary persons. All freedom fighters now reside in you. You are them. Every breath you inhale, they touch you. Feel it. Don't do injustice, do not tolerate injustice. You are the real heirs of independence. Be educated and knowledgeable not for yourselves only but for society.... Do hard work, no short cut to hard work, realize the strength within you. They regularly inspired the students to uphold the noncompromising spirit of fight against injustice of Subash Chandra Bose, Tagore's philosophy of universalism, and Mahatma Gandhi's praxis of truth and nonviolence with very simple language.

They regularly inspired the student to uphold the non-compromising spirit of Subas Chandra Bose, Tagore's philosophy of universalism and Mahatma Gandhi praxis of truth and nonviolence in simple language For the students, they were not only teachers during the school hours but also beyond. For these teachers too, and their relationship with the students extended beyond the school boundaries. These teachers professed their desire for an ideal India in tune with the dreams of the freedom fighters. They were explicitly against the caste prejudice, social inequality, illiteracy, conservatism and communalism. They were talking about the desh and the people. Their lectures and simple lifestyles encouraged the students to imbibe the spirit of patriotism with religious pluralism, sensitivity and respect for all.

This little boy was amazed to absorb and internalize such spirit from an early part of his childhood in India. He would repeat the story of the

freedom struggle, as told by his teachers, at home and in the neighbourhood. Even unconsciously, he gradually internalized the multicultural fabric of the village through everyday practice of rituals and religious festivals. He and other students and playmates from all caste and religious groups jointly celebrated *baro maser tero parban* (13 festivals in 12 months), visiting each other's houses, using *ittar* (special scent) and *kajal* and eating *semai* (sweets), *puli-pithe* (rural pie made of rice powder and corn) and other foods during all festivals.

Celebrations of Independence Day and Republic Day were special occasions for these children. They would collect tall bamboo and fine rope made of jute from the villagers to hoist the national flag to celebrate these occasions with simple but puritan sincerity. Many villagers would come forward to donate the tallest bamboo from their grove for these functions to encourage these adolescent children. He was very enthusiastic to ground himself in plural and secular practices with respect for each other, which he missed in East Pakistan. He and his classmates became proactive in minimizing the gap between prophesy in public life as propagated by the elders and practice in personal lives as observed by all. He and his friends after coming home deliberately mixed up all the three categories of glasses that were meant to serve water to three different categories of people of the village.

Resocialization in this village initiated him on a new horizon of plural fabric of rural India despite everyday frustration and sadness at home. His father was an ideal hero in his life. Despite the inspiring learning environment he found at school and love and care he found in the daily sacrifice of his mother, he always had in some corner of his heart the pain of missing his father. The pain became more intense in case someone enquired the well-being and information of his father and his brothers. This little boy had firm faith on his mother's utterance that his father was alive and he would come soon.

Breaking the Barriers of Isolation: A Letter via London from a Muslim Neighbour

This family was in vacuum and disdain in the absence of communication from their father, brothers and *Pishima* in East Pakistan for more than two years now. Now and then rumours were constructed in the village about the communal riots and torture on Hindus in the East Pakistan.

These rumours were sufficient to put this family to a higher degree of sadness, tension and uncertainty. His mother fell ill and lost her health. Many neighbours and relatives promised to do something. Even fortune tellers started getting extra attention in his house for a favourable prediction but without any result. Every day, they were getting frustrated. His mother had continued to write to his father with earnest expectation for a reply, but to no avail. However, despite all problems, she would visit the post office daily with one plea or the other.

It was in the middle of 1967 that they got a surprise letter addressed to the name of their mother from London. The local postmaster himself came to deliver this letter. There was a lot of suspense all around since such a colourful inland letter, that too from England, seldom came to this remote village. The sender was Zamarul, as it appended, a Muslim from London. There was intense curiosity. Some more villagers arrived. His second elder brother, who was studying in a college in the district headquarters, opened the envelope. Surprisingly, there was a small letter written in Bengali covering another envelope. After controlling all his emotion, he read it out:

> *Aadaab Naya Bhabijan*; I am Zamarul, the younger brother of Doctor babu's friend. The letter from Doctor babu is inside the envelope. All of them are fine with the grace of Almighty and are highly concerned about you all there. Write to me back soon. I will send your letter to my *Bhaijan* in East Pakistan who will pass on the same to Doctor babu. *Khuda Hafiz*.

It was a joyous and emotional moment for the family. Nobody could read out those letters fully then as these were being passed on from one hand to another. However, it was sufficient for them to get the information that their father, brothers and Pishima *were* alive in East Pakistan.

This letter brought a new sense of hope in them and gave them a lot of social recognition, among both the relatives and neighbours. This lonely family got a lifeline of communication through London with active engagement of his father's childhood Muslim friend and family. Henceforth, letter correspondence with his father continued via London for several months, even though it was very time-taking. This communication had remained a lived-in experience of Hindu–Muslim friendship, unity and reciprocity for these families. Over the months, they came to know that his father's friend and the Muslim neighbours played big roles not only to secure safely and security of their family in East Pakistan but also to get his eldest brother free, who was arrested while trying to cross over to India in 1966, from all charges framed against him as an antinational by the East Pakistani authorities. Subsequently, this Muslim family also made all the arrangements to send his other brothers to India and join their family in late 1968. Though his father started paying regular visits once the border was normalized thereafter, he declined to get settled in India because of his affection and commitment to his Muslim friend and neighbours and his obligation to his widowed sister.

Intersection with Lived-in History during Adolescence

Once this little boy joined the high school, he found more multicultural and multiethnic surroundings and a different kind of intellectual discourses from the young teachers than those of his primary school. A section of the teachers would gather the school children after the school hours and lecture them about class division, social inequality and the need for class struggle against the bourgeoisie for establishing a just society. They would try to inspire the students to take part in their activities and to form a new society as propagated by Marx, Lenin, Mao, Ho Chi Minh, etc. Some started providing a counter-thesis of independence, saying that India had got only a fake independence as the Government of India had not eradicated poverty, unemployment and economic and social inequality. He also keenly observed in the neighbourhood a lot of public processions and meetings organized by political leaders to gather support for their actions. In 1967, a non-Congress government was formed in West Bengal, and in 1969, the Naxalite Movement took place in the Naxalbari Thana in the Darjeeling district of West Bengal. Radical messages of the Naxalite movement started echoing in the wall writings in this village. A large part of the neighbourhood in the village got divided along political lines in terms of their association to one political party's ideology or the other. There were heated discussions in the village. The home environment had also changed substantively by this time as all his brothers were experiencing unemployment after completing their secondary level of study. A new environment was in the making in the village, whereby questioning domination, disparity, caste-based discrimination, etc., became part of regular discussion and collective action. For this little boy, these were matters of curiosity and learning and questioning.

They created the space to raise questions to the teachers, elders and even party activists about their plan of action on social transformation and nationality issues. Although many a time they were discouraged, they continued raising questions.

However, history took a new turn in March 1971. Sheikh Mujibur Rahman won the elections in East Pakistan and on 21 March 1971 declared independence from Pakistan. The discussion and debate on the Naxalite Movement, issues of equality and social justice got sidelined both at home and in the neighbourhood by this event in the neighbouring country. Everybody started talking about the liberation of Bangladesh. The school teachers of all neighbouring schools organized several marches of school children towards the Bangladesh border in support of liberation of Bangladesh. This family saw a new light of hope in this development. As military oppression increased in East Pakistan, the Indian border was opened for the East Pakistani refugees. Postal communication again got disrupted. The news of atrocities against the Bengali-speaking population in East Pakistan by the Pakistani military again brought worry for them. However, they were confident that their father would be taken care of by his Muslim friend and the neighbours. As expected, his father arrived after a few weeks in the third week of April 1971 along with his most time-tested reliable Muslim friend, undertaking a huge ordeal. However, his *Pishima* had decided to stay back in East Pakistan as per her conviction that India and Bangladesh would be one again. The family was very happy to get reunited. However, after a short stay, his father's friend left for London and came back after a few weeks to go back to Bangladesh to join the Bangladesh Liberation struggle. As the East Pakistani refugee influx increased enormously in that area, his father opened a medical dispensary for the treatment of the refugees and joined the relief work for them.

The Bangladesh Liberation movement invoked good deal of nationalist spirit in this village. As this village became a transit point of military activities in the month of November 1971, this little boy could see the dedication of the Indian Army for the nation very closely. All villagers started feeling united and linked to the nation, irrespective of their caste, tribe and religious divides. It was a great feeling of a consolidated collectivity which they never felt earlier. However, after India defeated the Pakistani force and Bangladesh became an independent country on 16 December 1971, his father decided to go back to Bangladesh in early 1972 after receiving a communication from his friend. There was also a lot of persuasion by his father's friend to get settled in Bangladesh permanently with the whole family as Bangladesh had become a secular country, the Treaty of Friendship was signed between Mrs Indira Gandhi and Sheikh Mujibur Rahman and peace and friendship would prevail for years to come. Although such returning had not taken place, the frequency of visits increased between the members of these two families living on two sides of the border.

However, newly liberated Bangladesh soon started experiencing the resurgence of religious fundamentalist forces within a few years of its existence. Across the country, fundamentalist groups became active to propagate the idea of an Islamic state instead of becoming a secular one. In many areas, the *Razakar*—a secret group of militia that opposed the creation of independent Bangladesh—got actively indulged in revenge killing. They started targeting the supporters of the Bangladesh Liberation movement. They also threatened his father as he was friendly with a Muslim who was a freedom fighter. Similar threats were also repeatedly given to his father's friend for his participation in the Bangladesh Liberation movement. However, his father and his father's friend ignored these threats, considering them to be childish and acts of frustration. His father was told by those fundamentalists to leave for India. However, his father was firm in his conviction to his friend. He told them that he would be in Bangladesh because of his love for his *matribhumi* (motherland) and local people in general and commitment to his Muslim friends in particular. However, such patriotic feelings had no meaning to the fundamentalists. The sectarian and communal politics had again started gaining ground in Bangladesh, prevailing over secular values as nurtured through the spirit of its independence movement. The sporadic incidences of killing by the *Razakar* also started getting covered in the newspapers, making the family living on the Indian side of the border quite tensed and anxious.

One rainy evening in July 1973, this boy was so happy to see that his father had arrived from Bangladesh. He rushed to him to grab the packet of sweets from his hand. He was surprised that this time there was no gift or sweet packet with his father. There was no smile on his face; he looked all grim as if he had encountered a big storm. All were surprised. His father was carrying a few bags and a marked brown stethoscope in his hand that was presented to him by his Muslim friend long ago. His father started sobbing and hid his face with both his hands. After a while, he said that his friend who supported him all through his life and the reliable lethel who was always with him were no more. They were killed openly in front of his eyes by the *Razakar* because of their participation in the Bangladesh Liberation struggle, and for giving shelters to Hindus like him. His father shouted: 'I have not been able to do anything for them. I was overpowered by those killers ... They are sectarians, fundamentalists— enemy of humanity. As my friends are no more alive in Bangladesh,

I have no desire to be there anymore'. The family was shocked and plunged in grief because of the brutal killing of lived-in symbols of Hindu–Muslim unity.

Defining Indian Identity in Adulthood: A Realization from Within through Bundle of Composite Experiences

After finally settling in India, his father took control of the family, started his medical practice and continued to socialize and enculture the children in a liberal and secular spirit. Very quickly, he became friendly and popular among all in this rural area. His father's dedication to hard work, sincerity to any commitment and disciplined ways of life became a reference point to most people there. As a liberal, he vehemently resisted the temptation of religious fundamentalists to become one for political gain. Once the sectarian forces of that area tried to project him as symbol of victimisation and oppression by the Muslims in the then East Pakistan and in the newly created Bangladesh. As they made his reference in a public meeting in that multicultural village, he publicly stopped them from making such depiction of him and also alerted people against the spread of communal hatred in the neighbourhood. He, however, was against making any public hue and cry as he had no political ambition to be a leader there. Through his regular interactions as a medical practitioner with the people, he always narrated that Muslims were his best friends and saviours all through the days of his crisis. He always said that he was made to suffer not by religious people but by religious fundamentalists and that he had vowed to resist communalism as a tribute to his friends. These people threatened his father to depose him to Bangladesh if he did not join their group. But his father remained firm on his conviction for religious tolerance and pluralism.

In the process of growing up and getting adulthood, this boy acquired a degree of maturity to be inclusive, liberal and accommodative. He became a mutually inclusive product of social phenomena and experiences that he gained with a lot of hardship like that of millions of rural selves. His father's public gestures and personal practice and a liberal culture at home, the overall plural liberal ambiance of his little village and the spirit of the independence movement and liberalism that he imbibed from the school teachers helped this young self to fix his identity as a patriot and a nationalist that was rooted in a liberal and plural order. He had experienced the plight of being a religious minority child in a theocratic fundamentalist country which had made him realize the plights of the religious minorities elsewhere who are made victims of forced alienhood, isolation, suspicion and apathy. He had also seen through the experiences of his family how communalism and religious fundamentalism as products of few vested interests engulf the feelings of common men. From his experience of the village life, he had realized that euphoria for binaries, alienhood, suspicion and apathy are constructed by a limited few to serve their immediate sectarian political interests. He had also realized that resistance to religious fundamentalists and communalists was possible both individually and collectively and was necessary for the fraternity and plural foundation of an Indian society that is founded on the tradition and realities of humanism, accommodation and tolerance. He acted accordingly both in the village and outside without knowing its specific implication and cost.

His village had remained a source of his learning and integrating with the plural fabric of the wider society. During his youth, he regularly organized the village boys to arrange help for fellow villagers for education, health and other societal needs by collecting contribution from other villagers and donors. Many a time, they even took the poor patients of this remote village to city hospitals for treatment. The village life, however, was also full of its own variety of negativity with poverty, unemployment, traditional domination, resurgence of sectarianism, etc. Added to this was the free movement of few notorious smugglers in this village because of its location near the Indo-Bangladesh border area. Villagers usually avoided acting against these smugglers, despite knowing their hidden activities, as they were from outside and had good relations with local politicians and administration. However, this boy took a risk.

A group of smugglers were regularly teasing and molesting some village girls. These, however, remained unreported as the parents of those girls were scared of those smugglers. Once those smugglers attempted to rape a poor Rajbanshi (a Scheduled Caste) girl in the village. When this victim along with her father was rushing around for protection and help, many villagers ignored them saying that the girl was of a 'loose character'. When this lad saw this, he along with his two friends chased the smugglers, risking their own lives. Being emotionally charged, they caught hold of these smugglers-cum–attempted-rapists and started beating them in public. This information spread very fast all over the village. Many villagers including women came out on the streets and joined these lads in their action. As local police were to be informed to hand over the smugglers, the incident took a communal turn. As one of the smugglers and attempted rapists was Muslim, a section of the Muslims claimed that it was a false allegation against a Muslim by a Hindu girl and that the Hindu people had conspired against an innocent Muslim. Murmuring started across the villages, several hundred people gathered and the villagers started talking in communal terms and tension increased. Few Hindu politicians also came forward aggressively to protect this lad and his friends in the name of protecting their religion. His father opposed this so-called divide and kept those criminals in his custody until police arrived. Sensing deliberate misrepresentation of the facts by a few communalists and the possibility of an immediate communal conflict, a Muslim teacher of this lad, who had taught him in his primary school, rushed to the spot along with several village seniors. They addressed the people, unequivocally criticizing the smugglers-cum-attempted-rapists and the misinterpretation of the facts by a few Muslim people there. They made it very clear that rapist smugglers and communalists have no religion and no patriotism. The father of this lad also came forward to congratulate these young boys who had taken the risk to save the dignity of village women. Villagers became mass witnesses to the crime committed by those smugglers and handed over them to the police for legal action and justice after public thrashing by men and women of all communities.

This young self had now acquired maturity to be bold enough to organize village boys against several social ills, including picketing against the opening of a liquor shop in the village. They organized protests against the regular harassment of innocent villagers by the police on several issues. Along with other village boys, he started a wall magazine in the village to share short stories, poetry, etc., written by the village boys and to share information on national and international events with the villagers. He also wrote skits, highlighting several social concerns, and organized plays during the village festivals to propagate messages for equality and justice in society.

Formalizing the Horizon in Institution of Higher Learning

As he went to college and university for his higher studies, he got himself introduced to formal and structured relationships between the student and the teacher, formal political party ideology-driven student politics, and a

Partition, Alienhood, Migration and Shaping Up of an Indian Identity 227

host of formal cultural and creative activities, which were much greater in number and magnitude than the informal activities he experienced in his village and in the village school. Through many ways, he found in these educational institutions sites of exercise of power and exhibition of affluence by various formal competing groups, where everybody was eager to shed the country touch and their simplicity. In the big unknown world widely conditioned by wishy-washy urban dualism, growing consumerism and explicit individualism, this youth found his nurtured ideals and social sensitivity to be misplaced baggage. Although he gradually introduced himself to a wide spectrum of multiculturalism, he could realize that there was inherent bias against rural students in these institutions. Besides getting ridiculed by the co-learners for his imperfect English pronunciations, oily hairstyle, traditional dressing patterns, unfamiliarity with Hindi cinema, etc., he was discriminated by a section of them because of his straightforwardness. Although he apparently became shaky to locate the relevance of inculcated rural idealism in a new set-up, he never gave up. He frequently remembered his village school teachers who taught him to be courageous to face the world: 'Realize your strength in you, it is there. You can realize your strength through hard work and tenacity....' This young man could realize shortly that as an average Indian, he was not alone in his conviction nor was he isolated. With some other students in the college and later in the university, he initiated a wall magazine to be reflective of their thoughts of cultural pluralism, liberty and secularism. They tried to provide an apolitical autonomous voice of criticality. Along with the popularity of their wall magazine, they also became popular for their autonomous thoughts. Simplicity, respect for pluralism and straightforwardness that he had learnt in the village life had always helped him to overcome many of the hurdles, to excel in academics and to assert his identity and autonomy in his own terms, standing against all odds, at times even upholding the tune of Tagore: '*ekla chalo re ...*' as taught by his inspiring village teachers.

Professional Identity in Formal Organization— A Folk Stands Alone against Multiple Threats

Identity cannot remain abstract; it needs its application and interlinkages with the wider society. This identity (or identities) effectively relates a person to the society through the organization where he works. Despite India becoming a knowledge superpower, a fast-growing economy, phenomenally modernized, global and a transitional society, it has substantially remained traditional in both action and attitude in many ways. While the traditional primordial institutions and identities based on caste, language, religion, region, etc., provide a plural framework for the society, these are also manipulated by sectarian forces even within formal organizations as tools to serve their interests. At places and occasions, the primordial identities are transfigured and are made to work as a divisive force to deny the weak social groups for getting access to quality formal knowledge and capacity, to assert as discriminatory arrangement, to prevent their entry in the formal organization and to segregate and marginalize them by denying opportunities and entitlements through several organized tactics. It was quite difficult for this rural young man to get entry in a formal organization and to find space for his mobility as he was devoid of the desire and capacity to be transfigured in those terms. Although due to his sheer perseverance, passion for hard work and sincerity, he got a position in a formal organization, his village training of straightforwardness kept him away from the lobbying forces in the organization tacitly operating in the name of regionalism, caste, religion and language. However, he showed endless courage to uphold the valued perception of him by his mother: 'He has a God, he has a father and he does not need a godfather'. Over the years, he became a self-made man in his profession and successfully upheld the cherished values of cultural pluralism, nationalism and patriotism even when encountering enormous threats and persecution of various forms.

In metro cities, in the wake of growing individualism and consumerism, social bonding has emerged to be very weak among colleagues in formal organizations. Majority wants instantaneous gratification and self-fulfilment, and some try to achieve this through extra-procedural means of lobbying. In organizational set-ups, they see each other more in competitive terms and less in complementary terms, until and unless they have common interests or are directed against a common 'other'. Within these organizational arrangements, lobbying is frequently done to influence the authorities to ensure mobility, to get favours in promotion and appointment and to remain close to the authority structure for gaining a sense of recognition. However, these are not necessarily ensured by respecting the established rules, norms and procedures, but by respecting social, economic and political equations, at times even at the cost of 'others'. The sources of this equation in formal organizations have emerged to be predominantly primordial, founded on region, religion, caste and linguistic ethnicity. Hence, it is not through the formal organizations that these officials/lobbyists relate themselves to the society; rather, it is through their primordial social arrangements that they make these formal organizations relate to the society. They try in many ways to convert the organization as their instrument of self-propagation where self is defined as a reflection of their limited primordial loyalty that has far wider social and political implications. Thus, through the activism of the lobbyists, the identity of these organizations gets parochialized in both the explicit and implicit expressions of their functioning. This neither separates primordial identities from the formal organizations nor shows equal treatment to all primordial groups working in these formal organizations. Now many formal organizations have developed the tendency to become implicitly strategic sites for the exercise of primordial power to provide service to society by developing favourable equations with established political parties.

As a result, varieties of extra-organizational actors explicitly form for themselves integrated gang of notorious opportunist's union within the organization to influence the organizational culture even at the cost of established rules and procedures to serve their interests and of their followers and adherents. They are always available in the corridors of power and authority. They become subdued as one authority becomes strong and resurface once the authorities are in transition or are weak. In an organized manner, they capture the associations of workers/staff/officers, etc., and either get co-opted by the administration, becoming an extension of the administration, or convert the administration into an extension of these associations, thereby signalling the death of impersonal objective collective bodies and ringing the alarm bell to notify the birth of demonizing undemocratic extra-organizational forces within a formal organization. They construct the consent of the so-called majority through coercion to assert their legitimacy as the representatives of the association and thereby get themselves represented in all decision-making bodies. They colonize each department of the organization as an octopus and impose a reign of terror to get the support of complacent middle-class employees who follow the established trail to avoid the possibility of victimization and political unconnectedness.

As part of his matured Indianness and citizenship, this individual asserts adherence to the rule of law and its equal application of for all without any prejudice towards class, caste, religion and region. In a world where simplicity is considered a sign of backwardness, straightforwardness is considered a language of arrogance and indiscipline, acts of breaking norms and rules are considered advanced modernity, and insensitivity and lack of commitment to the surroundings are considered marks of globalism, he only invites trouble and ruthless backlash from the lobbyists. He resists attempts to frame, name, shame and isolate people in the name of caste and religion by the lobbyists and stays firm on his earned conviction, remaining undeterred by the reaction and consequences of the lobbyists' actions. While the lobbyists are desperate to prove their hegemony over the organization, coerce to consent to toe their line of sectarianism and try to demolish disagreements and dissent, he raises his liberal voice and keeps on voicing his dissent as a citizen and as a patriot, even risking his life.

While the lobbyists shift their political affiliations/loyalty quickly from liberal to Left to Right or vice versa to develop alignment with political parties in power, he remains fixed to his commitment to pluralism and patriotism as taught to him by his village school teacher.

While they use all means including public and physical threats to demonize him, he keeps his firm stand on tolerance.

While they effectively influence the organization to initiate one enquiry after another against him on false charges, he makes them frustrated as no enquiry finds any substance in the charges framed against him and his commitment for truth gets vindicated.

While they influence the organization to take away and deny the position and recognition due to him in order to oblige their henchmen in violation of all rules, procedures and precedence, he accepts the denial with grace but by raising a voice.

To curtail his dissent and disagreement and to discourage him from participating in public discourse, they either ignore him or explicitly instruct him to 'remain within limit' while he would firmly make his point for the collective interests like a villager.

They often call his argument 'childish', to discourage from participating in public discourse. But he understands public discourse to be the power and would assert that let there be some child in the court of the king to say 'but the king has no clothes'.

While they pressurize him to change his conviction towards sectarianism, he suggests them to be inclusive, plural and accommodative to be Indian by conviction.

While they try to isolate him with the whims of primordiality, many come to his help as fellow friends to give strong indication that Indian society is essentially a plural, tolerant and accommodative.

While they try to corner him within the organization through whims, politicking and manipulation, he gets integrated with the wider world as a citizen.

While they feel that he is paying a cost for his dissent by way of getting isolated, denied and threatened, he feels enjoyment as he upholds his conviction for patriotism through everyday practice since his childhood. He does it consciously as a citizen, as one of the many patriots in the organization who relate themselves to the society and the nation through the organization where they work for the society and the nation.

Conclusion

The existence of individuals in society as citizens, nationals, patriots and members of ethnic groups is circumscribed by various forms of exercise of power. These identities not only criss-cross each others' boundaries, but also prevail over each other situationally in relation to the exercise of power. For a common man, power is derived out of everyday collective discourse, exercised in a given culture that is conditioned by social structure. It is very explicit that through uninterrupted participation in public discourse and by controlling the discourse, the dominant sections of society exercise power and condition the culture and structure of social relations. It also creates an environment of hegemonic control over the life, thought and action of common men in society. As identities are not fixed and they possess the differential probabilities, herein at time and places ethnic and primordial dimensions are brought into play to endure the hegemonic control. India has got a rich heritage of cultural pluralism with ethnic diversity becoming its immediate expression. While the nationalistic discourse develops an overarching unitary justificatory hegemonic discourse for varieties of social actions and tend to submerge the realities of cultural pluralism through the arousal of such spirit, and it is made subject to localized instrumentality by vested interest for immediate gain, they also encounter a counter-hegemonic force from below. The counter-hegemonic forces, many a time, emerge out of lived-in individual experiences and gradually get linked with varieties of individual and collective expressions. Such lived-in experiences make people reflexive. They are aware of their own strengths and weaknesses, motives and limitations of others, meaning and purpose of their own and others' actions, and produce a counter-discourse guided by lived-in acquired reflexivity. Their narratives are part of their lived-in history that expresses the relationship between individual, society and nation through their every action—actions that aim to uphold the spirit of patriotism even when paying a social cost.

The identity of the person described in this chapter is not only what the lived-in experiences has produced of him, but he also endeavours to shape the experiences and stand by the society through the experiences he has encountered and culture and practices he has imbibed. He is a product of the social environment in which he was socialized, nurtured, encultured and has taken a shape of himself. Many of his experiences and memories were not pleasant and may tend to overshadow the pleasant ones and vice versa. The chapter shows that despite such realities, if lived-in experiences and good memories are part of one's life support system even in moments of threat and crisis, they become guiding principles in one's social life for making independent choices. Here, he tends to forget the cost of being a patriot and enjoys being more of it.

Through his lived-in experiences, he has shaped in him a liberal patriotic identity of an Indian. The shaping up was not an easy process, but a hard-earned and composite one with varieties of sequences. He, along with his family, has experienced adverse situations of alienhood, migration and uncertainty because of his minority status in East Pakistan but has successfully overcome the challenges of separation, uncertainty, poverty and apathy through deep conviction in his own strengths. He has been deeply influenced by the strong adaptive and assertive personalities of his parents, has received selfless cooperation of Muslim friends and neighbours during their crises, and has been influenced by the patriotic spirit of his school teachers and the liberal environment of his village to develop a bold, liberal and adoptive identity in him. He has preserved this identity against all odds. His realization of India is founded on the ontology of other millions of Indians who believe in the unity of plural fragrance, give and take, sacrifice and trust for each other. It is a unity from within, not against 'others'. His is the identity of a patriot that has taken shape through his lived-in experiences with the plural cultural fabric of plural India.

In 1947, India had witnessed the ugly expression of religious fundamentalism that divided the country in the name of religion, bringing in unprecedented human tragedy for a vast section of population of the subcontinent. They experienced dislocation of their families, murder of their innocent family members, friends and neighbours, looting of their hard-earned property, unending uncertainty and humiliation as refugees for generations. Many are still paying the cost of this religious division. The pain of losing one's motherland, old memories and nostalgia for old associations still vibrate in the deep sighs and tearful eyes of many living on both sides of the border in India, Pakistan and Bangladesh. The trauma of this partition, however, has produced many identities that resonate beyond religion. It also gives a strong message to reckon with: while sectarianism and fundamentalism separates and kills, religious spirits and the civilizational ethos of cultural pluralism of India unites and accommodates. Here nationalism as a civilizational unity shows the reflexivity of unity in diversity.

Bibliography

Alavi, Hamza 1965. 'Peasants and Revolution'. In *The Socialist Register*, edited by Ralph Miliband and John Saville, 245–75. London: The Merlin Press.
———. 1973. 'Rural Bases of Political Power in South Asia'. *Journal of Contemporary Asia* VI (4).
Arnold, D. 1984. 'Gramsci and Peasant Subalternity in India'. *Journal of Peasant Studies* II (4): 155–77.
Australian Bureau of Statistics. 2006. 'Aboriginal and Torres Strait Islander People'. Canberra: Government of Australia.
———. 2010. 'Aboriginal and Torres Streit Islander People' Canberra: Government of Australia.
Bajpai, K. 2017. 'Fear and Loathing: Can India be Prevented from Becoming Another Pakistan?' *The Times of India*, 22 April, New Delhi.
Banaji, Jarus. 1994, January. 'The Farmers' Movements: A Critique of Conservative Rural Coalitions'. *Journal of Peasant Studies* 21 (2): 228–45.
Banerjee, A., P. Bardhan et al. 2002. 'Strategy for Economic Reform in West Bengal'. *Economic & Political Weekly* XXXVII (41): 4203–18.
Banerjee, S. 2002. 'Civil and Cultural Nationalism in India'. In *Competing Nationalism in South Asia: Essays for Asgar Ali Engineer*, edited by P. Brass and A. Vanaik. New Delhi: Orient Longman.
Barker, C., and D. Galasinski. 2001. *Cultural Studies and Discourse Analysis: A Dialogue on Language and Identity*. London: SAGE Publications.
Barth, Frederick, ed. 1969. *Ethnic Groups and Boundaries*. London: Allen and Unwin.
Bartelson, J. 2000. 'Three Concepts of Globalisation'. *International Sociology*.
Brass, P., and A. Vanaik., eds. 2002. *Competing Nationalisms in South Asia: Essays for Asgar Ali Engineer*. New Delhi: Orient Longman.
Beck, U. 2009. 'Losing the Traditional: Individualization and Precarious Freedom'. In *Identity in Question*, edited by A. Elliott and P. Gay. London: SAGE Publications.
Bell, D. 1976. *Coming of Post-Industrial Society: A Venture in Social Forecasting*. Harmondsworth: Penguin.
Bennett, J.M. 2015. 'Identity'. In *The Sage Encyclopedia of Inter-cultural Competence*, edited by M. Bennett Jannet. London: SAGE Publications.
Bennett, S. 1999. *White Politics and Black Australians*. Sydney: Allen and Unwin.
Beteille, A. 1999. 'Citizen, State and Civil Society'. *Economic & Political Weekly*, 34 (36): 2588–91.
———. 2008. 'Constitutional Morality'. *Economic & Political Weekly*, 43 (40): 35–42.
Bertaux, D. 1990. 'Oral History Approaches to an International Social Movement'. In *Comparative Methodology: Theory and Practices in International Social Research*, edited by E. Oyen. London: SAGE Publications.
Bhabha, H.K. 1994. *The Location of Culture*. London: Routledge.

Bhargava, R. 1998. *Secularism and Its Critics*. New Delhi: Oxford University Press.
Blumer, H. 1951. 'Social Movements'. In *New Outline of Principles of Society*, edited by A.N. Lee. New York, NY: Baines D. Noldi 1969.
———. 969. *Symbolic Interactionism: Perspective and Method*. Englewood Cliffs, NJ: Prentice Hall.
Bococks, R. 1993 Consumption, London: Routledge. 1969.
Bourdieu, P. 1984. *Distinction: A Social Critique of the Judgment of Taste*. London: Routledge. Available at http://www.powercube.net/wp-content/upload/2010/1/ Rautleon-016-JPS
———. 1986a. *Acts of Resistance: Against the New Myths of Our Time*. Translated by Richard Nice, Polity Press and The New Press, 1998.
———. 1986b. 'The Forms of Capital'. In *Handbook of Theory and Research for the Sociology of Capital*, edited by J.G. Richardson, 241–58. New York, NY: Greenwood Press.
Bourdieu, P., and L. Wacquant. 1999. 'On the Cunning of Imperialist Reason'. *Theory Culture and Society* 16 (1): 41–50.
Bradley, H. 2016. *Fractured Identities: Changing Patterns of Inequality*. Cambridge: Polity Press.
Brewer M.B. and Gardner W. 1996. Who is this 'We'? Levels of Collective Identities and Self representations. *Journal of Personality and Social Psychology*, 71: 83–93.
Bringa, Tone. 1993. 'Nationality Categories, National Identification and Identity Formation in "Multinational" Bosnia'. *The Anthropology of East Europe Review* 11: 69–76.
Byres, T.J. 1981. 'The New Technology, Class Formation and Class Action in the Indian Countryside'. *Journal of Peasant Studies* 8 (4): 405–54.
Calhoun, C. 1995. *Critical Social Theory: Culture, History, and the Challenge of Difference*. Oxford, UK: Blackwell.
Calma, T. 2007. *Reflections on Social Justice. Forty Years On: What Does The Yes Vote Mean for the Indigenous Australian?* Tasmania: Social Action and Research Centre.
Carr, E.H. 1961. *What is History?* New York, NY: Penguin Books.
Castells, M. 1983. *The City and the Grassroots: A Cross-Cultural Theory of Urban Social Movements*. Berkeley, CA: University of California Press.
———. 1996. *The Rise of the Network of Society*. Oxford: Blackwell.
———. 1997. *The Information Age: Economy, Society and Culture: The Power of Identity* Vol. II. Malden, MA: Blackwell Publishers.
Castles, S., and M.J. Miller. 2009. *The Age of Migration: International Population Movements in the Modern World*. New York, NY: Palgrave Macmillan.
Cerulo, Karen A. 1997. 'Identity Construction: New Issues, New Directions'. *Annual Review of Sociology* 23: 385–409.
Cerutti, F. 2001. 'Political Identity and Conflict: A Comparison of Definition'. In *Identities and Conflicts: The Mediterranean*, edited by F. Cerutti and R. Ragiorieri. New York, NY: Palgrave Macmillan.
Chandhoke, N. 1995. *State and Civil Society: Exploration in Political Theory*. New Delhi: SAGE Publications.
Chatterjee, P. 1994. *The Nation and Its Fragments: Colonial and Postcolonial Histories*. Delhi: Oxford University Press.
Chayanov, A.V. 1966. *The Theory of Peasant Economy*. Translated by D. Thorner, R.E.F. Smith, and B. Kerblay. Glencoe, IL: Irin.
Clark, J. 2008. *Aborigines and Activism: Race, Aborigines and the Coming of the Sixties to Australia*. Crawley, WA: University of West Australia Press.

CMIE. 2002. *Economic Intelligence Service: Agriculture*. Mumbai: CMIE.
Cohen, J. 1985. 'Strategy or Identity: New Theoretical Paradigms and Contemporary Social Movements'. *Social Research* 52 (4): 663–716.
Cohen, J.L., and A. Arato. 1994. *Civil Society and Political Theory*. London: MIT Press.
Coleman, S., and P. Collins, eds. 2004. *Religion, Identity and Change: Perspectives on Global Transformations*. London: Ashgate Publishing Limited.
Collins, Randall. 1974. *Conflict Sociology*. New York, NY: Academic Press.
Cooley, C.H. 1902. *Human Nature and Social Order*. New York, NY: Scribner.
Coombs, H.C. 1991. *Aborigines Made Visible: From Humbug to Politics*. Kenneth Myer Lecture I, National Library of Australia, Canberra.
Coser, Lewis. 1956. *The Functions of Social Conflict*. Toronto, Ontario: Collier-Macmillan Canada.
Crossley, N. 2002. *Making Sense of Social Movements*. Buckingham: Open University Press.
Curthoys, A. 2002. *Freedom Ride: A Freedom Rider Remembers*. Sydney: Allen and Unwin.
Dahrendorf, Ralf. 1959. *Class and Class Conflict in Industrial Society*. Stanford, CA: Stanford University Press.
Dasgupta, Biplab. 1974. *The Naxalite Movement*. Bombay: Allied Publishers.
della Porta, Donatella, and Mario Diani. 1999. *Social Movements*. Oxford: Blackwell.
Desai, A.R. 1976. *Social Background of Indian Nationalism*. Bombay: Popular Prakashan.
Devos, George, and L. Romanucci Rose, eds. 1975. *Cultural Continuities and Change*. Palo Alto, CA: Mayfield Publishing Company.
Dhanagare, D.N. 1983. *Peasant Movements in India, 1920–50*. Delhi: Oxford University Press.
Dickie-Clark, H.F. 1996. 'The Theory of the Marginal Man and Its Critics'. In *The Marginal Situation*, edited by H.F. Dickie-Clark. London: Routledge and Kegan Paul.
Drucker, P.F. 1994. *Knowledge Worker and Knowledge Society*. Available at http://www.kgs.havard.edu
Edwards, M. 2000. *NGO Rights and Responsibilities*. London: The Foreign Policy Centre.
Elliott, A., ed. 2015. *Identity: Critical Concepts in Sociology*. New York, NY: Routledge.
Elliott, A., and C. Lemert. 2006. *New Individualism: The Emotional Cost of Globalization*. London: Routledge.
Elster, J. 1989. *Nuts and Bolts for the Social Sciences*. Cambridge: Cambridge University Press.
Eminov, A. 2007. 'Social Construction of Identities: Pomaks in Bulgaria'. *Journal on Ethnopolitics and Minority Issues in Europe* 6 (2): 1–25. Available at http://www.ecmi.de/fileadmin/downloads/publications/JEMIE/2007/2-2007-Eminov.pdf
Encyclopedia Britannica. 1985. *Ethnic Group*. Vol. 4. Chicago, IL: Ethnic Group University of Chicago Press.
Eyerman, R., and Jamison. 1991. *Social Movements: A Cognitive Approach*. Cambridge: Polity Press.
Fanon, F. 1971. *The Wretched of the Earth*. Middlesex: Penguin Books.
Feree, M. 1992. 'The Political Contest of Rationality'. In *Frontiers in Social Movement Theory*, edited by A. Morros and C. Mueller, 29–52. New Haven, CT: Yale University Press.
Ferguson, M. 1992. 'The Mythology About Globalisation'. *European Journal of Communication*, 7 (1): 69–93.
Firth, R. 1946. *Malay Fishermen: Their Peasant Economy*. London: Kegan Paul, Trench, Trubner & Co.
Foucault, M. 1989. *The Archeology of Knowledge*. Translated by A. Sheridan. London: Routledge.

Bibliography 239

Francis, E.K. 1976. *Interethnic Relations: An Essay in Sociological Theory*. New York, NY: Elsevier.
Frank, A.G., and M. Fuentes. 1990. 'Civil Democracy: Social Movements in Recent World History'. In *Transforming the Revolution: Social Movement and the World System*, edited by S. Amin, G. Arrighi et al.
Gandhi, M.K. 1947. *India of My Dreams*, compiled by R.K. Prabhu. Ahmedabad: Navjivan Publishing House.
———. 1967. *Political and National Life and Affairs* Vol. II, compiled by V.B. Kher. Ahmedabad: Navjivan Publishing House.
Ghurye, G.S. 1963. *Scheduled Tribes*. Bombay: Popular Prakashan.
Germani, Gino. 1972. 'Aspectos Teoricos de la Marginalidad'. *Revista Paraguaya de Sociologia* 9 (30) (cf. Dickie-Clark, H.F. ed. 1996. *The Marginal Situation*. London: Routledge and Kagan Pauls).
———. 1980. *Marginality*. New Brunswick, NJ: Transaction Books.
Giddens, A. 1991. *Modernity and Self-identity*. Cambridge: Polity Press.
Giesen, B., and K. Eder. 2001. 'European Citizenship: An Avenve for the Social Integration of Europe'. In *European Citizenship Between National Legacies and Post National Projects*, edited by K. Eder & B. Giesen. Oxford: Oxford University Press.
Glazer, Nathan, and Daniel P. Moynihan, eds. 1975. *Ethnicity: Theory and Experience*. Cambridge, MA: Harvard University Press.
Goodall, H. 1996. *Invasion to Embassy: Land in Aboriginal Politics in New South Wales, 1770–1972*. Sydney: Allen and Unwin.
Gordon, Milton Myron. 1964. *Assimilation in American Life: The Role of Race, Religion, and National Origins*. New York, NY: Oxford University Press.
Gosewinkel, D. 2010. 'Citizenship'. In *International Encyclopedia of Civil Society* Vol. I, edited by H.K. Anheier and S. Toepler. Berlin: Springer.
Government of India. 1961. *Census of India 1961*. New Delhi: Ministry of Information and Broadcasting (MIB).
———. 1971. *Census of India 1971*. New Delhi: MIB.
———. 1981. *Census of India 1981*. New Delhi: MIB.
———. 1991. *Census of India 1991*. New Delhi: MIB.
———. 2001. *Census of India 2000*. New Delhi: MIB.
———. 2011. *Census of India* 2011. New Delhi: MIB.
———. 2013. *Report of the National Sample Survey*. New Delhi: GoI.
Gramsci, A. 1998. *Selections from the Prison Notebooks*. Chennai: Orient Longman (Reprint).
Greenfield. 1993. *Five Roads to Modernity*. Cambridge, MA: Harvard University Press.
Guha, R. 1998. *Dominance Without Hegemony: History and Power in Colonial India*. New Delhi: Oxford University Press.
Gupta, Dipankar. 1988. 'Country–Town Nexus and Agrarian Mobilisation: The Bhartiya Kisan Union as an Instance'. *Economic & Political Weekly* 16 (37).
———. 2005. 'Wither the Indian Village: Culture and Agriculture in Rural India'. *Economic & Political Weekly* XL (8).
Gusfield, J.R., ed. 1971. *Protest, Reform and Revolt: A Reader in Social Movements*. New York, NY: John Wiley & Sons.
Haberle, R. 1972. 'Types and Functions of Social Movement'. In *International Encyclopedia of Social Sciences*. New York, NY: Macmillan Company Free Press.
Haberle, R. 1951. *Social Movements*. New York: Appleton Century-Crofts.
Habermas, J. 1975. *Legitimation Crisis*. Boston, MA: Beacon Press.

Haebich, A. 2001. *Broken Cycles: Fragmenting Indigenous Families 1800–2000*. Fremantle: Fremantle Art Centre Press.
Hegedus, Z. 1990. 'Social Movements and Social Change in Self-creative Society: New Initiatives in the International Arena'. In *Globalization, Knowledge and Society*, edited by M. Albrow and E. King. London: SAGE Publications.
Hall, S. 1990a. 'Cultural Identity and Diaspora'. In *Identity*, edited by J. Rutherford. London: Lawrence and Whishart.
Hall, S. 1990b. 'The Question of Cultural Identity'. In *Modernity and Its Future*, edited by S. Hall, D. Held, and T. McGraw. Cambridge: Polity Press.
———. 1996. 'Who Needs Identity?' In *Questions of Cultural Identity*, edited by S. Hall and P. du (Du) Gay. London: SAGE Publications.
Hardt, M., and A. Negri. 2000. *Empire*. Harvard: Harvard University Press.
Hobsbawm, E.J. 1990. *Nation and Nationalism Since 1780*. Cambridge: Cambridge University Press.
Hochschild, A. 1997. *The Time Bind: When Work Becomes Home and Home Becomes Work*. New York, NY: Metropolitan Books. Horowitz, Donald H. 1985. *Ethnic Groups in Conflict*. Berkeley, CA: University of California Press.
Ignatieff, M. 1993. *Blood and Belonging: Journeys to New Nationalism*. Toronto: Oxford University Press.
Jasper, J. 2010. 'Strategic Marginalizations, Emotional Marginalities: The Dilemma of Stigmatized Identities'. In D. K. SinghaRoy (ed.), *Surviving Against the Odds: Manginalised in a Globalizing World*. New Delhi: Manohar Publications.
Jenkins, C. 1983. 'Resource Mobilisation Theory and the Study of Social Movements'. *Annual Review of Sociology* 9: 527–53.
Jenkins, C., and C. Perrow. 1977. 'Insurgency of the Powerless: Farm Workers Movements (1946–1972)'. *American Sociological Review* 42 (2): 249–68.
Jenkin, Richard. 2007. 'Ethnicity'. In *Blackwell Encyclopedia of Sociology*, edited by G. Ritzer, Vol. 111. Oxford: Blackwell.
Jessop, B. 2003. 'The Future of State in an Era of Globalisation'. *International Politics and Society*.
Jones, and Hill-Burnett. 1982. 'The Political Contexts of Ethnogenesis: An Australian Example'. In *Aboriginal Power in Australian Society*, edited by M. Howard. St. Lucia, QLD: University of Queensland Press.
Kautsky, K. 1899. *The Agrarian Question*. London: Zwan Publications (Reprinted 1988).
Kaviraj, S. 1995. Religion, Politics and Modernity. In Upendra Baxi and Bhikhu Parekh (eds), *Crisis and Change in Contemporary India*. New Delhi: SAGE.
Khilnani, S. 1997. *The Idea of India*. London: Hamish Hamilton.
Kroeber, A.L. 1948. *Anthropology*. New York, NY: Harcourt, Brace & World Inc.
Langman, L. 2000. 'Identity, Hegemony and the Reproduction of Domination'. In *Marx, Weber and Durkheim*, edited by R. Altschuler, 238–90. New York, NY: Gordian Knot Press.
Larana, E., H. Johnston, and R. Gusfield. 1984. 'Identities, Grievances and New Social Movements'. In *New Social Movements: From Ideology to Identity*, edited by E. Larana, H. Johnston, and R. Gusfield. Philadelphia, PA: Temple University Press.
Lawler, S. 2008. *Identity*. Cambridge: Polity.
Lenin, V.L. 1972. *Selected Works*. Moscow: Progress Publishers.
Levine, David P. 1999. 'Identity, the Group, and the Social Construction of Reality'. *Journal for the Psychoanalysis of Culture and Society* 4 (1, Spring): 81–91.

Bibliography 241

Lewis, Oscar. 1996. 'The Cultural of Poverty'. *Scientific American* 215 (4): 19–25.
Lind, J., and I.H. Moller. 1999. *The Labour Market in the Process of Change? Some Critical Comments* (CID Studies No. 22).
Longman, L. 2010. 'Global Justice as Identity: Mobilisation for a Better World'. In *Dissenting Voices and Transformative Actions, Social Movements in Globalising World*, edited by D.K. SinghaRoy. New Delhi: Manohar Publication.
Luhmann, N. 1982. *Differentiation of Society*. New York, NY: University of Columbia Press.
Madan, T.N. 1997. *Modern Myths, Looked Hinds, Secularism and Fundamentalism in India*. New Delhi: Oxford University Press.
———. 2006. *Images of the World, Essay on Religion, Secularism and Culture*. New Delhi: Oxford University Press.
Maddison, S. 2009. *Black Politics: Inside the Complexity of Aboriginal Political Culture*. Crows Nest: Allen and Unwin.
Mead, G.H. 1913. Social Self. *The Journal of Philosophy, Psychology and Scientific, Method* 1 (14); 374–80. Reproduced in Elliot, A. and Pitt, N. eds 2015. Identity: Critical Concepts in Sociology 2015. London: Routledge.
Marx, Karl. 1852. Excerpts from 'The Class Struggle in France 1848–1850' and 'The Eighteenth Brumaire of Louis Bonaparte'. In *Selected Works* Vol. 1, edited by K. Marx and F. Engels. London: Lawrence & Wishart (Reprinted 1974).
———. 1976. *Selected Writings*. Moscow: Progress Publication (Reprint).
Marx, Karl, and Frederick Engels. 1748. 'Manifesto of the Communist Party'. In *Selected Works* Vol. I, edited by Karl Marx and Frederick Engels. Moscow: Progress Publishers (Reprinted 1972).
McAdam, D. 1982. *Political Process and the Development of Black Insurgency*. Chicago, IL: University of Chicago Press.
McCarthy, J., and M. Zald. 1977. 'Resource Mobilisation and Social Movements'. *American Journal of Sociology* 82 (6): 1212–41.
McDonald, K. 2002. 'From Solidarity to Fluidarity: Social Movements Beyond Collective Identity: The Case of Globalisation of Conflict'. *Social Movement Studies* 1 (2): 109–278.
Melucci, A 1992; Frontier Land: Collective Actions between Actor and System in Maria, D. and Eyerman, R. eds. Studying Collective Action. London: SAGE Publications.
———. *Challenging Codes: Collective Action in the Information Age*. Cambridge: Cambridge University Press.
———. 1996b. 'The Symbolic Challenge of Contemporary Movements'. In *Social Movements: Perspectives and Issues*, edited by S.M. Buechler and F.K. Cylke Jr. Mountain View, CA: Mayfield Publishing Company.
Merlan, F. 2005. 'Indigenous Movements in Australia'. *The Annual Review of Anthropology* 34: 473–94.
Meyrowitz, J. 1989. The Generalized Elsewhere. *Critical Studies Mass Communication*, 6(3): 323–34.
Mill, J.S. 1861. *Consideration of Representative Government*. New York, NY: Liberal Arts Press (Reprinted 1958).
Moller, I.H. 1998. *On the Spoor of Conceptual Clarification*. Paper prepared to the INPART study. See Moller, I.H. 2002. *Inclusion, Marginalization and Exclusion*. www.eurozone.com/understanding-integration-and-differentiation....
Moore, B. 1966. *Social Origins of Dictatorship and Demography: Lords and Peasants in the Making of the Modern World*. Middlesex: Penguin Books.

Moore, S. 1988. 'Getting a Bit of the Other: The Pimps of Postmodernism'. In *Male Order*, edited by R. Chapman and J. Rutherford, 165–87. London: Lawrence and Wishart.
Morris, A., and C. McClurg Mueller. 1992. 'Master Frames and Cycles of Protests'. In *Frontiers of Social Movement Theory*, edited by A. Morris and C. McClurg Mueller, 133–55. New Haven, CT and London: Yale University Press.
Mosca, Gaetano. 1939. *The Ruling Class*. New York, NY: McGraw Hill.
Mukherjee, R.K. 1957. *Dynamics of a Rural Society*. Berlin: Academic Verlag.
Mukherji, Partha. 1979. 'Naxalite Movement and the Peasant Revolt in North'. In *Social Movements in India*, edited by M.S.A. Rao. Delhi: Manohar Publication.
Mukherji, P.N. 1994. 'The Indian State in Crisis? Nationalism and Nation-Building'. *Sociological Bulletin* 43 (1): 21–49.
Mullaly, B. 2007. 'Oppression: The Focus of Structural Social Work'. In *The New Structural Social Work Up*, edited by B. Mullay, 252–86. Don Mills: Oxford University Press.
Nag, S. 1993. 'Multiplication of Nations? Political Economy of Sub-Nationalism in India'. *Economic & Political Weekly* 28 (29/30): 1521–32.
Nairn, T. 1977. *The Break-up of Britain*. London: New Left Books.
Naisbitt, J. 1986. *Reinventing the Corporation: Transforming Your Job and Your Company for the New Information Society*. London: Nicholas.
Nandi, A. 2006. 'Nationalism, Genuine and Spurious: Mourning Two Early Post-Nationalist Strains'. *Economic & Political Weekly* 41 (32): 3500–04.
National Sample Survey Organisation. 1956. *Report of the National Sample Survey*. New Delhi: Government of India (GoI).
———. 1962. *Report of the National Sample Survey*. New Delhi: GoI.
———. 1972. *Report of the National Sample Survey*. New Delhi: GoI.
———. 1982. *Report of the National Sample Survey*. New Delhi: GoI.
———. 1992. *Report of the National Sample Survey*. New Delhi: GoI.
———. 2002. *Report of the National Sample Survey*. New Delhi: GoI.
———. 2003. *Report of the National Sample Survey*. New Delhi: GoI.
———. 2013. *Report of the National Sample Survey*. New Delhi: GoI.
Nehru, Jawaharlal. 1955. *An Autobiography*. London: The Bodley Head.
———. 1983. *An Anthology*, edited by S. Gopal. Delhi: Oxford University Press.
Norman, Heidi. 2009. 'Land Rights At Last!' *Cosmopolitan Civil Societies Journal* 1 (2).
Ochs, L. 1993. Constructing Social Identity: A Language of Socialization Perspective. *Research on Language and Social Interaction*, 26(3): 287–306.
Olzak, S. 2007. 'Ethnic, Racial and Nationalist Movements'. In *Blackwell Encyclopedia of Sociology*, edited by G. Ritzer, Vol. 111. Oxford: Blackwell.
Oommen, T.K. 1994. 'Demystifying the Nation and Nationalism'. *India International Quarterly* 29 (4): 259–74.
———. 1985. *From Mobilization to Institutionalisation: The Dynamics of Agrarian Movement in 20th Century Kerala*. Bombay: Popular Prakashan.
Park, Robert E. 1982. 'Human Migration and the Marginal Man'. *American Journal of Sociology* 33 (6): 881–93.
Persons, T. 1969. *Polities and Social Structure*. New York: Free Press.
Parsons, Talcott, and Edward A. Shills. 1954. *Toward a General Theory of Action*. Cambridge, MA: Harvard University Press.
Pelizzon, A., K. Gough, and B. Nicholson. 2010. *A Story of Sandon Point*. Thirrul: SPATE.
Pizzorno, A. 1978. 'Political Exchange and Collective Identity in Industrial Conflict'. In *The Resurgence of Class Conflict in Western Europe Since 1968*, edited by C. Crouch and A. Pizzorno, 277–98. London: Macmillan.

Planning Commission. 2001. *Tenth Five Year Plan 2002–2007*. New Delhi: Planning Commission, GOI.
Powel, B.H. 1957. *The Indian Village Community*. New Haven, CT: HRAF Press (Reprint).
Pradhan, T. 2002, August 19. *Kantapuri Andolan Kon Pathe* (Bengali) [Direction of Kantapuri Movement]. *Ajkaal*.
Prakash, A. 2017. 'Nations, Nationalism in the 21st Century'. *The Hitavada*, March 20, Raipur.
Prasad, P. 1973. 'Production Relations: Achilles Heel of Indian Planning'. *Economic & Political Weekly* VIII (19): 869–72.
Raghuramaraju, A. 1993, July, 3–10. Problematizing Nationalism. *Economic & Political Weekly*, 8 (27–28): 1433–35, 1437–38.
Redfield, R. 1956. *Peasant Society and Culture: An Anthropological Approach to Civilisation*. Chicago, IL: University of Chicago Press.
———. 1959. *The Folk Culture of Yucatan*. Chicago, IL: University of Chicago Press.
Renan, Ernest. 1992. 'What Is a Nation'. Conference delivered at the Sorbonne on 11 March 1882. In *Qu' est-ce qu' une nation?* edited by Renan Ernest, translated by Ethan Rundell. Paris: Presses-Pocket.
Rowley, C.D. 1973, March. 'From Humbug to Politics: Aboriginal Affairs and the Academy Project'. *Oceania* XLIII (3): 182–97.
Rucht, D., and F. Neidhardt. 2002. 'Towards a Movement Society? On the Possibilities of Institutionalising Social Movements'. *Social Movement Studies* 1 (1): 1–30.
Runciman, W.G., ed. 1978. *Weber: Selections in Translation*. Cambridge: Cambridge University Press.
Rustow, D.A. 1972. 'Nation'. In L. Sills David (ed.), *International Encyclopedia of Social Sciences*, 11: 7–13. New York: Macmillan and Free Press.
Sahliyeh, Emile. 1993. 'Ethnicity and State Building: The Case of the Palestinians in the Middle East'. In *Ethnicity and the State*, edited by Judith T. Toland, 177–200. London: Transaction Publishers.
Sarkar, S. 1985. *Popular Movements and Middle-Class Leadership in Late Colonial India: Perspectives and Problems of a History from Below*. Calcutta: Centre for Studies in Social Sciences.
Sartre, J. 1960. *Questions de Methode*. Paris: Gollimerd. *See* Bertaux, D. 1990. 'Oral History Approaches to an International Social Movements'. In E. Oyen (ed.), *Comparative Methodology*. London: SAGE.
Sassen, S. 1996. 'Whose City Is It? Globalisation and Formation of New Claims'. *Public Culture* 8: 205–23.
Savarkar, V.D. 1923. *Hindutva: Who is a Hindu?* New Delhi: Bharatiya Sahitya Sadan (Reprinted 1989).
Schuurman, F.J., ed. 1993. *Beyond the Impasse*. London: Zed Books.
Scott, A. 1991. *Ideology and New Social Movements*. London: Unwin Hyman.
Scott, J.C. 1990. *Domination and the Art of Resistance: Hidden Transcript*. New Haven, CT: Yale University Press.
Sen, A. 1998. *Social Exclusion: A Critical Assessment of the Concept and its Relevance*. A paper prepared for the Asian Development Bank, Manila.
———. 1999. *Reasons Before Identity*. New Delhi: Oxford University Press.
Shanin, T. 1984., ed. *Peasant and Peasant Societies*. New York, NY: Penguin Books.
Singh, P.V. 2016. *Pluralism and Its Contestations: A Sociological Study of Gorakhnath, Kabir and Nanak* (Unpublished PhD thesis). New Delhi: Centre for the Study of Social Systems.

SinghaRoy, D.K. 2001. 'Critical Issues in Grassroots Mobilizations and Collective Action'. In *Social Development and Empowerment of the Marginalized Groups: Perspectives and Strategies*, edited by D.K. SinghaRoy. New Delhi: SAGE Publications.
———. 2004. *Peasant Movements in Post-Colonial India: Dynamics of Identity and Mobilisation*. New Delhi: SAGE Publications.
———. 2005. 'Peasant Movements in Contemporary India'. *Economic & Political Weekly* December, 24, 40 (52): 5505–13.
———. 2010. 'Changing Trajectory of Social Movements in India: Search for an Alternative Analytical Perspective'. In *Dissenting Voices and Transformative Actions, Social Movements in Globalising World*, edited by D.K. SinghaRoy. New Delhi: Manohar Publication.
Smelser, Neil J. 1976. *The Sociology of Economic Life*. Englewood Cliffs, NJ: Prentice-Hall Inc.
Smith, Anthony D. 1971. *Theories of Nationalism*, First Edition. London: Duckworth.
———. 1981. *The Ethnic Revival in the Modern World*. Cambridge: Cambridge University Press.
———. 1986. *The Ethnic Origins of Nations*. Oxford: Basil Blackwell.
———. 1991. *National Identity*. Harmondsworth: Penguin.
———. 1995. *Nations and Nationalism in Global Era*. Cambridge: Polity Press.
Smith, P.J., and E. Symthe. 1999. 'Globalisation, Citizenship and Technology: The MAI Meets the Internet'. *Canadian Foreign Policy* 7 (2): 83–105.
Spencer, P., and H. Wollman. 1998. 'Good and Bad Nationalisms: A Critique of Dualism'. *Journal of Political Ideologies* 3 (3): 255–74.
Sorokin, Pitirim. 1959. *Social and Cultural Mobility*. New York, NY: The Free Press.
Soysal, Y. 1994. *Limits of Citizenship, Migrants and Post National Membership in Europe*. Chicago, IL: Chicago Press.
Srinivas, M.N. 1952. *Religion and Society Among the Coorgs of South India*. Bombay: Asia Publishing House.
———. 1978. *The Changing Position of Indian Women*. New Delhi: Oxford University Press.
———. 1992. *On Living in a Revolution and Other Essays*. Delhi: Oxford University Press.
Stavenhagen, Rudolfo. 1970, June. *Marginality, Participation, and Agrarian Structure in Latin America* (Bulletin 7).
Stone, J., and B. Piya. 2007. 'Ethnic Group'. In *Blackwell Encyclopedia of Sociology*, edited by G. Ritzer, Vol. 111. Oxford: Blackwell.
Streten, P. 1998. 'The Contribution of Non-governmental Organisations to Development'. *Political Economy Journal of India* 6 (2): 111–21.
Stryker, S. 1980. *Symbolic Interactionism: A Social Structural Version*. Menlo Park, CA: Benjamin/Cummings.
———. 1990. 'Identity Theory'. In *Encyclopedia of Sociology* Vol. 2, edited by E.E. Borgatha and M.L. Borgatha. New York, NY: Macmillan Publishing.
Stewart, A. 2001. *Theories of Power and Domination*. London: SAGE Publications.
Sundarayya, P. 1985. *Telangana People's Arm Struggle 1946–51*. New Delhi: National Book Centre.
Sydney Morning Herald. 2004, July 31.
———. 2011, April 08.
Tagore, R. 1958. *Nationalism*. Delhi: Macmillan.
Tarrow, S. 1998. *Power in Movement: Social Movements and Contentious Politics*. Cambridge: Cambridge University Press.

Thapper, R. 2016. *Indian Society and the Secular: Essays*. New Delhi: Three Essays Collectives.
The Christian Science Monitor. 2010. *Australia Aboriginal Youths 28 Times More-Likely to End Up in Jail*. http://updatednews.ca/2010/03/27/australia-aboriginal-youths-28-times-more-likely-to-end-up-in-jail/
Therborn, G. 2000. 'Globalizations: Dimensions, Historical Waves, Regional Effects, Normative Governance'. *International Sociology* 15 (2): 151–79.
Thompson, E.P. 1963. *The Making of the English Working Class*. London: Victor Gollancz.
Thorner, Daniel. 1980. *The Shaping of Modern India*. New Delhi: Allied.
Tilly, C. 1985. 'Models and Realities of Popular Collective Action'. *Social Research* 52 (Winter).
Toffler, A. 1980. *The Third Wave*. London: Pan Books.
Tonnies, F. 1957. *Community and Society*. East Lansingh, MI: Michigan State University Press.
Touraine, A. 1981. *The Voice and the Eye: An Analysis of Social Movements*. Cambridge: Cambridge University Press.
Turner, R. and Killian, L. 1957. *Collective Beharous*. Englewood cliff, NJ: Prentice Hall.
Turek, J. 2003. 'Review of Maurell Castell's Publication'. *The Information Age*. Available at www.capimu.de/fgz/reviews/30.php (accessed in August 2010).
UNDP. 1993. *UNDP and Civil Society*. New York, NY: UN.
———. 1995. *Declaration of the Social Development Summit, Copenhagen*. New York, NY: UN.
———. 1997. *Human Development Report*. New Delhi: Oxford University Press.
———. 2001. *Human Development Report 2001*. New Delhi: Oxford University Press.
———. 2005. *Human Development Report*. New Delhi: Oxford University Press.
———. 2015. *Human Development Report*. New Delhi: Oxford University Press.
Stewart, A. 2001. *Theories of Power and Domination*. London: SAGE.
Urry, John. 2000a. 'The Importance of Social Movements'. *Social Movement Studies* 1 (1): 185–203.
———. 2000b. 'Mobile Sociology'. *British Journal of Sociology* 51 (1): 185–203.
Verma, P.K. 2017. 'India's Politics of Fear'. *The Times of India*, April 6, New Delhi.
Wacquant, L. 2005. 'Habitus'. In *International Encyclopedia of Economic Sociology*, edited by J. Basket and Z. Hilan. London: Routledge.
Wallerstein, I. 1990. 'Antisystematic Movements: History and Dilemmas'. In S. Amin, G. Arrighi et al., *Transforming the Revolution: Social Movement and the World System*. New York: Monthly Review Press.
Weeks, J. 1990. 'The Value of Difference'. In *Identity*, edited by J. Rutherford, 88–100. London: Lawrence and Wishart.
Wieviorka, M. 2005. 'After New Social Movements'. *Social Movement Studies* 4 (1): 1–19.
Wilson, J. 1973. *Introduction to Social Movements*. New York, NY: Basic Books.
Winnicott, D.W. 1965. 'Ego Distortion in Terms of True and False Self'. In *The Maturational Process and the Facilitating Environment: Studies in the Theory of Emotional Development*, 140–57. New York, NY: International Universities Press.
Wolf, E.R. 1984. 'On Peasant Rebellions'. In *Peasant and Peasant Studies*, edited by T. Shanin. Middlesex: Penguin Books.
Wolff, Kurt H. Trans. 1950. *The Sociology of Georg Simmel*. Glencoe, IL: The Free Press.
World Bank. 1997. *World Development Report 1997*. New Delhi: Oxford University Press.

Xara, V. 2005. 'Politics of Language, Religion and Identity Tribes in India'. *Economics & Political Weekly* 40 (13): 1363–74.

Zald, M., and J. McCarthy. 1987. *Social Movements in an Organizational Society: Collected Essays*. New Brunswick, NJ: Transaction Books.

Web Resources

http://www.glalc.org.au/Achievement.aspx
http://en.wikipedia.org/wiki/Indigenous_Australians
http://www.austlii.edu.au/au/orgs/car/m2000/quickguidewalk.htm
http://www.ethicaltraveler.org/2010
http//:www.apo.org.au/audio/wild-rivers-act-debate
http://www.hrlrc.org.au
http://www.culturalsurvival.org
http://old.sandon-point.org.au

Index

Aboriginal Land Rights (Northern Territory) Act 1976, 102
aboriginal people, 100, 104, 113, 115, 119
acceptability of behaviour, 2
acquiring meaning process, 14
adhiar, 76
adult franchise, 78
age set, 13
agrarian conflict, 58
agrarianism, 68
agrarian society in India, changes after independence, 8, 78–83
Agriculturalists Movements Against Land Acquisition, 90
alienhood, 6
  in East Pakistan, 10
All India Kisan Sabha, 87
alternative identity, 3
Andhra Pradesh Civil Liberties Committee (APCLC), 58
Antajas, 77
Anti-Arrack Movement, 58
anti-institutional identity formation, 52–54
atomization, 41
autonomy, individual, 41

Bada Kisan, 76
bai, 34
Bardoli Satyagraha (1928), 79, 87
beef bans, 187
beef eating, attack and killing of Muslims over, 187
beldar, 34
Bengal Kisan Sabha, 87
Berlin Wall, 188
bhagchashi, 76
bhaiya, 34
Bharatiya Janata Party (BJP), 93, 188
Bhuswami, 76
Civil Rights Movements, in US, 100

blogs, 29
Brexit, 188
Buddhism, 191
  by economic determinism, 22

caste, 2, 4, 5, 7, 13, 75–78
  landholding by, 84
  segregation, 69
Champaran movements (1917), 79, 87
change, 1
chashi, 76
Chauri Chaura movement in 1922, 58
choice, 16, 17
  multiplicity of, 41
Christianity, 191
Citizens Forum, 58
citizenship, 13, 192
  elements of, 178
  rights and obligation, 179
  vs primordial collective identities in India, 179–181
civic nationalism, 186
class, 13
  conflicts, 47, 50
  consciousness, 17
  -for-itself, 21, 22
  -in-itself, 22
CNN, 27
collective actions, 7, 21, 45–46
  constructs space for transformation, 22
  direct participation
  impact of, 22
collective conscience, 17
collective identities, 7, 38, 46
  formation in social movements, 69
  Marxian analysis transformation in, 22
  objective realities of economic exploitation, 69
collective mobilization, 67, 69
collective ontology, 1

colonization, 5, 24, 25
communalization, 68
Communist Party of India (CPI), 93, 94
Communist Party of India (Marxists) (CPIM), 93
Community Development Employment Projects, 104
community living, 16
complexity, 11
compulsive consumerism, 28
concrete identities, 3
conflict, 7, 9, 44, 65
construction, identity as, 16–21
construction of identity, emergence in India, 5–6, 18
contestation to domination, 6
control, 28, 71
conventional social bondage, 189
Convention on the Elimination of All Forms of Racial Discrimination, 104
conversions, 187
coolie, 34, 76
corporate capital, valorization of, 33
Corroboree 2000, 103
Council for Aboriginal Reconciliation (CAR), 103
counting process, 3
countrymen, 13
CPI Maoist, 94
creativity, 41
cultural de-recognition, 32
cultural identity, 20
cultural isolation, 3
culturally eclectic hybrid identity, 20
cultural movement, generation of low level of institutional awareness, 54
cultural pluralism, 184
cultural significance of identity, 18
cultural solidarity, 18–19
cultural subordination, 8
cultural symbols, 18–19
culture, 15, 27, 43, 50, 90, 120
   aboriginal, 110
   homogenization of, 4
   indigenous, 6, 108
   intergenerational transmission of, 162
   of collective mobilizations, 69
   political, 120
   postmodern, 20
   shared, 160, 163
   specific to social groups, 17

decentred identity, 20
democratic liberation, 68
democratic revolution, 176
discontinuity, 9
discontinuous identity, 20
disempowerment, 3
disorientation, 9
dispersed identity, 20
dominant institutions, 31
Durkheim collective conscience, 24
dyadic/relational self, 39

East Pakistan, alien religious minority in, 10
economic dispossession, 8
economic globalization, 9
economic momentum, 9
economic neoliberalism, 9
employment, 106
   rate among SC, ST and OBC in rural areas, 85
   seasonal, 71
   shifts towards non-agricultural activity, 83
Enlightenment project of Western Europe, 159
environmental dispossession, 8
essential, identity as, 16–21
essentialization process
   of identity, 1, 5–6
   of primordial identities, 26
ethnic groups, 161
   continuity of, 163
   exclusivity of, 163
ethnicity, 13, 192
   and nation, relationship between, 162–164
   as response against domination, 184
   characteristics of, 160
   foundation of, 10
   identification of, principles for, 161–162
   increasing fluidity and connectivity through, 184

Facebook, 29
falsehood
   identity, 19
   revelation of, 18
false self, 19
farmers, 13, 23, 59, 65, 76, 191
Fascism, 24
feudal domination, 68
fluidification identities process, 66
fluidity, 41
   in identity, 4, 30, 56

Index

forced assimilation, 8
formation of identity process, 19
formation process, 1
former identities, 25
fragmented identity, 20

Gandangara Land Council, 99
Gemeinschaft, 17
gender, 2, 13, 18, 22, 59, 66
  differences among peasants, 91
  equality, 46
  inequality, 69
  oppressions, 177
  segregation, 152
generalized elsewhere, identity creation
    through, 29
ghar wapsi, 187
globalization, 6, 7, 24, 25, 27, 30, 68
global village, 130
Gorbachev, Mikhail, 188

habitus, concept of, 15, 17
Hinduism, 191
Hindu nationalism, 188
Hindutva, 190
horizontal mobility of peasants, 8
human mind, 41
Human Rights and Equal Opportunity
    Commission (HREOC), 102

identity(ies)
  as a means to end, 35–37
  as an expression of itself, 35–37
  as meaning, 14
  as self-discovery, 13–14
  as self-reflexive project, 4
  as social expressions, 2
  as social roles, 13–14
  based on primordial considerations, 2
  change and transformative agency of
      structured entity, 11
  changing contours of, 37–42
  changing trajectory in India, 57–59
  characteristics of, 1
  construction of, 54–57
  dimensions of, 14
  dynamics of, 3, 5, 11
  expression of solidarity, 1
  formation, 16, 43
  formed within structural arrangements, 2
  Foucault views on, 15

fundamental nuances of, 6
fuzziness and fluidity in, 5
interaction in plural situation, 13
multiple, 4
old, 1
perspective, 48–53
pre-existing, 27
reconstruction process, 3
social constructs, 2
Indian National Congress, 93
Indigenous Land Corporation (ILC), 102
indigenous people, life and culture of, 99
indigenous people of Australia
  condemnation of blemish chapter and
      apology to, 102
  consolidation of land claim, 100
  contestation of identity, 119–126
  cooption of identity, 121–126
  dispossession of, 99
  farming of solidarity among, 100
  recent acrimony, 103
  sand mining through WLLC, 115
  Sandon Point (McCauley Beach), 112
indigenous people, life and culture of, 99
individual identity, 3, 15, 28, 38
individualization, 41
individualization in identity, 28
individuals, as rational beings, 3
individual self, growth of, 2
individuation, 14
Indo-Pak war in 1965, 10
industrialism, 68
industrialization, 25, 176
informationalism, 33
information and communication technologies
    (ICTs), 2, 3, 4, 27, 56
  and fluidity identity, 158
  connectivity, 8
  driven globalised world, 30
  expansion process, 63–66
  nature of work participation 141
  penetration of, 5, 6
  proliferation of, 9
information society, 130
informationalism, 33
inherited primordial collective identities, 3
institutionalized mobilization, 64
integrations
  of indigenous people, 97
  of individualized individuals, 2, 28
  with broader networks, 5

interconnectivity, 12
interconnectivity between individual and collective selves, 38–39
Islam, 191

Jainism, 191
Jala Sandhana Samithi, 58
Jotedar, 76

Kantapuri peasant movement, 94
Kheda Satyagraha (1918), 79, 87
kisan, 76
knowledge economy
  emergence of, 5
knowledge society, 6
  brings despair and hope in Indian society, 9
  characteristics of, 9
  construction of identity in, 9
  discontinuity with past, 133
  emerging, 144
  envisioned as progressive, planned and rational society, 132
  features of, 129
  human beings transformation, 131
  ICTs and globalization use, 132
  in India, shifting direction towards, 136
  mass production of knowledge, 129
  new opportunities and networks, 152
  patterns of integration with, 148
  restructuring and alteration in pre-existing arrangements, 133
  shaping on pre-given foundation, 134
  traditional workforce replacement, 131
knowledge workers, 9
krishak, 76
krishi, shramik, 76

landholding
  among SC, ST and OBC in rural areas, 85
  by caste and ethnic background, 84
land–man ratio 8, 70
  declining trend of, 81
language, 13
legitimizing identity, 31
liberation, space for, 41
little community, 17
localization, 68
love jihad, 187
lucid identity, 133, 155

Madiga Reservation Porata Samithi (MRPS), 58
Madiga (a group of Scheduled Castes), 58
Mahatma Gandhi (Father of the Nation), 174
main workers in India, 83
majdoor, 76
majur, 76
Malik, 76
marginal identities
  in rural areas, 34
  in urban areas, globalisation and reproduction of, 33
marginal identities in urban areas, 33
marginality, 34, 128
  multiple, 94, 96
  reproduction of peasants, 8
marginalization, 10
  definition of, 71
  denials and deprivations as operational dynamics of, 72
  hierarchy, domination and insecurities for sustenance, 71–72
  protests as products of, 73
  uses of, 71
marginal workers in India, 83
mass email, 29
mass media, 9
mediatization, 27
migration, 4, 32, 34, 66, 90, 125
  re-socialization, 6
  to urban areas, 34
Mill, J.S., 165
mobility, 9, 29, 34, 37, 54–56
  horizontal, 8
  imbalanced, 67
  of people, 12
  political choice through, 32
modernity
  constructs new identities, 25
  reconstructed new identity, 3
  transform various of social universe, 26
modernization, 5, 24, 25
modeshi, 34
Moplah rebellions, 58
multidimensional identities, 69
multiple identities
  construction of, 66–67
multiple manifestations of identity, 32

Nandigram, land acquisition issue, 90
nation, 13, 165–168, 194

Index **251**

National Apology to the Stolen Generations, 104
National Congress, 94
National Guideline for Land Reform (1971), 79
national identity, 6
   against colonial forces, 3
   ethnicization of, 182
nationalism, 24
   evolved from cultural folkloric, 193
   origin of, 167
nationalism in India
   critiquing ideal of commonness, 171–172
   foundation of, 170–171
nationality, 165–168, 192
nationalization, as imaginary construction, 10
Naxalbari peasant movement, 89
Nehru, Jawaharlal, 175
neonationalism, 188
new collective identities, 4
new culture, emergence of, 7
new media, 4, 9, 27
new networks, 9
News Corporation, 27
new social movement, 53, 67
new tyrannies phenomena, 16
non-acceptability of behaviour, 2
normative integration, 47
Northern Territory National Emergency Response Bill 2007, 104

occupational choices, 9
   of economic globalization, 127
old identities
   consolidation of, 5
   fragmentation and rejuvenation of, 37
   rejuvenation of, 4
Oommen, T.K., 55
Organization for the Protection of Democratic Rights, 58
Other Backward Classes, 77, 84
otherness, 4
Oudh, peasant agitation in, 58

pait, 76
Panchayati Raj, 78
partition of India, migrations after, 10
peasants
   academia, 73
   definition of, 76
   engagement in other activities, 76

identities, changing trends of collective mobilization, 92
   in contemporary India, transition of, 70
   in political action, 74–75
   isolated entities, 78
   marginalization of, 70
   movements, 79
   multi-dimensional identities, 92–94
   new identities, formation of, 95
   new identities innovation and fragmentation, 94
   small or marginal size of land, 77
   social identities, 74
   transformation in independent India, 83
   transformation of movement, 95
peasant society in India, 5
   political mobilization of, 8
   physical annihilation, 8
planetarianization, 7
plasticity of identity, 18
plurality, 16
political entrepreneurs, 48
political powerlessness, 64
political representation, 33
political segregation, 3
political significance of identity, 18
political subordination, 8, 69
post-modernist critics on identity, 19–21
power, 15–16
primary groups, 17
primordial
   bondage, 16, 46
   collectivities, 23, 179
   credentials, 184
   expression, 159
   identity, 30, 34, 177
   informal affiliations, 25
   reconfiguration of collective identities, 7
   subordination, 182
primordially, significance within organizations, 183
production of identity process, 28
project identity, 31

race, 2, 13, 18, 19, 41, 46, 50, 71, 160, 163, 165
Racial Discrimination Act 1975, 104
radical peasant movement, 92
Reagan, Ronald, 188

reality TV, 28
reasoning, 16
reasons, 17
recognition, 14
reflexive self-identity, 9
reflexivity, 1, 12, 27
  arousal of, 11
  in identity, 27–28
  issues of, 6
reformative peasant movement, 92
rejuvenation of identity in India, 5–6
religion, 2, 4, 13, 18, 26, 30, 35, 41, 46, 95, 163, 166, 170
religious
  affiliation, 3, 181
  indoctrination, 175
  minorities, 77
  reformation, 176
resilience, 1
resistance identity, 31
re-socialization, 6
resonance, 1
responsibility, 41
Revolutionary Socialist Party (RSP), 93
role performance, 14
rythu, 76
Rythu Seva Samithi, 58
Rudd, Kevin, 103
rural household, distribution by landholding size, 80

sarva dharma sambhava, 191
Scheduled Castes, 77, 84
Scheduled Tribes, 77, 84
secularization, 27, 68, 174, 176, 181
seduction, 27
self-actualization, 2, 28
self-as fluid identity, 20
self, changing contours of, 37–42
self-conscious identities, 69
self-consciousness, 42
self-denial, 18
self-destruction, 34
self evolving, 38
self-identity, 41, 42
self-perception, 14
self-planning, 2, 28
self-reflexivity, 4, 27
self-reinvention, 2, 28
Sikkhim, 191

Skype, 29
social analysis, 11
social anti-movements, 56
  emergence of, 23
social bondage, 25
social choices, 9
social collectivities, 12
  exist as essential categories, 21
social collectivity, 22
social conflicts, 65, 69
social construction, of identity, 19
social control, 2, 15, 22, 33, 47
social divisions, 9
social entities, 17
social groups, 2, 5, 17, 26, 27, 30, 35, 39, 74, 76, 85, 167, 186, 191
social identity(ies), 1, 38, 69, 184
  construction process of, 21
  contemporary research on, 22
  in public space, 4
  pre-existing in Western world, 24
social inequalities, 3, 176
social integration, 9
social interactivity, 25
social isolation, 64
social liberation, 68
social life, 12
social living, 2
social media, 6, 27
social mobility, 30, 64, 65
social movements, 5, 22–24
  as collective social actors, 43
  autonomous character of, 67
  collective identities, 47–53
  constructing contestation, 44–46
  core of social dynamics, 7
  importance of, 43
  in India, changing trajectory, 63–65
  institutionalization of, 66–67
  negated as disruptive agencies, 43
  revolutionary, 68
  routinization of, 66
  transformation of, 54–57
  typology of, 53
  ushering news ideas and identities, 44–46
social networking, 9
social organization, 24, 173
social personae, 12
social progression, 43
social reality, 11

social relationships, changing contours of, 37–42
social role relationship, 37
social segregation, 32
social solidarity, 12, 25, 29, 37
   nature of, 37
social statuses, 12
social structural arrangements, 15–16
social structure, 2, 5, 13, 15, 20, 21, 39, 42
social transformation, 12, 24
social transitions, 42
social we-ness, 17
societal arrangements, 7
socio-cultural decontextualization, 24
solidarity, 11, 14, 22, 35, 56, 184
   class, 96
   common, 164
   in identity, 30
spatial mobility of peasants, 8
speed dating, 28
statism, 33
structural arrangement of society identity, 12
subsistence cultivators, 73
Sudras, 77
sustenance, 1

Telangana Rashtra Samiti (TRS), 94
taporis, 34
Tata Motors, 90
Tebhaga peasant movement (1946–47), 58, 59, 79, 87
Telangana peasant movements (1948–52), 58, 79, 87, 88
Telugu Desam Party, 94
Them Home Report (1997), 100
therapy culture, 28
Thudum Debba (a militant organization of Scheduled Tribes), 58
transformation, 1
   of identities, 22–24
transinternationalization, 33

transnationalization of space, 4
tribes in India, 78
Trinamool Congress (TMC), 90, 93
Twitter, 29

UN Committee on the Elimination of Racial Discrimination (CERD), 104
UN Declaration on the Rights of Indigenous Peoples, 104
unemployment, 32, 34, 64, 86
urban connectivity, 70

virtual communities, 29
virtualization, 27
Vishwa Hindu Parishad, 94
vishwa kutumbakam, 191

Weber, Max, 160
we-ness, notion of, 17
westernization, 3, 5, 25
WhatsApp, 29
Worimi Local Aboriginal Land Council (WLLC), sand mining through, 113–115
workers, 13, 41
   disadvantaged, 33
   indigenous, 106
   low-or-medium-skilled, 33
   marginalized, 33
   mobile educated, 33
   rights, 46
   rural, 59
work participation
   change in agriculture since 1951, 82
   peasants and changing patterns of, 82

Yahoo, 27

zamindars, 76
Zoroastrianism, 191

About the Author

Debal K. SinghaRoy, MA, MPhil, PhD, is Professor of Sociology at the Faculty of Sociology, School of Social Sciences, Indira Gandhi National Open University, New Delhi. He is a recipient of the Australian Government Endeavour Fellowship, 2010, at the University of Technology Sydney, Australia, and the Commonwealth Fellowship at The Open University, the United Kingdom (2006–07). Furthermore, he is a fellow with the Alternative Development Studies Programme, Netherlands (2003); a visiting research fellow at the University of Alberta, Canada (2001); and a visiting scholar at the la Maison des Sciences de l'Homme, Paris (1999 and 2007). His academically acclaimed publications include *Towards Knowledge Society: New Identities in Emerging India*, *Peasant Movements in Post-Colonial India: Dynamics of Mobilization and Identity*, *Social Development and the Empowerment of the Marginalised Groups: Perspectives and Strategies* (ed.), *Women, New Technology and Development: Changing Nature of Gender Relations in Rural India*, *Women in Peasant Movements: Tebhaga, Naxalite and After*, *Social Movements: A Course Guide*, *Dissenting Voices and Transformative Actions: Social Movements in Globalizing World* (ed.), *Interrogating Social Development: Global Perspectives and Local Initiatives* (ed.) and *Surviving Against Odds: Marginalized in a Globalising World* (ed.). Professor SinghaRoy has published several research papers in nationally and internationally reputed journals and contributed chapters on 'Social Movements in India' and 'Peasant Movements' in the *Wiley-Blackwell Encyclopedia of Social and Political Movements*, 2013.